DELIBERATE
CALM

DELIBERATE
CALM

HOW TO LEARN
AND
LEAD IN A
VOLATILE WORLD

JACQUELINE BRASSEY, AARON DE SMET, AND MICHIEL KRUYT

McKINSEY & COMPANY INC.

**HARPER
BUSINESS**

An Imprint of HarperCollinsPublishers

HarperCollins books may be purchased for educational, business, or sales promotional use. For information, please email the Special Markets Department at SPsales@harpercollins.com.

FIRST EDITION

Designed by Nancy Singer

Library of Congress Cataloging-in-Publication Data

Names: Brassey, Jacqueline, author. | De Smet, Aaron, author. |
    Kruyt, Michiel, author.
Title: Deliberate calm: how to learn and lead in a volatile world /
    Jacqueline Brassey, Aaron De Smet, and Michiel Kruyt, McKinsey &
    Company Inc.
Description: First edition. | New York, NY: HarperBusiness, [2022] |
Identifiers: LCCN 2022026058 (print) | LCCN 2022026059 (ebook) | ISBN
    9780063208964 (hardcover) | ISBN 9780063208971 (epub)
Subjects: LCSH: Leadership. | Adaptability (Psychology) | Learning. |
    Executive ability.
Classification: LCC HD57.7 .B7277   2022 (print) | LCC HD57.7 (ebook)
    | DDC 658.4/092—dc23/eng/20220609
LC record available at https://lccn.loc.gov/2022026058
LC ebook record available at https://lccn.loc.gov/2022026059

---

22 23 24 25 26 LSC 10 9 8 7 6 5 4 3 2 1

For my dear husband, Nicholas; our precious twins,
Josephine and Samuel; and for all the others who inspired
and supported me on my journey to Deliberate Calm; and
for everyone who is willing to give it a try.—Jacqui

For my wife, Naina, and my three children, Kailey, Blaze, and
Zoravar, with whom I continue to learn and grow every day.—Aaron

For my parents, Jan and Ellen, who through their
example of curiosity and interest inspired my lifelong
love for learning and growth.—Michiel

CONTENTS

PART IV
<u>THE DELIBERATE CALM PROTOCOL</u>

INTRODUCTION

Leaders are more powerful role models
when they learn than when they teach.
—ROSABETH MOSS KANTER

In 2009, Captain Chesley Sullenberger illustrated what it means to practice Deliberate Calm in the midst of a crisis. When a bird strike cut both engines of his commercial flight soon after takeoff, he was facing the unknown, and the stakes could not have been higher. But he did not panic and, perhaps even more important, he did not rely on a standard playbook or protocol to give him a false sense of security. Instead, he recognized the situation he was in, mastered his internal response, and made the difficult yet necessary decision to reject the advice from air traffic control to return to the airport and to instead land the plane in the Hudson River.

This is Deliberate Calm in action.

As leaders, this may seem at face value like an unrelatable scenario. Most of us are not flying planes, nor do we have hundreds of lives in our hands. But more and more, we are tasked with the difficult job of balancing our emotions with a rational and deliberate thought process in the midst of chaos and uncertainty, if not in an actual crisis. When we are able to do this, we can catch early internal signals of distress, doubt, or fear without acting out a stress response that often makes the situation even worse. For a leader facing a complex business challenge, this can be the difference between adapting as needed to rise to the occasion and failing to adapt, missing opportunities to innovate, or worse. For Captain Sullenberger, it was the difference between life and death.

Deliberate Calm is not merely another book about a new or "better" style of leadership. The problem with claiming that one type of leadership behavior is more effective than another is that different styles are better suited to certain situations. But most leaders select their styles based largely on personal preference, on the latest fad, or worse, unconsciously, on ingrained patterns and habits. What we need, instead, is the ability and tools to thoughtfully address the situation and select the behavior that is best suited to our particular challenge or opportunity. This ability is becoming increasingly important, particularly when we need to learn and adapt. As the world has become more turbulent and volatile, adaptability has emerged as the number one critical capability for leaders.[1,2]

However, it is difficult to adapt, and it is even more difficult precisely when it matters most. Adaptability, learning, innovation, and creativity are most challenging in high-stakes, uncertain situations—exactly when they are most needed.[3] The human brain is wired to react to these situations with the exact opposite of learning and creativity, and this threatens to undermine our performance in the most critical moments.

Deliberate Calm is the solution. It is not a leadership style or behavior. Rather, it is a personal self-mastery practice that provides leaders with the awareness and skills to avoid reacting ineffectively and to instead *choose* the mode of thinking and acting that is most effective based on their current circumstances.

This book is evidence-based and combines cross-disciplinary research insights from neuroscience, leadership development, and team effectiveness. At its core, however, Deliberate Calm is a unique combination of four sets of skills applied to the context of leaders: adaptability, learning agility, awareness, and emotional self-regulation. Each of these skills is critical to the success and performance of leaders, but this is the first time they have been combined to help us learn and lead differently when it matters most.

A recent meta-analysis of empirical studies found that adaptability and learning agility were the top predictors of individual leader performance and potential. Coming in at number two was IQ or general intelligence, followed by job experience.[4] Another meta-analysis of forty-three empirical studies found that leaders with higher levels of awareness and emotional self-regulation practices drove better job performance from their teams above and beyond other factors like personality and personal leadership style.[5]

As far as we know, there is no existing research on what happens when leaders are taught adaptability, learning agility, awareness, and emotional self-regulation at once because outside of our work no such program exists. But the results of our work with leaders and organizations around the world are extremely compelling. When we deployed a program with 1,450 leaders at a global pharmaceutical company and compared their results to a control group, participating leaders showed an improvement that was three times higher than the control group's on a number of factors including performance in their role, successful adaptation to unplanned circumstances and change, optimism, and the development of new knowledge and skills. Furthermore, their well-being improved seven times more than the control group's. Best of all, the participating leaders only engaged in this program for thirty minutes a week over three months to achieve these results, which were based on self-reported data and assessments by colleagues.

Practicing Deliberate Calm is more important than ever. Our world is changing rapidly, forcing us to deal with unprecedented levels of uncertainty and volatility, both individually and collectively. More and more, we are tasked with making high-stakes decisions when our old methods and success models are not fit for the new challenges we are facing. Often, we don't know what will work or if a solution will ever be discovered, just as Captain Sullenberger could not have known whether or not his radical plan to land in the Hudson River would succeed.

This unfamiliar context is what we call the Adaptive Zone. In order to succeed in this zone, we must adapt, break free of our established patterns and habits, open our minds, learn new things, and even find new ways of learning and collaborating. In the Adaptive Zone, there is a tremendous opportunity for creativity, growth, innovation, and true transformation, but there is also risk of failure and stagnation if we fail to learn and change. It all depends on how well we navigate this zone and if we can avoid the natural tendencies that are likely to keep us stuck.

The circumstances that push us beyond what is known, safe, and predictable and into the Adaptive Zone often evoke feelings of fear. We are likely to unconsciously feel threatened and react by clinging tightly to our old ideas, success models, opinions, beliefs, and habits, all of which might not work in this new situation. In this contracted state, we tend to blame other people or circumstances for our problems and expect them to change instead of looking at how we can open up and adapt to the new situation, challenge, or opportunity.

It is not wrong to react this way. In fact, our brains and bodies are wired to interpret unfamiliar or unknown situations as potential threats, particularly if we perceive the stakes to be high. It is natural in the face of uncertainty and pressure to seek out the safety and familiarity of our established patterns and success models. However, just because we are wired this way doesn't mean it is effective. Our natural impulse to contract when facing challenges in the Adaptive Zone can lead to serious unintended consequences when circumstances require us to adapt. Ironically, *the exact circumstances that require us to adapt and learn make it more difficult for us to do so.*

Thankfully, it is possible to experience the Adaptive Zone differently—to expand, embrace ambiguity, open our minds to novel ideas and methods, learn something new, and even ultimately find new ways of learning. This not only helps us achieve our goals regardless of what is going on around us, but it is also better for our health and well-being. The ability to recognize when the challenges you are facing are in the Adaptive Zone and to use it as an opportunity to learn and grow instead of reacting with outdated and ineffective patterns lies at the heart of Deliberate Calm. *Deliberate* because the practices will make you aware that you have a choice in how you experience a situation and respond; and *Calm* because it will enable you to stay focused and present under pressure and amid volatility without being swept away by your instinctive reactions.

This book is written for people who want to enhance their capacity to face challenging situations with an open mind, to adapt as individuals, and to have a positive impact on our increasingly volatile world so they can lead in a sustainable way. Practicing Deliberate Calm can help anyone navigate challenges with courage, creativity, purpose, authenticity, and adaptability, precisely at a time when it is most difficult to do so. Based on our decades of work supporting executives facing everyday stressors, their biggest, most complex challenges, and full-blown crisis situations, we have developed a unique approach to observing our external and internal worlds and to opening our minds and learning despite the chaos around us. We have found that this creates an extraordinary multiplier effect for both our inner growth and our ability to lead in the midst of volatility and complexity.

While this work is relevant for anyone, we focus on leaders because of the critical role that Deliberate Calm plays in enabling effective leadership and the disproportionate influence that leaders can have on the lives of the people and communities they lead. When leaders get stuck, often their teams, organizations, and families get stuck, too. Our work has an exponential impact when we help those leaders uncover the unproductive patterns and beliefs that are keeping them from realizing their full potential.

We also believe that anyone can be a leader. Positions of authority are not required for great leadership, and many influential leaders have no formal or positional authority at all. They simply have the ability to rally those around them to rise to the occasion, often through their own individual acts of courage, creativity, and kindness.

While each of us came to this work with unique backgrounds, experiences, and expertise, we are equally passionate about using Deliberate Calm to facilitate individual growth as well as broader societal change.

Jacqueline (Jacqui) suffered from low-grade anxiety for a large part of her life before it manifested as a crisis of confidence at mid-career level that eventually started to impact her well-being and limit her potential. At a critical point, she began to research self-confidence and anxiety as well as the related neuroscience. This led her to earn a medical master's of science in affective neuroscience later in her career and to publish her book, *Authentic Confidence: Advancing Authentic Confidence Through Emotional Flexibility: An Evidence-Based Playbook of Insights, Practices and Tools to Shape Your Future.*[6]

Along the way, Jacqui developed a research- and evidence-based toolkit that she used on her own path to healing and brought to McKinsey and other organizations.[7] This work provides Deliberate

Calm's foundation in neuroscience. All of the tools and practices are based on the latest and ever-evolving research. After obtaining her PhD in leadership and diversity effectiveness, Jacqui combined her professional work with complementary academic research. She is currently McKinsey's chief scientist, director of research science in the area of people and organization performance, a global leader with the McKinsey Health Institute, and a part-time academic, researching sustainable human development and performance. Previously she led the learning and development of McKinsey's top six hundred most senior leaders, among others, and served on the Firm's global Learning Leadership Team. While she still struggles with moments of anxiety and self-doubt, the tools in this book have been true game changers for her well-being, career and personal fulfillment, healing, learning, acceptance, and awareness.

Aaron initially came to this work through his training as an organizational psychologist and organization development practitioner in the 1990s. His doctoral dissertation at Columbia University was on the effects of self-awareness on leadership effectiveness and team performance. Although he studied dual awareness and Deliberate Calm for decades and practiced it in his professional life for many years, he was wholly unprepared for the adaptive challenges that confronted him in his personal life when his family faced the tragedy of addiction.

The more Aaron's family spun out of control, the more tightly he clung to old ways of solving problems, including throwing himself into work, micromanaging every aspect of the household, and carefully executing elaborate schemes to make the addict quit. He became a workaholic, suffered from anxiety and depression, and developed an eating disorder. The worse the situation got, the more he "took charge" using the same brute-force tactics that weren't working. And the more he took charge, the further his family descended into chaos and dysfunction. It turns out it's much harder to demonstrate Deliberate Calm when the stakes are really high, and although work had always been important, it was his family that really mattered most. When that was threatened, he had to figure out a new way of learning and adapting. He now uses what he has learned to help transform clients, to effectively lead his own teams, and to cultivate calm and serenity at home with his wife and three children.

Michiel came to this work after experiencing a runaway thyroid while he was part of the executive team at a business in the middle of a market disruption. Instead of treating it with medicine, he chose to look into the psychosomatic reasons behind this condition. He discovered several blind spots, becoming aware that he was applying leadership success models that worked well for him in the past but had stopped working in the industry disruption his company was facing.

This was a life-changing experience for Michiel, as the process of uncovering and working through these blocks guided him toward the newfound purpose of helping executive teams develop the ability to spot their blind spots and work through disruptive transformations. This led him to become a partner and one of the leaders of the Organization Practice at McKinsey and Company and cofounder and comanaging partner at Aberkyn, a pioneer specializing in performance transformations, culture change, and executive team and leadership development. Currently Michiel is CEO of Imagine, which supports companies in their transformations toward a net positive business.

Together, we have drawn from a unique and powerful combination of psychology, neuroscience, consciousness practices, and practical learning from our work as leaders and consultants to many of the world's top leaders and organizations to create a book that can help anyone gain awareness of when they are in the Adaptive Zone and use these moments as a stimulus for growth and development. All of the examples and case studies that you will read throughout the book are based on real clients and real situations, with names and identifying details changed for anonymity. Many of these stories show a leader being coached by a mentor or consultant or other "expert," but it is not necessary for you to hire anyone to incorporate these practices into your life and create real growth and change. Our hope is that this book becomes your coach as you begin your journey toward Deliberate Calm.

In part one of the book, you will learn the Deliberate Calm Promise: why this practice is so important and how it can help you evolve your development and leadership effectiveness. This includes information about the different zones that we find ourselves in and the multiple ways that we can show up and perform within those zones. We also discuss the intricate connections between the brain and the body that determine how we react under stress and why, along with tools that we can use to regulate our response and remain aware and calm under pressure.

In part two, you will discover the Deliberate Calm Way: the invisible drivers that lead to our habitual behaviors and how you can uncover and adapt them. This includes how to tap into a powerful sense of purpose to reframe stressful situations as part of a larger journey, the five different levels of internal and external awareness that we may travel through as we practice Deliberate Calm, and the importance of adequate and holistic recovery to keep our batteries charged so we can more easily navigate the Adaptive Zone when needed.

In part three, you will come to understand the Deliberate Calm Practice: how to take this work from an individual practice to one that can radically change how you interact with others at all levels of your personal and professional life. This includes methods to transform interpersonal dynamics and communication and raise group trust and awareness to create innovative and collaborative Deliberate Calm teams.

Finally, you will get a chance to begin to walk the walk by creating a personal operating model through a four-week Deliberate Calm Protocol with daily practices to help you increase awareness of your external environment and your internal state, where you can reframe challenges as opportunities for growth, adopt new and more effective mindsets, and begin to navigate the Adaptive Zone with ease. At the end of four weeks, you should have a new perspective on yourself, your leadership, and the people around you. But Deliberate Calm is a journey, not a destination. We teach and test and live these practices ourselves, as we are passionate practitioners and students of life, and we still find ourselves reverting to old patterns of behavior or being swept away by our emotions more often than we would like. Self-acceptance and forgiveness are important parts of this journey and are powerful by-products of increased awareness and accountability.

Our hope is that throughout this book, you will increase your ability to learn and lead through volatile and difficult situations with Deliberate Calm—a skill that is in high demand in our increasingly complex world. Deliberate Calm offers guidance when the need to transform ourselves, our institutions, and our world has never been more pressing. We are so grateful to be able to bring these practices to you and are filled with hope about the things it will help you accomplish.

PART I

THE DELIBERATE CALM PROMISE

CHAPTER 1

WHY DELIBERATE CALM MATTERS

No pessimist ever discovered the secrets of
the stars, or sailed to an uncharted land, or
opened a new haven to the human spirit.
—HELEN KELLER

Jeff is the head of sales for a lighting company located in Northern California. He has a good relationship with his boss, Janice, who is the owner of the company, but she puts a lot of pressure on him to deliver. A hard-driving, charismatic people person who is determined to succeed, Jeff has been with the company for a long time, and he knows that Janice relies on him as her "second-in-command." He takes that responsibility seriously. Jeff's relationships within the company are important to him, but at the end of the day, no matter what is going on externally or within the company, Jeff knows that his job is to sell. Period, no matter what.

So, when changes in the industry start to negatively impact the business, Jeff gets pretty stressed. Their company relies on imports from China, and the combination of manufacturing shutdowns overseas and shipping issues has thrown their production timeline into chaos. On top of that, competing companies have begun offering technologically advanced lighting systems that have quickly come to dominate the market. It seems like everything is changing all at once, and they simply can't keep up.

The company is in real trouble when Janice calls Jeff into her office. "We're way off on our targets *again* this quarter," she tells Jeff. Of course, this isn't news to him. He was up all night before this meeting worrying about their sales volume and what Janice would say. "How are we going to get these numbers to where they need to be?"

Jeff is breathing rapidly as he wipes his sweaty palms against his pants. His inner voice is screaming, *"I don't know!"* He desperately wants to leave the room and avoid this conversation completely, and instead focus on fixing the problem rather than explaining things he doesn't yet have an answer for, and deep down he knows that there are no easy answers. But Jeff feels that Janice is counting on him and that he can't let her down. "I've got this," he tells her with determination in his voice. "I'm gathering my team now and will let them know that they have to deliver. Don't worry, I'll fix it."

This is a pivotal moment for Jeff. Janice's question was a good one: "How are we going to get these numbers to where they need to be?" Jeff could have responded to this question in many different ways: by offering new solutions, by brainstorming with his boss, by saying he would brainstorm with his team and get back to Janice later, or by responding honestly, "I don't know." Jeff didn't do any of these things. Instead, he reverted to the pattern of behavior that has served him well up until this point—to feel pressure, take it on his shoulders, and promise to fix it.

THE TIP OF THE ICEBERG

Jeff is certainly not alone. Each of us has our own patterns that we rely on to function in everyday life. We find it helpful to use the metaphor of an iceberg as a simplified explanation of a complex and dynamic interaction between the brain and body. Take a moment to picture an iceberg. Only roughly 10 percent of it is visible as it breaks through the surface of the water, while the other 90 percent lies beneath the waterline—invisible, mysterious, and unknown. Our own patterns are very similar. Only our behaviors themselves are visible to an outside observer (and even at times to ourselves), but underneath the "waterline" and making up the bulk of our iceberg lie our thoughts, feelings, beliefs, mindsets, and core identities, which are comprised of our values, needs (both met and unmet), hopes, dreams, fears, and life purpose.

While some of our own thoughts and feelings are apparent to us, many of these deeper aspects of our personalities lie only partly within our conscious awareness, with some elements completely obscured even to us. *Yet, whether or not we are aware of it, these deeper, largely unconscious layers are constantly driving our visible behaviors.* Our hidden iceberg below the surface of the metaphorical water is at the root of our ongoing patterns of behaviors and actions, our decisions, and how we navigate the world throughout our lives.

If we want to navigate life better, become more likely to deliver desired results, shift unhelpful or ineffective patterns, and/or achieve our goals and aspirations, we must become aware of what is lying beneath the waterline, and address and often transform our hidden icebergs. We can only do this by diving beneath the surface and taking a clear and honest inquiry into these layers and where they come from.

Our existing iceberg patterns may not always be the best fit for our goals and aspirations, but they are not in any way "wrong" or "bad." In fact, they serve an important function. In a complex world, they

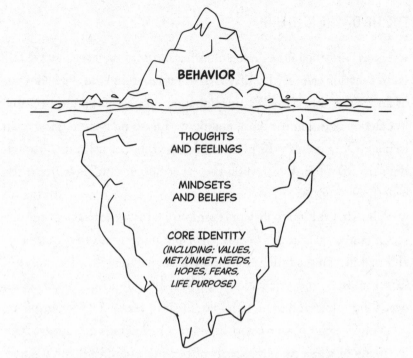

FIGURE 1.1: The iceberg

help us to effectively live our lives. Instead of analyzing every situation before deciding how to act, the habits buried within our icebergs allow us to take shortcuts and simplify decision-making. This saves us time and frees up our mental capacity for other less routine tasks. When facing familiar circumstances and challenges we have already mastered, these patterns often serve us very well. That's precisely why they become habitual in the first place. For instance, Jeff has done very well for himself and for the company with his success model of taking ownership of problems, pushing his team, and demanding results.

The problem is that Jeff has not experienced or mastered his current challenge before, and relying on his habitual behaviors prevents him from attending to this novel challenge with an open mind and potentially a new response. Indeed, the very habits that help us operate more efficiently can also hold us back when they keep us from consciously choosing the most effective behavior in any given moment. Jeff's habit of saying "Don't worry, I got this, I will fix it" is likely not a helpful approach in his current situation. Jeff does not know how to increase sales amid the changes that are taking place in his industry, and now he has possibly made things worse for himself by making promises that he cannot keep. The success model that has worked so well for Jeff until now is no longer working, exactly at the crucial moment when he needs to perform at his best.

This is not a moral failing on Jeff's part. His established habitual patterns simply do not work for the complexity of the situation he is facing. Yet, beyond his stress, Jeff is largely unaware of the feelings, mindsets, beliefs, fears, and needs buried deep within his iceberg that are driving and reinforcing his behavioral habits. If Jeff had been aware of the fact that he was reacting with behaviors stemming from his hidden iceberg, he might have been able to put himself in a position to choose a different response. Because, like most of us, he is unaware of his iceberg and what is beneath the surface driving his behavior, he is stuck reacting in the same old ways as always, mistakenly expecting what has worked in the past to continue working now. And the stress created by this challenging situation makes it even harder for him to change. As the poet John Dryden says, "We first make our habits, and then our habits make us."

We are biologically wired this way. When facing stress, pressure, uncertainty, and/or complexity, we often feel threatened and act to protect ourselves and our core identities at the root of our icebergs. Along the way, we are apt to lose access to the parts of our brains that help us to think creatively, collaborate productively, and discover new ways of doing things. We close our minds, move to tunnel vision, and blame others or circumstances for our problems. Some of us just check out. In this fearful, threatened state, our natural tendency is to seek the comfort and familiarity of those well-established habits, and we become unable to open our minds to new ideas. We get locked even more tightly into the old patterns of behavior that have worked for us in the past but fail us at this critical juncture. This can lead to serious unintended consequences when our circumstances require us to adapt in order to come up with new solutions.

We call this the paradox of adaptability, and it is the ultimate irony for those of us who aspire to high levels of performance: *At the very moment when we most need to break free from our habitual patterns and creatively engage with an unfamiliar, complex, or uncertain situation and choose a new and innovative response, it is that very unfamiliarity, complexity, and lack of certainty that render us unable to do so.*

When under pressure, Jeff's default behavioral pattern is to promise to fix things and work harder. But what is driving that pattern? Beneath the surface of his iceberg, Jeff believes that in order to succeed and be liked by his boss, he must deliver results. This belief leads him to feel fearful and out of control when facing novel problems that he does not have solutions for. His inner voice is saying, *I cannot fail; I cannot let her down; I have to have an answer.* Whether or not he is aware of it, in his mind, Jeff's employment, his reputation, his relationships with his boss and his team, and ultimately his identity as a trusted performer and a provider for his family are all under assault. In this threatened, fearful state, telling his boss that he'll fix the problem feels safe and familiar. It is his way of trying to create a sense of control by asserting what he desperately wants to believe instead of fully accepting the reality of the situation.

Where does this behavior lead Jeff? After his meeting with Janice, he gathers his team in the conference room. "I need you guys to step up and do better," he tells them in a no-nonsense tone of voice. "We've missed our targets for the past few quarters, and we've got to nip this in the bud before it gets out of control. Janice is counting on us, and we need you to deliver." He sets new, aggressive sales targets for each of his regional sales reps for the upcoming quarter and ends the meeting with no further discussion.

The next year is tough for Jeff and his team. He stays on their backs, constantly asking for updates on their sales numbers, and they grow more and more frustrated. A few of them come to Jeff to try to discuss the changes in the marketplace and how those changes are impacting sales, but he doesn't want to hear it. "You are accountable," he tells them. "Don't bring me problems; bring me solutions."

Feeling this intense pressure to perform at all costs, some of Jeff's team members get desperate. They offer extreme discounts and rebates, driving down their profit margins just to try to meet their quarterly targets. But they are not open with each other about which strategies they are using, leading to rumors and backstabbing within the team instead of collaboration. And it's still not working. In meeting after meeting, Jeff digs his heels in even more deeply and hammers the team on why they're not delivering, but everyone is too afraid to speak up and openly discuss what is really going on.

Jeff may sound like a bad guy and a toxic leader at worst and an ineffective leader at best, but he is acting out of good intentions based on what has worked for him in the past. And he is putting in the same kind of hard work that he is demanding from his team. In fact, it is possible that Jeff is working *too* hard. He is totally absorbed by what is going on at work, forgoes his regular evening jog and early bedtime, and spends late nights and weekends in his home office going over the numbers. When his family tries to engage him, he gets snappy and tells them that he has to work. But all of this hard work on Jeff's part and on the part of his team isn't leading to any results because it's coming from a place of fear and stress instead of creativity, an open mind, and engagement. As time goes on, there is less trust and more fear and insecurity among the team, making it harder and harder to open up and admit that new and different solutions are needed.

Meanwhile, Janice consistently follows up with Jeff. While he's tempted to admit that he doesn't really have a solution, he keeps promising her that he will handle it. His inner belief is that he has to solve this all on his own, and he is afraid of failing. He keeps telling Janice what he thinks she wants to hear—that he's on top of it and will find a way to turn things around. By now, even he knows it's not true. Some of Jeff's team members have started calling in sick, the numbers are way down, a culture of fear has crept into the team, and the camaraderie they once shared is long gone. A year after that first meeting in Janice's office, the company is in a real crisis.

Like Jeff, many leaders believe that the best way to motivate their people is to create a "burning platform," a way of scaring them out of complacency. This can work to motivate people to do something that they already know how to do. But in a case like Jeff's where his team must change their behavior, a burning platform tends to backfire (pun intended) because instilling fear drains their energy and keeps them reacting with old patterns instead of learning new behaviors.

Obviously, Jeff made a lot of mistakes along the way, but every one of them stemmed from his invisible iceberg that kept him stuck in habitual patterns instead of adapting his success model to meet the complexity of the current moment. Perhaps his biggest mistake was failing to realize that his current dilemma required a new response. This type of situation is all too common, not only at work but in every part of our lives. We subconsciously react to uncertainty and change in our environments with behavior that we have experienced and learned in the past, missing opportunity after opportunity to continue learning and evolving in the face of challenges.

This can cause a lot of pain, damage to relationships, and

frustration, not to mention the cost of failing to grow as individuals, teams, organizations, and nations to keep up with a changing world. There is a particularly high cost for senior leaders who are making high-stakes decisions and whose emotions and behavior have a ripple effect on their organizations and teams.

But what if, instead, we had the ability to open our minds at these critical moments instead of shutting down? What if we could respond with the curiosity, creativity, and collaboration that novel circumstances require? This is exactly what we can gain from Deliberate Calm: *Deliberate* because it builds our awareness of both the external environment in which we are operating and our inner environment (our thoughts, feelings, mindsets, and beliefs) and how they impact each other, allowing us to act with a more neutral, objective situational awareness; *Calm* because with that awareness, we can pause under pressure and intentionally choose how to best respond and engage without being swept away by our emotions and reverting to habitual patterns of behavior.

Think about an iceberg and how hard and rigid it is when frozen. This is the perfect metaphor for our own behavior when we are reacting out of stress and fear. Like frozen water, we literally cannot bend to meet the present challenge. We cannot learn, cannot open our minds to new ideas, cannot think creatively, and cannot implement a new way of doing things. Instead, we revert to blaming others or circumstances, we disengage, or we withdraw from the challenge. We are stuck, frozen in that iceberg like a fossilized animal that has lost the ability to thrive in the current environment. Sadly, Jeff is that fossil, acting rigidly based on the past because his inner iceberg is frozen.

Yet, when we are aware of the hidden iceberg that holds our habitual patterns, we can melt it so that our iceberg becomes fluid and malleable like water itself, which can change its shape and transform at any time into something new and different. In this fluid state, we can more objectively read our external circumstances and what they require of us, become aware of the related feelings inside ourselves, imagine alternative responses and innovative solutions, learn new things, collaborate creatively, and shift our behavior to adapt as needed. This doesn't mean that we won't face challenges, feel stressed, or experience intense, even negative emotions. We can't always change our external environment, but Deliberate Calm gives us a choice in how we respond.

DUAL AWARENESS

Don't we all wish we could have our own "sliding doors moment" when we go back and see how our lives might have been different if we had changed course at one pivotal moment? Luckily for Jeff, we can do that here. Let's see how the outcome might have been different for Jeff, his company, and his team if he had approached the problems they were facing while practicing Deliberate Calm.

Jeff 2 (as we'll call him) and his situation start off the exact same way. The company is suffering due to rapid industry changes, and Jeff 2 is feeling intense pressure. Janice calls him into her office and asks, "How are we going to get our numbers to where they need to be?"

This time, instead of reacting right away with his default answer, Jeff 2 takes a breath and for just a few seconds scans his body, thoughts, feelings, and emotions. It is as if a part of him is looking down from a giant skylight in the ceiling, observing himself. As objectively and nonjudgmentally as possible, he monitors his inner world—his physical sensations, his emotions, and his thoughts—without identifying with them.

In simple terms, we can think of this as being detached from our feelings and thoughts rather than attached. When we are attached, there is only one "us," and we identify with our feelings and thoughts. The version of us that is having an experience and the version of us that is observing us having that experience are one and the same. For example, in this state of being attached, instead of experiencing feelings of incompetence, we *are* incompetent. Instead of having thoughts about letting our boss down, we *are* letting our boss down.

When we are detached from our feelings and thoughts, however, we can observe ourselves having an experience and we can observe our feelings and thoughts. We still feel emotions, and we still may think negative or hurtful thoughts, but we can notice and accept our thoughts without fully identifying with them. In this state, we *have feelings of failure* instead of being a failure. We *have feelings of anger* instead of being angry. As long as there is a part of ourselves that remains a separate observer, we are in a position to choose a response instead of fully identifying with and getting swept away by our emotions and reacting out of habit.

The first step to detaching from our feelings and thoughts is to practice Dual Awareness, or the integrated awareness of both our external and internal environments and how they impact each other. With this awareness, we are able to access a state in which we can act with intention and perform at our best no matter what is going on around us. The ability to do this in the midst of changing, complex circumstances is the first step toward mastery in leadership, athletics, and other human endeavors.

Jeff 2 is well practiced in Dual Awareness. He recognizes that the challenges he is facing require something other than his typical leadership behavior. As he observes himself from that skylight, he notices that his palms are getting sweaty and that his breaths have quickened. He is aware of his inner voice screaming, *"I don't know!"* He is aware of his feelings of uncertainty, fear, and frustration. And he recognizes the temptation to tell Janice that he'll take care of it and end the conversation. Jeff 2 also knows that he didn't sleep well the night before, and he may be extra vulnerable to being swept away by his emotions. As a result, he does not react right away. He pauses. He notices how uncomfortable and out of control he is feeling and how worried he is about not delivering and letting himself and Janice down.

Before he acts, Jeff 2 works on accepting the situation and his feelings about it as they are instead of judging them or wishing they were different. Jeff 2 also becomes aware of how the circumstances are affecting him internally and how his own fear and anxiety might in turn be affecting Janice, and therefore having an impact on his external environment. And that brief pause opens up the space for a different response.

Unlike Jeff 1, Jeff 2 has the skills to buy time before giving Janice a definitive answer that he might regret later. "Let me get back to you," he says to Janice. "There are multiple changes taking place right now, some in our own supply chain and some in the industry more broadly, and we don't have a handle on it yet. I can't promise that we'll be able to deliver on these targets, but I will come back with some ideas."

Jeff 2 takes a moment to absorb Janice's disappointed expression. He imagines that she is disappointed in him, but he also has the awareness to realize that he might be projecting his own fears and anxieties onto her. It's possible that she is simply disappointed in the situation, not Jeff himself. He has never spoken to her with this type of brutal honesty about potentially not delivering before and wants to address the tension in the room, knowing that she might react to the dropping sales numbers out of emotion.

"I imagine that you're feeling anxious, and I am, too," he tells her. "There are a lot of things going on that we've never faced before. But

I'm confident that with my team we can identify the biggest challenges to address and come up with some solutions that will move us in the right direction."

The change in Jeff 2's behavior this time around is deceptively simple. But in reality, it is extremely difficult to shift away from our habitual behaviors, particularly when we are feeling threatened. It requires a great deal of practice. So, let's break down exactly what Jeff 2 does differently this time that allows him to choose this new and different response.

The first and perhaps most important thing that Jeff 2 does differently is to pause, begin practicing Dual Awareness, and quickly become conscious of what is happening to him both externally and internally. He realizes that he is in new territory, where his proven success model likely won't work. He also knows that he is feeling threatened by this uncertainty and that in this state he is likely to shut down and react with his habitual behaviors instead of opening up his mind to new possibilities. By taking a pause and applying the tools he has available in the moment, he manages to keep an open mind and respond in a way that is far more effective.

This is Deliberate Calm in action. It keeps Jeff 2 from being swept away by emotion, helps him realize that the changes in his environment most likely require a novel approach, and gives him the simple yet profound choice to try something new.

Jeff 1, as you know, experiences the same thoughts and feelings as Jeff 2. They both experience rapid breathing and sweaty palms, two clear signs of stress. They both hear the same inner voice, feel the same fear, and have the same instincts about what to say to Janice. But Jeff 1 is unaware and attached to his thoughts and feelings, while Jeff 2 practices Dual Awareness and can observe himself from a distance while remaining detached. In this state, he is able to see things as they truly are and recognize that his usual way of doing things will not solve this particular challenge. Only then can he apply tools to change the course of action.

This is a key skill for leaders: to read the external reality as objectively as possible, relate it to how we feel, reflect on the decisions that need to be made, and choose how to best respond and engage. We might be triggered to push our uncomfortable emotions under the surface, drowning them in our subconscious, but proactively facing our uncomfortable emotions head-on without reacting to them is necessary if we want to evolve and grow as humans and leaders.

When we become aware of them without attaching to them, we can recognize that our intense feelings are actually gifts. They are messages telling us that our typical behaviors may not be the best fit for the situation we are facing. Instead of shutting down or getting swept away by our emotions when this happens, we can recognize that this is a moment that encourages new learning.

Where does this lead Jeff 2? Before calling in his team, he takes some time to set an intention about what he wants to accomplish in this pivotal meeting. How does he want his team to feel, and what does he want them to do? How should this be different from what he's done in the past?

After reflecting, Jeff 2 realizes that in the past, he always believed that the best way to get results from people was to push them hard. He expected others to react to pressure the same way he did—by just "handling" it. But now he sees that he might get better results if he chooses a different tactic. The intention he sets is to take his team from one that follows his orders and looks to him for answers and direction to a team that figures out together what is required of them. At the end of the meeting, he intends for the team to feel motivated, responsible, and open to discussing challenges while creatively problem solving. And he wants to give them the confidence to know that together, they can win.

Once Jeff 2 has set his intention, he calls his team in to look at the numbers. Right away, he can tell that they are nervous. Every single one of them is behind on their targets. Even the best regional sales rep on the team is behind by 10 percent. His team likes Jeff 2, but he has always pushed them hard, and they know his pattern: he doesn't like to hear excuses; he just wants to see results. This time, they don't know how to deliver those results, so they feel threatened. Yet, Jeff 2 can also see that they still care.

Instead of diving into the numbers as usual, Jeff 2 opens the meeting by saying, "I know you're probably not feeling good, and honestly, I feel the same way. I just had a discussion with Janice, and I had to tell her that we're still behind on our numbers." Jeff 2 looks at his team and notices that their worried, stressed expressions are softening ever so slightly. "I explained to her that with so many changes in the marketplace, we haven't found a way to get back on track yet. I have to admit that I don't have an easy answer, so I'm feeling worried. This is stuff we've never faced before. But I also feel excited because I am confident that with this team, we can find a way to address these challenges and come up with solutions."

With that, the team starts to speak up. They discuss what they are seeing in their individual markets, which strategies have been working well for them and which ones have failed to generate results. Jeff 2 has helped alleviate their feelings of being under threat and needing to know all the answers, so they are able to problem solve and collaborate without feeling threatened and reverting to their own default behaviors.

This is incredibly important. As we saw with Jeff 1, a leader who is feeling threatened can create the same feelings in everyone around them, leading to a total breakdown in collaboration and communication. By remaining open, Jeff 2 engenders the same thing in his team. Instead of leaving that meeting feeling demoralized, helpless, and pressured, they feel empowered and confident that they are working to create a better future for the company. This makes them eager to work together to find solutions instead of falling into a destructive pattern of attack and defend.

However, the problems they are facing don't go away overnight. Every month, Janice calls Jeff 2 into her office and asks how he's going to get the numbers up. At the end of the first quarter, they are still significantly behind. Before each of these meetings, Jeff 2 recognizes that he's going to feel pressured and challenged and sets an intention to connect with Janice and remain open and honest. At the end of the first quarter, he tells her, "I understand that you're feeling angry and disappointed that we're not making our targets. I feel the same way, too." He is showing vulnerability, and he's also breaking the cascade of Janice's stress. While Jeff 1 cascades her stress onto his team, Jeff 2 is a change agent who stops it there and then, which is hugely powerful.

There's another difference. Because Jeff 2 isn't reverting to his old pattern of taking the problem entirely onto his own shoulders, he is willing to ask Janice for help. "The numbers are telling us pretty clearly that in order to keep up, we have to start selling products with software built in," he tells her. "We can keep giving discounts, but so far they're not really getting the boxes out the door. There are just too many competitors offering something we don't have."

Just like that, Janice becomes part of the solution. She and Jeff 2 openly discuss the pros and cons of acquiring a small lighting company that is already offering these products versus speeding up their own innovation cycle so they can start offering their own software-enhanced products more quickly. By opening up and asking for help, Jeff 2 is using his expertise to make positive changes within the company. As a next step, Jeff 2 agrees to have his team identify specific products that are most relevant for their customers, while Janice reaches out to the business development team about moving from a yearly innovation cycle to a quarterly cycle. This also starts a positive chain reaction. When his team sees Jeff 2 asking Janice for help, they become more likely to ask for help, too.

Jeff 2 is working just as hard as Jeff 1. But because he's not keeping all of his emotions inside and trying to fix everything on his own, he is more open with his family about what is going on. With more context about what Jeff 2 is facing at work, his family is more understanding and there is far less tension in the house. He has stopped cascading his stress onto them, too. One night, Jeff 2's kids beg him to take a break and play outside with them, and he relents, realizing that the company won't spiral into bankruptcy if he takes a couple of hours to play with his kids.

The next morning, Jeff 2 arrives at work with fresh energy. He notices that he feels more alert and content than usual, and he remembers that he used to feel that way after taking his regular evening run, which he gave up when the situation at work got so precarious. Jeff 2 reincorporates that run into his routine and starts to use that time to reflect on the day that has just ended and the one he will face tomorrow.

As he runs, Jeff 2 thinks about how he acted during moments when he felt threatened. When did he revert to his default behaviors, and when was he able to stay fluid and learn something new? What external factors affected his behavior? Thinking about the day ahead, he asks himself when he is most likely to feel threatened and thinks about how he would like to respond. These runs become an integral part of Jeff 2's recovery and serve as a meditation in action.

At the end of the year, Jeff 2's company has sped up their innovation cycle, they've acquired a small tech-savvy company, and the team is more empowered and able to adapt. They are still facing challenges, and there are certainly still moments when Jeff 2 feels anxious and incapable, shifts into autopilot, and loses his ability to respond in the way he had intended. The problems that he is dealing with are complex, and at times Jeff 2 gets overwhelmed and carried away by his strong emotions. Like all of us, Jeff 2 is human and imperfect. But more and more, he is able to practice Dual Awareness, stay fluid, and make choices that he feels are best for him, the company, and his team, even during the most challenging moments.

———

Take a moment to think about the endless number of situations in your own life, both personal and professional, that you could more effectively navigate from a state of Deliberate Calm. Throughout this book, we will do the work to develop Dual Awareness and gain the tools you need to anticipate and adapt to meet challenges, keep up with a world that is changing more and more rapidly, and learn and lead more productively than ever during uncertain times. You will find yourself moving from victim to agent, from inflexibility to discovery, and from fear to hope. We hope you are ready and excited to move on and get started.

PRACTICING DUAL AWARENESS

The idea of observing yourself while in action may seem abstract, so let's practice making this theoretical concept practical and physical. We will begin with a solo meditative practice, and over time you will be able to apply this practice to a dynamic experience when you are interacting with others.

To start, picture a skylight in your ceiling. Perhaps you can see the blue sky above, a few clouds, or the sunlight streaming in through the window. Now imagine that you are actually up above, looking at yourself through that skylight. You see yourself in your surroundings. You see yourself interacting with other people in the room. Just become aware of this: you in your environment, completing tasks or interacting with others. Notice that you can both engage in whatever task you are doing and be in the skylight observing yourself at the same time.

Now, observe a bit more and become aware of how you physically feel. What is the temperature in the room? Can you feel the fabric of your clothes against your skin or the feedback of the floor against your feet? What about your emotions? Are you anxious or excited or scared or bored? Can you observe your thoughts, the ones you would not share openly with the others in the room? Take a moment to name at least one emotion you are feeling and one thought that is passing through your mind.

You just experienced the basic foundations of Dual Awareness by observing yourself in your environment. This awareness is always available to us, but it can be difficult to access the "skylight" during stressful, challenging times when you are focusing all of your attention and resources on the situation at hand. However, the more you practice Dual Awareness in non-stressful moments, the better you will be able to do so while under stress. With time, you will be able to practice this during intense, heated, high-pressure moments—the moments when it matters most. This will help you gain freedom from your hidden iceberg and the impact that external circumstances have on your ability to succeed and perform, and you will be increasingly able to come up with the innovative responses that are required to handle complex new challenges.

CHAPTER 2

THE ZONES

Listen to the whispers, and you won't
have to hear the screams.
—CHEROKEE PROVERB

Raymond is the CEO of a regional energy company that plays an important role in his tight-knit local community. His company is a major employer in the area, often providing jobs for multiple generations of the same family. For four years, Raymond has confidently led the company through a series of incremental improvements and felt that they were on a good path. He shows up as a strong CEO when he is running the daily business and motivating the executive team. He is also a larger-than-life figure in the community and highly visible in local politics and charitable initiatives and events.

In his private life, Raymond socializes with a close circle of family friends. Although he works long hours, he makes sure to set aside ample time with his family, and he is a present and loving husband and father. He and his family spend much of this downtime with the families of two of his executive team members, Dave and Cecily. Their three families and a few others vacation together, their kids go to school together and play on the same sports teams, and they often feel like one big extended family. They spend many weekends together at Raymond's lake house, kayaking, barbecuing, and enjoying one another's company.

Of course, Raymond faces a range of stressful moments on a daily basis, but overall, he is able to balance things well. That is, until the business environment around Raymond begins to shift. Regulations are changing significantly, and so is the company's customer base and competitive landscape. Raymond realizes that in order to adapt and thrive amid these changes, the company will need to transform its business and much of the organization.

Raymond has his greatest insights regarding the company's transformation while he drives to and from work on his regular route. Because the roads are so familiar, his mind is free to think about how to transform the company, and he experiences many "aha moments" during these drives. Eventually, the challenges facing the company crystallize for Raymond, and he realizes that the company needs to make three key changes: significantly enhance digital go-to-market capabilities, radically lower costs, and invest in new technologies and markets.

Making these changes is a huge undertaking and will have a big impact on the organization and its people. But Raymond feels sure that this is what's required. He confidently communicates his new vision for the company to the board and his executive team, and then to the entire management staff. He has always shined when inspiring his team. The response overall is very positive, and Raymond feels sure that he has the support he needs for this difficult transformation to succeed.

Raymond is encouraged by the fact that Dave and Cecily seem very enthusiastic about his vision and his plans for the transformation.

Both in executive meetings and outside of work, they assure Raymond that they will take the reins to lead their teams through the necessary changes. In addition to being his friends, Cecily and Dave are respected leaders within the company who have always delivered. They also lead the two divisions with the most revenue and the largest number of employees. Those divisions also require the greatest amount of change. Raymond knows that he needs Cecily and Dave for this transformation to succeed, and he is grateful to have them on the team.

The messages Raymond is sending are difficult because of the huge amount of change that will be required, but company leaders rally, and the transformation gets off to a great start. Employees are able to honor the past while recognizing that change is required to secure a good future for the company.

However, a month after launching the transformation with great fanfare, the company is not making the progress that Raymond had expected. Things appear to be operating like business as usual, and he isn't sure why. At their biweekly executive team meetings, everyone says that they are taking all of the necessary steps to support the transformation. But things aren't moving. Most worryingly, progress seems to be at a standstill in the two divisions that need the most change—the ones led by Cecily and Dave.

After another few weeks, Raymond starts to hear rumors that when Cecily and Dave speak to their individual teams, they are not as positive about the transformation as they claim to be in board meetings or in executive meetings with Raymond. In fact, they appear to be running their organizations in the same way they always have. At first, Raymond simply cannot believe that his closest friends aren't supporting him and his vision. It would be such a deep betrayal, and he refuses to accept it despite seeing more and more signs that they are not really on board.

Over time, it becomes increasingly obvious that the lack of progress is real. The transformation is stuck, and the delay is in fact stemming in large part from Cecily's and Dave's divisions. Raymond has also gathered more and more information suggesting that Cecily and Dave are actively giving direction to their teams not to execute on the difficult but necessary decisions needed to create change.

Raymond doesn't know how to face the truth, so he continues to ignore his growing suspicions of betrayal, hoping the situation will improve. He tells himself that their organizations are big and complex and difficult to turn quickly. They just need more time. Of course, this allows the pattern to repeat itself. Cecily and Dave vocally support Raymond in meetings, and everyone, including Raymond, acts as if everything is fine. But outside those meetings, Dave's and Cecily's departments aren't budging, and the transformation remains stalled.

Soon, Raymond can see business performance starting to slip. He believes that the challenges they are facing pose an existential threat to the company. He's more convinced than ever that his vision and transformation plan are the best way, and perhaps the only way, to save the company. Yet the company isn't just changing too slowly; it now appears not to be changing at all.

Even more frustrating, when people in other parts of the organization see that two of the largest divisions of the company are only paying lip service to the transformation, overall support starts to wane. The gap between what Raymond and the other executives are saying publicly and what they are actually doing is becoming evident to the entire organization. Raymond feels more and more stressed as this starts to get under his skin. He is sleeping less and drinking more at night and avoids a few family weekends in a row at the lake house. He claims that he's just too busy, but in part he is avoiding a confrontation with Dave and Cecily.

Meanwhile, his wife is now hearing rumors and concerns about the company and starts asking Raymond about what is going on at work. Not knowing how to answer, he grows irritable and defensive. Now, even his home life has become a source of stress, and Raymond feels his emotions unraveling as he remains at a loss about what to do.

THE FAMILIAR ZONE AND THE ADAPTIVE ZONE

As we face situations throughout our lives, we oscillate between different contextual "zones." Broadly speaking, we find it helpful to group these into two main zones: the Familiar Zone and the Adaptive Zone. What is required of us in order to successfully navigate and thrive each zone is markedly different.

The Familiar Zone is exactly as it sounds—an external environment that is familiar and known. We are typically well prepared for the tasks and challenges that we face in this zone. We know the landscape and the "rules of the game," we have built up a repertoire of responses, approaches, and behaviors that are appropriate for the situation, and we more or less know what we need to do in order to succeed.

The Adaptive Zone, however, is an external environment that is new territory or "uncharted waters." Our context is unfamiliar, uncertain, or unpredictable in some important way. Once we find ourselves in this zone, the patterns, methods, and solutions that have worked for us in the past will likely be insufficient and in order to succeed we must learn something new. Here, we don't know what it will take to achieve a good outcome or whether or not we are up to the task.

The primary focus of Deliberate Calm is learning to identify when we enter the Adaptive Zone and how to best navigate it so we can choose the most effective response instead of reverting to old patterns or getting swept away by our emotions. This is the first half of Dual Awareness: recognizing what zone we are in and what the situation requires of us in that particular moment in order to achieve our goals and aspirations.

We have a lot to lose if we lack this awareness, are slow to realize that we are operating in the Adaptive Zone, and continue to rely on habits and patterns that are simply not a fit for our current circumstances. On the other hand, when we learn to navigate this zone with greater ease, there is tremendous opportunity in the Adaptive Zone for discovery, innovation, and true transformation.

As the world becomes increasingly volatile, uncertain, complex, and ambiguous (VUCA), we are finding ourselves in the Adaptive Zone more and more frequently, facing new, never-before-seen challenges without an established toolkit to rely on. It is more important than ever for us to learn to successfully navigate the Adaptive Zone. The constant introduction of disruptive technology, the rapid democratization of information, an increased demand and competition for new talent, and the changing needs of stakeholders, among other current challenges, all demand swift changes and new, innovative solutions from both organizations and individuals. In this context, continuing to rely on our old playbooks can lead to disastrous results, while taking the opportunity to create new ones can open up space for personal and organizational growth.

Raising the Stakes

Within each zone, it is important to gain clarity on what is at stake for us and the people around us. Sometimes these stakes are objective, such as in the case of an existential threat. Other times, the stakes are more subjective, such as in the case of a challenge or opportunity that is particularly meaningful to us for personal reasons. Whether the stakes are objective or based on our own subjective interpretation, they influence the amount of stress or pressure we feel, how we tend to react, and the best possible response in the moment. Particularly when we perceive the stakes to be high, our natural response is often not the best response for our context. Practicing Dual Awareness allows us to intentionally match our internal response to the demands of our external environment.

The Familiar Zone

When we are in the Familiar Zone and the stakes are low, it is a good time to coast or function on autopilot, to relax and enjoy the situation, or to recover and recharge. It can be a safe place to practice and hone our existing skills. We are also free in this context to have fun, socialize, and enjoy a state of play. For instance, Raymond is in a low-stakes, Familiar Zone when he is driving to work along a familiar route and when he is relaxing with his family and friends at the lake.

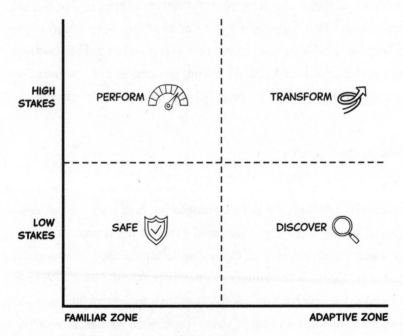

FIGURE 2.1 The Dual Awareness Framework

A low-stakes, familiar environment is what we often think of as our "comfort zone," but we are intentionally avoiding that term here because this terminology combines two elements that are separate and distinct—our external environment and our internal experience. It is quite possible to be in a familiar and objectively safe environment yet feel stressed and uncomfortable, often because our hidden icebergs are triggered.

For instance, those with a history of trauma often find that small, mundane cues in the environment can trigger an extreme internal stress response, even when the external environment is safe. In these instances, the issue is not necessarily the extent of the external threat or danger but the severity of the underlying trauma and the internal fear that has been triggered. But we all experience internal triggers to some extent, regardless of whether or not we have a history of trauma, and may at times feel unsafe even in a safe, familiar environment.

That said, the most natural response in a low-stakes Familiar Zone is to relax. Although many leaders struggle to let themselves function on autopilot, relax, or make time for recovery even in a low-stakes familiar context, these activities play a crucial role in our overall performance and our ability to lead. In particular, coasting has a negative connotation, but it can be beneficial to coast when the situation calls for it because it frees up our cognitive and energetic resources for other things, allowing our mind to take a break and conserve energy for when we are facing higher-pressure situations.

Coasting can also be productive in and of itself. Like Raymond, many of us may experience moments when we let our minds wander in the shower, when doing the dishes, or while we are completing some other mundane tasks, and we suddenly have a "eureka" breakthrough insight. Others use these "coasting" situations to reflect, take stock, or passively explore and learn, such as while listening to an audiobook or podcast during a commute. This is a version of coasting that allows us to take a break and can also help us replenish our resources and bolster our awareness.

Likewise, recovery, or creating a safe and comfortable space and healthy routines to recharge our physical and emotional batteries, is a beneficial activity when we are in a low-stakes Familiar Zone situation. When we are in recovery, we can replenish ourselves because we are not exerting effort to perform or adapt under pressure. Making adequate time for holistic recovery is so important to our performance and ability to navigate the zones that we dedicate a full chapter to it later in the book.

Finally, a low-stakes Familiar Zone context is a good time to practice or rehearse our existing skills. Our circumstances do not require us to learn something new, and we are not facing the pressure of performance. We are able to work on improving at the things we already know how to do in a safe and known environment. Top-performing athletes and musicians, for example, often have intense daily practice routines interspersed with intentional recovery in the low-stakes Familiar Zone to keep their skills in peak form.[1]

When the stakes are higher in the Familiar Zone, we are under pressure, but we have the existing skills or methods that we need to succeed and perform and meet the challenge at hand. This is when it is time to execute. Ideally, in this context we are pushing ourselves to the very edge of our abilities in a state of peak performance. At times like these, when Raymond is in his element and at the top of his game, he is able to make good decisions, translate his strategic vision into a compelling call to action for the organization, illuminate and inspire others, and empower them even as he makes big decisions to help steer the company to success.

In a high-stakes Familiar Zone, we can get into a state of flow, which requires deep, single-minded concentration. According to psychologist Mihaly Csikszentmihalyi, a flow state has the following characteristics: we have clear goals, time speeds up or slows down, the experience is intrinsically rewarding, we experience effortlessness and ease, there is a balance between our challenge and skills, our actions and awareness are merged and we lose self-conscious rumination, and we feel a sense of control over the task at hand.

In this state, we are comfortable because our environment is familiar and aligned with our expectations and capabilities. We do not need to adapt in this moment in order to succeed. Although we might face challenges, we can rise to them. We have already done the necessary learning to face the challenges and opportunities that are in front of us, and now it's time to perform.

Because our skills are unique, the activities and environments that elicit a state of flow in each of us are highly individualized. Leaders may enter a state of flow when they are inspiring their teams or imagining their companies' future. Artists may enter a state of flow when they are inspired and completely focused on whatever they are creating. And athletes often enter a state of flow when they are on the field, using the skills they have practiced and perfected over many years.

In each of these cases, the person in flow is working hard, but it doesn't look hard. To the untrained eye, the athlete's motions, the movement of the artist's paintbrush, or the CEO's speech appear effortless. In reality, we are extremely effortful in this state, but it is also gratifying to be completely engrossed in what we are doing and demonstrating the full extent of our expertise.

One reason elite athletes regularly experience heightened states of flow when performing is that they are able to spend significant portions of their lives preparing themselves physically and mentally (ideally in a low-stakes, familiar context) to perform at their very best when the big competition finally comes and the stakes are higher. When it is time to perform, the rules of the game are known and don't change mid-game. The court or field is exactly as they expect, and the size and height of the tennis net or basketball hoop are standardized.

When a negative surprise like a small mistake knocks an athlete out of flow, the best thing they can do is forget about it and get back to doing what they have prepared for.[2] They can and should make adjustments to their performance based on how their opponents are playing, but they are still adjusting within the realm of their established expertise. They are not learning a totally new technique in the middle of a game as they would be required to do in the Adaptive Zone.

In his classic book, *The Inner Game of Tennis*, Timothy Gallwey talks about how top athletes reduce the mental interference that often derails peak performance. In the Familiar Zone, the primary "interference" to overcome is often less about external obstacles and comes in the form of anxiety, rumination, self-doubt, ego, and so on. As Gallwey says, "The inner game takes place in the mind of the player, and it is played against such obstacles as lapses in concentration, nervousness, self-doubt and self-condemnation. In short, it is played to overcome all habits of mind which inhibit excellence in performance."

The Adaptive Zone

Of course, our ideal responses in the Adaptive Zone are quite different than they are in the Familiar Zone. In the Adaptive Zone, we don't already know what will work to help us succeed, so simply executing and minimizing interference is not sufficient.

When the stakes are low in the Adaptive Zone, we have an opportunity to freely explore without the pressure that comes with needing to solve a pressing challenge. Here, we can get creative and discover new things. This is the context in which many inventions are discovered—think of the proverbial inventor tinkering around in her garage or laboratory. While the low-stakes Adaptive Zone is not necessarily low effort, it does tend to be low stress, simply because the stakes are low and therefore fear and risk tend to be minimized. This is also a good time to learn something new to add to our repertoires, whether it is a hobby that brings fulfillment or a new skill set that is not necessarily required to solve a current problem.

As the stakes rise in the Adaptive Zone, we face unique demands, risks, and opportunities. We are in unfamiliar territory, and there is real pressure to get it right. In this context, we are facing challenges that require us to do something new that isn't easy or natural for us to do, and if we fail, there are real consequences. The circumstances have outgrown our existing capabilities, and our normal habits, patterns, and behaviors no longer work for us the way we need or want them to.

In order to succeed and achieve our goals in this context, we are challenged to let go of our established success models and learn something new in the midst of intense pressure and the often-frightening unknown. Yet, as we will explore further, the natural human response to an uncertain, high-stakes situation is the exact opposite—to defend, protect, and revert back to what we already know. This gives rise to the adaptability paradox—the moment when we most need to transform and adapt (the high-stakes Adaptive Zone) is when our typical biological response is one of fear and protection, causing us to revert to old patterns instead of learning new ones.

When he is performing the daily tasks of CEO, Raymond is most often in the Familiar Zone. He is working hard, and at times the stakes are high, but he can handle these challenges and get his needs met with his existing patterns. Then, Raymond begins to face multiple Adaptive Zone situations, and these patterns no longer serve him. Now, in order to get his needs met, he must change his behaviors and likely the underlying beliefs, mindsets, thoughts, and feelings that drive them.

Leading his company through a massive transformation is a more complex challenge than Raymond has ever faced before. It requires him to innovate and try new things, which puts him squarely in the Adaptive Zone. And he knows it. But as he begins to experience conflict with Dave and Cecily, his awareness becomes clouded by wishful thinking, which leads him to a state of denial. His emotions are so intense and uncomfortable that he does not want to face them. He keeps pushing them away, unable or unwilling to take a hard look at the reality of what's happening and how he actually feels about it.

Like Raymond, when we are in the Adaptive Zone, we often feel stress, anxiety, and discomfort, particularly when the stakes are high. These feelings may be unpleasant, but they are also valuable information and an invitation to gain awareness and become more masterful as we develop the new patterns that we need in order to thrive. If we do not accept that invitation, we run the risk of missing opportunities to evolve and grow. We may not see situations clearly, fall into complacency, fail to meet challenges by hanging on to old, ineffective beliefs, or miss big opportunities because we cling to what feels comfortable and safe. Often, reverting to old behaviors only makes our current problems even worse.

LEARNING VERSUS PROTECTION

As the transformation remains stalled, Raymond starts showing up to work with deep circles under his eyes. At their executive committee meetings, Dave and Cecily keep saying that they support the transformation, and time and time again Raymond cannot get himself to address the elephant in the room. This allows mistrust and doubt about Raymond's leadership to creep into the rest of the team. They start rolling their eyes in meetings as they observe this cycle repeating itself again and again.

It is obvious to everyone else that Raymond needs to hold Dave and Cecily accountable. Some of the other executive team members even try to talk to Raymond about it. While he acknowledges that what they are saying might be true, it is as if he cannot really hear them. He is in such a deep state of denial that he cannot see the objective reality of the situation.

As time goes on, Raymond feels more and more helpless. During his restless nights, he often decides to take action and talk to Dave and Cecily the next day. But when the new day arrives, he can't bring himself to do it. During the few conversations he has with them, they say that they just have some challenges to solve in their divisions before they can get traction on the transformation. Raymond lets them off the hook because he so badly wants to believe them.

Both the company's transformation and the situation with Dave and Cecily are Adaptive Zone challenges with similarly high stakes. The company's future is at risk. What causes Raymond to react so differently to these two high-stakes challenges? The simple answer is that he feels safe when creating a strategy for the company's transformation, but he interprets the lack of buy-in from his teammates as a threat to his core identity sitting at the root of his iceberg. Feeling safe versus under threat puts him in two very different emotional, psychological, and mental states while navigating these issues.

This brings us to the second piece of Dual Awareness: recognizing which emotional, psychological, and mental state we are in internally and whether or not it is the best fit for our current external circumstances. While there is a wide range of states that represent how we may show up and operate in whichever zone we are in, it is most important to learn how to move between the two states that we are most likely to shift into when we are in the Adaptive Zone: protection and learning.

Protection

Protection is the state we are in when we feel threatened, whether or not that potential threat is real or simply the way our brains and bodies interpret our current circumstances. As humans, we tend to interpret unfamiliar, unknown situations as threats. This leads us to react in ways that we believe, either consciously or unconsciously, will protect us, including our ideas, our livelihoods, our opinions, our jobs, our friends, our families, and our communities.

In the midst of this uncertainty, we crave the comfort of familiarity, so we revert to what has worked for us in the past. This leaves us frozen in our iceberg patterns and easily swept away by our emotions and gives rise to the adaptability paradox. The exact circumstances that create an Adaptive Zone environment and require us to find novel ideas and solutions also create fear and anxiety that lead us to retreat and execute outdated tactics rather than to learn, explore, innovate, and adapt to the situation. While we may perceive threats and shift into a state of protection regardless of our context, the higher the stakes are and the more our circumstances require us to adapt, the more likely we are to shift into protection, rendering us incapable of doing so. *In other words, the more our circumstances require us to adapt, the more difficult it is and the less likely we are able to do so.*

However, personal triggers can shift us into protection even when we are in the Familiar Zone and there is no true need to adapt or there is no existing threat of any kind. In this case, we experience something that we subjectively *perceive* as threatening, largely because of our own hidden icebergs. The main thing to fear in this situation is fear itself.

In a truly high-stakes Adaptive Zone situation, three elements work together to shift us deeper and deeper into protection. First, the situation is likely to include personal triggers, so we must be aware of and manage our own internal response. Second, there is a real challenge to contend with, which makes it even more important to be in a state of learning *and* more difficult to remain in this state. Finally, an Adaptive challenge is likely threatening not only to us but also to the people around us, so being a Deliberate Calm leader is more important—and more difficult—than ever.

Once he feels threatened by Cecily and Dave's potential betrayal, Raymond shifts into a state of protection. He cannot see past it and recognize that his circumstances require a new or different response. All of his attention is sucked into the issue at hand, and he has none left over to observe and become aware of what is happening to him internally. He reverts to his old patterns and exhibits classic protection behaviors: controlling, overpowering, self-victimization, overly rational behavior, and avoidance.

This is normal. As we enter a state of protection, we hunker down, contract, and become primarily concerned with protecting our identities, opinions, stories, and inner logic. We defend and cling tightly to them instead of considering an alternative perspective or the possibility of trying or learning something new.

There is a great deal of research to show that raising the stakes in the Adaptive Zone often leads to less innovation. In one experiment, participants were given a candle, a lighter, and a box of tacks and asked to arrange the candle in such a way that the burning candle and wax stayed at least ten centimeters above their desks. The task required them to break free from conventional problem-solving methods and experience the creative breakthrough of using the box from the tacks to hold the candle and collect the dripping wax. In other words, the participants were in the Adaptive Zone.

One group of participants was given a financial incentive to complete the task within twelve minutes, while another group was given no incentive. In other words, the group with the financial incentive experienced higher stakes within the Adaptive Zone. These higher stakes affected their creativity negatively. They were less likely to successfully solve the problem than the group that was facing lower stakes.[3]

It is important to note that it is our internal response to our external circumstances that can trigger us into protection, so our internal environment plays a key role in how likely we are to enter this state. When our inner resources are depleted because we don't sleep enough, don't eat well, or push ourselves too hard without recovery, our bodies become stressed. This makes us more likely to interpret external triggers as potentially threatening, which can more easily tip us over the edge into protection. Indeed, when Raymond starts drinking more and sleeping less, he becomes more easily triggered into protection.

Being in a state of protection may sound terrible, but it is a part of the human condition. In the rare instance when we are facing an existential threat, it can save our lives. Our goal is not to always avoid being in protection. Life happens, and our natural reaction is to shift to a state of protection when we sense for whatever reason that we are under threat. The key is to develop the awareness and tools that we need to navigate our way into the state that best serves us in the moment.

While in general we can and should aim to spend less time in protection, we should not judge ourselves for the behaviors we exhibit in this state. We teach these skills to leaders and unfortunately still find ourselves exhibiting protection behaviors at times—perhaps more often than we would like to admit! Likewise, when Raymond is in protection, he is not a bad person. He is just ineffective. His closed mind renders him incapable of solving his current problem, but it doesn't have to be that way.

Learning

When we are in a state of learning, we can adopt a curious, beginner's mindset, relate to others and consider their points of view, and explore new possibilities and approaches. Things aren't necessarily perfect. We may still be under stress, we may still feel intense emotions, we may still be facing the unknown, and we still may not have the knowledge or the skills that we need to solve our current problems. But in a state of learning, we are comfortable with that discomfort because we do not perceive it as a threat. We are aware that our context includes uncertainty and requires us to learn new things or adopt different mindsets, and we can frame it as an opportunity to grow. This allows us to respond effectively and gain the skills we need to succeed.

With Dual Awareness, we can recognize what the external situation demands of us and enter an internal state of learning consciously. When we do, we are at choice about how we relate, engage, and respond. Perhaps most important, in a state of learning we maintain an inner locus of control. We stop waiting for our external circumstances to change, accept them for what they are, and fully embrace our own power to change the situation or adjust how we experience the situation. We recognize that only we can determine how we respond to our thoughts, emotions, beliefs, and behaviors, and therefore we determine our own outcomes. With this awareness, we can do the necessary work to create the new mindset and behavioral patterns that will best serve us in the present moment.

It is possible to dramatically increase the amount of time we stay in learning versus protection by melting and transforming our inner icebergs. This fundamentally reduces the number of things that feel threatening to us. In a low-stakes, familiar environment in which we are truly safe, mastering our internal triggers is often sufficient to help us stay in learning. As the stakes get higher in the Familiar Zone, we are more likely to shift into protection. In this context, it is helpful to use physiological tools to calm our nervous systems so that we can perform at our peak. When we want to learn and lead in an increasingly volatile world, many of our challenges will be in the Adaptive

Zone. Practicing Dual Awareness and using Deliberate Calm tools can help us shift into learning in these moments when it matters most. We will learn these tools throughout the book.

DANGER

When we experience trauma or burnout, are in an immediate crisis, or remain in a state of protection for too long, we may enter a state of danger. This is an extreme stress response, and we typically respond by becoming either hyper-mobilized (an extreme version of the "fight" stress response) or hyper-immobilized (an extreme version of the "freeze" stress response). In this state, we can no longer function properly. We may pass out, become paralyzed, or experience other physical symptoms as our bodies dip into their reserve resources. This is not a sign of weakness. It is a physiological response to an extreme threat.

We typically enter this state when our lives are in danger, but psychologically, when our core identity is under threat, it can feel very much the same. This is one reason that social media can be so debilitating, especially for teenagers. When we are attacked or bullied or even just ignored online, it may feel like a threat to our identities. Without awareness and the ability to self-regulate, it is possible to feel that threat so intensely that we enter a state of danger.

Our bodies cannot sustain this state for long. When we experience chronic stress, we often oscillate between protection and danger. In protection, we feel anxious and ruminate. It can be deeply uncomfortable. As we move toward a state of danger, our bodies flood with adrenaline and cortisol to prepare us to fight or flee. When we remain in protection for a long time, those floods of adrenaline and cortisol can feel normalizing, as if something is missing without them. If this continues for too long, it can become a dangerous and addictive cycle that can repeat until we reach a state of clinical burnout, where our bodies decide that we can no longer actively participate in our day-to-day lives. It is difficult to come back from this without an extended period of recovery.

In general, we do not enter a state of danger often, but it is important to know that it exists, particularly if you are under extreme or long-term stress or pressure. It is essential to take care of yourself, rest, and plan time in recovery. If you have experienced trauma, we recommend seeking professional help to address any lingering symptoms of PTSD and to fully heal.

SHIFTING INTO LEARNING

At this point in Raymond's journey, we joined his company as a source of external support for certain aspects of the transformation. Right away, some of the executive team members started to talk to us about what was going on with Dave's and Cecily's divisions. They wanted to see if we could help get through to Raymond. We sat down with him and discussed the situation.

It seemed like Raymond understood rationally what was going on. He saw and acknowledged the lack of progress and support, especially in Cecily's and Dave's divisions. He also knew that this was slowing down the whole organization. However, he was in a state of protection and continued avoiding the tough decisions he needed to make regarding Dave and Cecily's behavior. Our first step was to help Raymond create more awareness about why he was not taking action by exploring what was going on in his iceberg.

Sitting around the conference table with Raymond and his chief human resources officer, we asked if he was willing to explore the challenge in a slightly different way. He agreed to play along, so we asked him to close his eyes and relax. When we saw his breath slow down, we asked him to imagine himself arriving at the office on Monday morning, after a relaxing weekend at the lake. Then we asked him to imagine himself walking into the boardroom to start his executive team meeting. As he scanned the room, he could see everyone gathered, except for two empty seats. Cecily and Dave were not there.

We saw a smile spread across Raymond's face and asked him, "How do you feel?"

"Relieved," Raymond said. "It feels like with the two blockers gone, we can finally move forward with the transformation and discuss the real topics again."

We asked him to open his eyes.

"What does this mean? Is there anything you can do to create this situation you just visualized, where you can move forward without two team members blocking progress?"

"There's nothing I can do," Raymond said with resignation. "It's gotten too heated. It's too late for them to turn around and support me, and they're not being open with me, so I can't trust their feedback."

"Well," we asked him, "if you don't believe they will change, what else can you do?"

Raymond let out a deep sigh and shook his head. "I think about this so often. The only alternative I have is to remove them, but I can't fire them. It will ruin our relationships and will cause too much devastation to all of our families. I feel like I am a prisoner of the situation. There is nowhere to go with this."

It was clear to us that Raymond was in deep protection because he was so threatened by the idea of potentially damaging his friendships. This kept him from developing an objective awareness of his context and his inner reaction, leading to a dangerous blind spot that was limiting his effectiveness as a leader. He could not see a way out of this situation because he was putting his friendships and social circle above everything else.

This time we asked, "If you are not able to address this issue, what will the consequence be?"

"The transformation won't happen," Raymond said decisively. "The company will suffer."

"And what would that mean for the nine thousand employee families that are depending on this company?"

"Well, we'd probably have to cut salaries," Raymond said. "We might have to let even more people go."

"What impact will this have on the local community?" we asked. "And what weighs more heavily, that result or potentially ruining your friendships?"

Suddenly, it was as if Raymond had stepped out of a fog. He sighed deeply, opened his eyes, and looked at us with clarity and upset on his face. "I have been prioritizing the wrong things," he said. "Of course, the future of the company is more important. I have a responsibility to all of my employees, not just them."

As we talked further, it became clear that beneath his behaviors was Raymond's belief that if he removed Dave and Cecily, it would threaten not only their family relationships but also his core identity as their friend and as a prominent community member.

If Raymond had practiced Dual Awareness, he likely would have come to this realization much sooner, potentially allowing him to solve the issue and get Dave and Cecily on board before it was too late. This is one reason it's so important to practice Deliberate Calm: it enables us to hear the whispers from our external environment and internally from our minds, hearts, and bodies that our status quo isn't working anymore. When we fail to hear those whispers, they often get louder and louder until they turn into full-blown screams.

When Raymond experienced this "aha moment" and saw that he

needed to put his company before his personal relationships, he realized that his protection behaviors of avoidance and denial were not serving him. In order to save his company, he needed to stop acting from a state of protection and dismantle his deeply held belief that he couldn't take action to change the current dynamic. Through this work, he was able to shift into a state of learning.

The next week, Raymond had tough conversations with Cecily and Dave. In those conversations, Raymond expressed both his disappointment in their actions and his understanding of their perspectives. They felt threatened by the changes happening around them and had reacted in turn from their own state of protection. But it was too late to go back and change that now. Ultimately, Dave left the company and Cecily was moved to another role within the company.

As Raymond predicted, this did negatively affect their friendships, at least for a while. Ironically, Raymond ended up jeopardizing and even harming the very relationships that he was so determined to protect. This often happens in a state of protection. As the saying goes, "What I fear, I create."

At this point, being able to move on without Dave and Cecily came as a huge relief to Raymond. Now that he had finally become aware of how his behaviors were contributing to the problem, he could face his feelings instead of stuffing them down, and it felt like a huge weight had been lifted off him. Raymond was exhausted from the whole ordeal, so the first thing he did was go to the lake for the weekend without Dave or Cecily; just the family relaxing and enjoying themselves and preparing for the next step forward.

Raymond returned to work on Monday feeling rejuvenated. He realized how constrained he had felt when he kept telling himself that he did not have a choice. Now he was free to take ownership of the situation. Without the resistance from Dave and Cecily, the transformation began to move forward. As the rest of the team saw real leadership commitment from Raymond to support the new vision for the company, they started to increase their ownership as well.

Deliberate Calm is not a "one and done" thing. It is a lifelong practice of navigating the Adaptive and Familiar Zones with awareness and choice so we can lead with purpose for the organizations and societies that we serve, achieve our goals, and become our authentic selves. As we practice Deliberate Calm, we build our ability to recognize and predict the moments when we are in protection and make a conscious choice to instead shift into the state that best suits us in that moment.

We continued working with Raymond to help him practice awareness and reframe his beliefs so that he could break free of the mindsets and behaviors that were not serving him any longer. He started taking better care of himself and developed daily practices that brought him more awareness about his external environment and its challenges, as well as the inner thoughts, beliefs, and emotions that were driving his iceberg behaviors. Over time, Raymond regained the trust and support of his team and they were able to open up, collaborate, explore, and learn new things together. Ultimately, he became a transformational leader for the new version of his company that he was creating. It's no coincidence that the changes within the company flowed smoothly from there.

WHAT ZONE ARE YOU IN?

The different zones and states may seem theoretical, so let's take a look at how they play out in your own life. To start, take a moment to reflect on the top three challenges or opportunities you faced today.

After reflecting on your day, answer the following questions for each of the challenges:

1. Is this challenge or opportunity primarily in the Familiar Zone or in the Adaptive Zone? What was it about this challenge or opportunity that makes it either familiar or adaptive?
2. Are the stakes you are facing with this challenge or opportunity high or low?
3. When facing this challenge or opportunity, how much of your time were you in a state of protection? What do you believe triggered you into this state?
4. When facing this challenge or opportunity, how much of your time were you in a state of learning? What do you believe allowed you to access this state?

This is just the very beginning of developing Dual Awareness so that you can remain conscious of what zone you are in and what circumstances trigger a protection or learning state in you. Later, you will master the ability to move fluidly between states so that you can adapt and thrive in changing circumstances, surpassing your current potential.

CHAPTER 3

THE BRAIN-BODY
CONNECTION

Between stimulus and response, there is a space.
In that space is our power to choose our response.
In our response lies our growth and our freedom.
—VIKTOR FRANKL

Reshma is the communications director for an international software company. She takes a lot of pride in her work and her career is extremely important to her. Reshma grew up in a large family, where she often felt that she was ignored or just got lost in the crowd. The only way she felt that she was able to stand out was through her academic performance, so her work has become a huge part of her core identity.

Reshma has only been at her company for about a year, and so far she hasn't had much face-to-face time with the company's CEO, Monika. Now, she is about to present her work about a new company initiative to Monika for the first time. Reshma has heard from her colleagues that Monika can be tough in these types of meetings. If she likes the work, she asks difficult questions and really pushes the person who is presenting. If they are up to the challenge, this is where they can really shine.

If Monika doesn't like the work, however, Reshma has heard that she just shuts down. With this in mind, Reshma has prepared for this meeting to the utmost. She's spent countless hours making sure her presentation is perfect and readying herself to answer the most challenging questions.

On the day of the meeting, Reshma gives the presentation her all, but the whole time, Monika seems distracted and tuned out. It looks like she's holding back, as if there's something she wants to say, but she remains quiet. Reshma notices her checking the clock and frequently looking down at her phone.

As this continues, Reshma feels a pit forming deep in her stomach, she starts sweating, and her heart begins beating faster and faster. But she keeps trying to press on and engage Monika by highlighting the best parts of the work she has done. Nothing she says seems to make a difference. Monika isn't asking any questions and seems totally disinterested.

Reshma is feeling antsy and even a bit panicky. She taps her leg and rolls her neck while her inner voice begins to spiral. *I've lost her,* she thinks. *She doesn't care at all. This is my first real chance to impress her, and I've totally blown it. Will I even get a second chance after this?* When Monika abruptly ends the meeting early just a few minutes later, Reshma rushes into the nearby restroom and bursts into tears.

While working on the presentation, Reshma had been saving up her vacation days. After the meeting, she takes some time off and goes away. Even while on vacation, though, she has a hard time relaxing. Reshma continues to ruminate about the presentation, trying to pinpoint exactly what she had done wrong and why Monika was so disinterested in her work. Her inner voice tells her that her work just wasn't good enough and that Monika will probably end up replacing her on the project or just canceling the initiative completely. If she manages to stay on the project, Reshma decides that she will put a lot more time and effort into her presentation before sharing it with anyone again.

Shortly after she returns to work, Reshma runs into Monika in the company's cafeteria. Unlike on the day of the presentation, this time Monika seems totally alert and present. But just seeing her brings back that pit in Reshma's stomach. Her heartbeat quickens and her palms get sweaty. It's as if she's right back in that conference room, desperately trying to engage a tuned-out Monika as the whole presentation goes down in flames.

"Hi, Reshma," Monika says, approaching her. "I wanted to follow up with you about that project you were working on."

Uh-oh. Reshma freezes, her fists clenched at her sides and a nervous expression on her face. She hasn't worked on the presentation at all since the day of their disastrous meeting, and she knows that Monika wasn't happy with her work. Now what? Reshma wonders how bad it will be when Monika realizes that she hasn't made any changes to the presentation or to the project plan.

"Oh, I'm so sorry," Reshma replies, avoiding eye contact with Monika and stammering a bit. "I haven't made any progress. I didn't think . . . well, I thought . . . I guess I just need more time."

Monika looks confused, and then it seems like she's starting to tune out again, and Reshma kicks herself internally. *I've done it again,* she thinks. *I just keep messing this up.* The only way she can redeem herself, she believes, is to completely redo the presentation, and maybe even change her whole approach to the project. Monika had clearly been unimpressed with what she shared before.

Reshma asks Monika for another month to work on her presentation. Once again, Reshma dives in, revamping the approach and the presentation. But two weeks later, Monika tells her that they are moving on, as new priorities have emerged. This project seems a lot more complicated than they first thought and must be far off track if Reshma needed another month just to share her approach.

TRIGGER AND RESPONSE OR PREDICTION ERROR

There are two main views on how the human brain and body respond to a perceived threat that could explain what happened to Reshma both in the boardroom with Monika and again later when she sees her in the cafeteria. In the view that most of us are familiar with and is presented in many current books on this topic, when faced with a threat we shift into a heightened state of stress and protection in a process of trigger and response. Something happens that we perceive as a threat, and as a result of that stimulus, we experience a stress response. The classic example is of a lion chasing us, and in response our brains and bodies prepare us to fight, flee, or freeze.

The dominant explanation in existing popular books is that once the amygdala, which is located at the base of the brain, registers an imminent potential danger, it sends a distress signal to start this stress response. This activates the sympathetic nervous system, which leads to the release of multiple stress response chemicals that prime the body to focus its resources on survival. In particular, adrenaline increases blood flow so that we are ready to react quickly. This is why the heart rate increases under stress—it needs to pump faster. In addition, cortisol floods the body with glucose, an energy source to activate and fuel our large muscles.

Simultaneously, this process inhibits the parasympathetic nervous system, which is important to support the body's functions when it is at rest in non-stressful situations. The prefrontal cortex, an important part of the brain that is involved in executive functions like planning, working memory, emotion processing, and cognitive flexibility, becomes challenged as stress response chemicals push us to quit *thinking* about things and start *doing* something, *now* (fight or run away).

We have neuropeptide receptors for these chemicals in our brains and throughout our bodies so that different parts of the body can pick up the signal that we are under threat and respond as needed.[1] Many receptors for these stress response chemicals are also in our stomach—our gut—so we literally have a "gut feeling" when we sense or predict that something might be going wrong, and can even feel nauseated and queasy as a result.[2] However, we also might misinterpret a nauseous feeling that is the result of being sick or eating something bad as a gut feeling that something is wrong.

All of this explains Reshma's mental and physiological response to the "threat" of a disapproving boss. She is antsy during the meeting and has a racing heart, sweaty palms, and a stomachache. And she cannot think clearly enough to ask Monika an open-ended question to try to figure out what is really happening. In the cafeteria, she clenches her fists, begins to sweat, and her mind goes blank again. This all happens because her body is primed to fight, and her mind is flooded with fear, along with the chemicals that tend to accompany a fear response, simply because an external stimulus triggered her into a state of stress.

In his book *Emotional Intelligence*, Daniel Goleman refers to this process as the "amygdala hijack."[3] At face value, it is an easy explanation of why we shift into a state of protection when we are stressed, but it is incomplete and doesn't do justice to this amazing part of the brain. The amygdala is so much more than just a fear center. The full picture, with insights that continue to evolve in real time as we learn more and more about how the brain works, is far more profound and more nuanced.

CONSTRUCTING OUR EMOTIONS

There is an emerging scientific view that has been getting more attention lately thanks to the work of many experts, particularly Lisa Feldman Barrett, professor of psychology at Northeastern University.[4] This view explains that we do not simply shift into a state of protection because of an external trigger. Obviously, there was no lion or any other objective threat in that conference room or in the cafeteria with Reshma. And we get stressed out all the time when our lives are not literally in danger. How can this be possible if the stress response is a simple matter of trigger and response?

The complicated truth according to this view is that we actually construct our own emotions, including fear.[5] This does not happen as a reaction to an external trigger. Instead, it is a result of our brains' *predictions* about what is going to happen to us next. Primarily, our emotions are based on our predictions about whether or not we are in danger or will soon be in danger, if risky outcomes might be around the corner, or if we are confident that everything is going to work out and we are and will remain safe. When our brains predict that we are safe and will stay that way for the foreseeable future, we are easily able to remain calm and access a state of learning. If we predict that we are or will soon be in danger or even just facing the unknown, we shift into protection.

Let's look at how this prediction process works. One of our brains' primary functions is to keep us safe, and they focus on this task all day long. To do so, they are constantly alert, scanning our environments both internally and externally through our senses. The information about what is going on both inside and outside us is integrated in our insula, a central hub in our brain.[6] Our brains then use this information to adjust our bodily functions accordingly.

For instance, if those "scanners" pick up on the signal that we are safe and that we are about to eat, our brains will in turn send a signal to our bodies to produce saliva to help digest our food. But if they pick up on a potential threat, a process unfolds to respond as needed and bring us back to a place of safety as quickly as possible. When Reshma's presentation starts spiraling, her scanners pick up on a threat signal and her brain primes her body to fight or run away through increased heart rate, activated muscles, and a focus on the potential danger to keep her safe.

So far, this is not dissimilar from the idea of an "amygdala hijack." However, to save time and energy and make sense of the world quickly and efficiently, our brains make those predictions about what is going to happen based primarily on our past experiences, how we physically feel in the moment, and the context in which we are operating. Our brains are the most "expensive" organs in our bodies, using 20 percent of our total energy resources.[7] So, any time our brains can take a shortcut and save energy, they jump at the chance. This is why they like to rely on our established patterns of behavior.

Thanks to these shortcuts, when we encounter something that is similar to what we have experienced before, we are able to make sense of it without wasting time or energy. When we encounter anything, good or bad, billions of neurons in our brains sift through our past experiences looking for something similar. Our brains then *predict* what will happen based on how we felt mentally, emotionally, and physically the last time we encountered a similar person, place, thing, or situation.

When our brains receive information about something that matches with past feelings of safety, we are able to remain in our state of learning. When our brains receive information about something that matches with a previously experienced threat, we move into protection. Our brains may then interpret it as a source of potential danger and prepare the body to respond. They are beautifully built to be ready and respond very fast when we are in danger and need to get ourselves to a safe place.

Think back to Reshma in the cafeteria. Again, there is no lion. Monika is simply following up with her about the project she cares so much about. But Reshma's brain matches this experience with her last threatening encounter with Monika and predicts that she is once again potentially under threat. Her body then focuses her resources on her survival and getting back to a place of safety, not on impressing her boss with a well thought out response.

When our brains sift through our prior experiences and do not find a match because we are facing something new or uncertain, they will remain alert for threats simply because they have never encountered anything like this before and are uncertain about our safety in this new situation. This explains why we often feel stressed when we are facing new experiences, even those that are mostly positive, like taking on a new role or presenting a new project that we are excited about. Our brains will remain alert until one of three things happens: we interpret the situation as safe, we have used our past experience and knowledge to make sense of the situation, or we have learned something new. Then that new information becomes the baseline for future predictions about the same thing.

This process serves an important purpose that keeps humans alive. In situations where we are literally in danger, there is no time to waste by responding with curiosity or creativity. However, because our brains work through a process of prediction, they respond to new situations with "old" knowledge, and they cannot always decipher between a real threat like a lion and a perceived threat like a disappointed boss. Of course, when we are in real danger, it's useful for our bodies to respond quickly. But in the latter scenario, it would be far more effective for us to remain open-minded and calmly try new things. It is in these situations that we most need to access a state of learning and leverage the executive thinking part of our brains, but because our brains are not sure whether or not we are safe, we often get stuck in protection instead, reacting with knee-jerk, fear-based behaviors.

This is unfortunately what happens to Reshma. Even worse, it was entirely avoidable because in reality, Reshma isn't facing a threat at all. In fact, it is Reshma's own brain that predicts she is under threat, and that is what leads her to go into a state of protection and creates the unfortunate end result. The real danger in this case simply does not exist.

How is this possible? Well, let's look at the same exact situation from Monika's point of view. Before the initial meeting, Monika is excited about Reshma's presentation and is really interested in learning more about the new initiative that she is working on. But right before the meeting, Monika receives a call from her daughter, who is in the midst of a medical crisis. She believes that she has appendicitis and might need emergency surgery.

Monika's daughter lives in another city. She decides there is no point in rushing to catch a plane to be with her. She wouldn't get there in time before the surgery, anyway, so she decides to stay put and wait for news. Just as Reshma's presentation begins, Monika receives a text from her daughter's husband, saying that she is indeed being wheeled into surgery and that he will send her an update as soon as he has one.

Of course, for the rest of the meeting, Monika is very distracted. Consumed with worries about her daughter's health, she cannot concentrate on anything that Reshma is saying and distracts herself even more by constantly checking her phone for an update. If she could pay attention, Monika would be impressed by the work that Reshma is sharing. But her own overwhelming emotions make it impossible for her to focus. She barely hears anything that Reshma is saying.

By the time Reshma leaves for her vacation, Monika's daughter is recovering well from surgery. Monika realizes after the fact that she hadn't been paying attention during Reshma's presentation, but she is still really interested in the project. She makes a note to herself to follow up with Reshma as soon as she sees her back at work.

So, Monika is excited when she runs into Reshma in the cafeteria. But she immediately notices and is confused by Reshma's reaction to her follow-up. She doesn't remember Reshma being so nervous and unsure of herself and of her own work in the meeting, but Monika also recognizes that she wasn't really paying attention.

Reshma's reaction and then her request for another month to work on the presentation significantly dim Monika's confidence in her. Assuming there are major problems with the entire initiative that she had been unaware of, Monika decides to forget it and just move on.

MEANING-MAKING MACHINES

Now we can see that in that conference room, there is no objective threat. It is Reshma's brain that creates the feelings of being threatened as it makes predictions and tries to make meaning out of the world around her. With their use of predictions, our complex brains are basically meaning-making machines. This is evidenced in our rich storytelling history. Our propensity for storytelling is one of the greatest things about us as humans. In many ways, it is what sets us apart from other animals. We tell ourselves stories, or personal narratives, to explain to ourselves how the world works and where we belong. The downside is that some of the stories that our brains make up and that we believe to be true are actually complete and utter works of fiction.

We create these personal narratives out of our life experiences, and they can color our entire lives as our subconscious constantly searches for evidence that they are true and they feed into our continuous prediction process. Imagine a child who has been told that he was adopted as an infant. He may take this to mean that his birth mother didn't want him. He may take this one step further to mean that he is not wanted in general. He may take this another step further to mean that he is not good enough to be wanted. And that story can easily become a deeply held belief that freezes into his iceberg. Now, as an adult man, he may feel threatened when his interpretations of events make him feel unwanted or not good enough. Something as simple as not being invited to a meeting may kick-start his personal narrative about not being wanted and cause him to shift into protection.

Our brains also use predictions to interpret other people's emotions. When we think we are detecting someone else's feelings, it is actually our own brains making a guess based on our interpretation of that person's facial expression. But facial expressions have no intrinsic meaning. They can mean many different things depending on the circumstances. It is our meaning-making machines that attach a story to the other person's expression, based on the context and our past experiences.

We see this happen to Reshma when she observes Monika looking bored and disinterested. What she really sees is Monika panicking about her daughter. But behind the scenes, Reshma's brain is busy at work sifting through past experiences looking for a similar expression. When it finds one, it immediately attaches a meaning to it—bored. Then Reshma's brain creates the story around that emotion and tells her that Monika is bored with her because her work isn't good enough.

Because of her family history, this reinforces Reshma's subconscious idea that she is easy to overlook or ignore based on the personal narrative she has told herself throughout her life. This is exactly why Monika's reaction is so deeply threatening to Reshma. Her work is the one thing that she believes will help her stand out, and now that, too, is being ignored. Reshma subconsciously interprets this as a threat to her very identity.

To Reshma's subconscious brain, this is no different from a real threat to her existence, and it responds in kind. But we can see from the outside looking in that this threat does not actually exist. As we know, Monika is not displeased with Reshma's work. She is simply unable to pay attention. Reshma is in a high-stakes Familiar Zone situation. The presentation and its outcome are important, but she has the tools that she needs to succeed. However, her internal triggers prevent her from performing at her peak and instead shift her into protection.

Even when it comes to our personal narratives, our brains and bodies are intricately connected. In one experiment, researchers divided hotel room attendants into two groups. They told the members of one group that the work they did was good exercise and in line with the recommendations for an active lifestyle. They didn't tell the other group anything about their job or exercise or lifestyle. They measured the weight, blood pressure, body fat, and waist-to-hip ratio of both groups, instructed them not to make any lifestyle changes, and measured them again after four weeks. The group that was told their work was good exercise showed significantly different health outcomes. They simply perceived that they had gotten more exercise, and all of their health measures improved compared to those of the other group.[8]

According to Stephen Porges's polyvagal theory,[9] a central nerve called the vagus nerve runs from our brain stem to our gut and has many side branches. This nerve plays an essential role in regulating stress in our body in response to what is going on both inside and around us. The ventral vagal pathway, one of the vagus nerve's many branches, plays an important role in social engagement. It develops from a very young age, starting with the bond between mother and child. This pathway is connected with facial and mid-ear muscles and is quickly activated and engaged in social interactions when we pick up cues of safety. This process is called neuroception: the body scanning its environment for danger. In these situations, the vagus nerve has a positive regulating effect.

When we pick up cues that our life is in real danger, the dorsal vagal pathway is activated and engaged instead. This causes us to shut down, become numb, and disconnect from others. Importantly, these messages are not objective. They are again based on our instincts and conscious or unconscious interpretations and meanings that we attach to what is happening to us internally and externally. These are based on our personal narratives and past experiences.

Think about Reshma's stomachache. When Reshma feels her stomach begin to hurt, she tells herself the story that she is so stressed that it's literally making her sick. In this case, the stress not only exacerbates her feeling of nausea but also leads her to interpret that nauseous feeling as being entirely stress related. This in turn causes her to feel even more stressed. But of course, the story Reshma is telling herself may or may not be true. Perhaps she is simply coming down with a stomach bug.

Our interpretations both affect and are affected by our awareness. When we are in a state of protection like Reshma was, our awareness is fully absorbed in the experience. But when we are able to keep part of our attention in external observer mode, we gain a more objective awareness of the reality of the situation, how we are interpreting the situation, how the situation is affecting us internally, and vice versa.

In reality, Reshma has no idea why her stomach hurts, but her brain interprets the signals it receives to mean that she is in danger. Then when she runs into Monika in the cafeteria later, she feels that stomachache again because her brain predicts that a similar threatening situation is going to unfold. Of course, this prediction that her encounter with Monika is going to go badly turns into a self-fulfilling prophecy.

Indeed, many of our personal narratives go on to become self-fulfilling prophecies. Just look at the story Reshma tells herself about Monika being disinterested and disappointed in her work. While this is not initially the case at all, it becomes true because of how Reshma reacts to the situation from a state of protection. And she keeps herself in that state by continuing to look for evidence that her story about Monika's disengagement is true.

If Reshma had practiced Dual Awareness, she would have been able to look down at herself during her presentation through that skylight in the ceiling. She may have noticed how checked out Monika seemed to be and how nervous and desperate she felt to engage her. And she might have become aware of the story she was telling herself about why Monika was tuned out. This could have opened her mind to new possibilities.

If Reshma had left that initial meeting and told herself, *There may be five different reasons that Monika seemed so disinterested. I won't make any assumptions and will just leave it open for now,* the entire outcome could have been different. When she encountered Monika in the cafeteria later, she likely wouldn't be so nervous and act so awkwardly and defensively about her work. Maybe she would be able to calmly ask Monika about what had happened during their meeting. And if Reshma was able to react differently, then Monika, whose brain is making up its own stories about Reshma's reaction in the cafeteria, might not assume that the project is way off course.

LEARNING AND DOPAMINE

Another chemical that plays an important role in our ability to learn and adapt is the neurotransmitter dopamine. But instead of activating a stress response, dopamine is associated with feelings of pleasure and motivation. It is a key part of our brain's reward process. When something positive happens, dopamine is released, it feels good, and we are motivated to keep going.

Based on what we know about our brain's prediction process, we can use dopamine to help us access a state of learning. We are now aware that as far as our brains are concerned, there is no such thing as an objective "good" thing that can happen to us and stimulate dopamine release. Anything can be good or bad, depending on how we look at it, and we create these positive moments based on our own interpretations.

We can leverage Deliberate Calm skills like intentionally adopting a mindset of gratitude around whatever challenges we are facing to increase our dopamine levels and, along with them, the energy we need to continue learning. Or, if we are working on a long-term project, celebrating milestones along the way can lead to dopamine release, which can give us the motivation we need to keep going. Truly enjoying and embracing challenges and viewing them as opportunities to learn also leads to an increase in dopamine and has the positive benefit of changing the predictions we will make the next time we are in a similar situation.

However, when we constantly chase excitement and accomplishments without sufficient recovery time, we deplete our resources by putting our dopamine levels in imbalance. After a big accomplishment and the feelings of excitement that come with it, we often experience a low. This is the result of our dopamine rebalancing, and it is a sign that we need to recover. If we keep chasing the high instead, it can be dangerously addictive.[10]

CHANGING THE NARRATIVE

The outcome of Reshma's story is unfortunate, but having an understanding of what is going on in her brain and body as it unfolds reveals the many moments when she could have intervened to shift into learning instead of protection.

We can learn to pivot from protection to learning by changing our personal narratives and opening our minds to new interpretations. This helps us to perceive fewer things as threatening. When we melt our icebergs and update our mindsets and the thoughts and feelings they drive, we can make better predictions. Our past, our personal narratives, and our emotions no longer control us, and we gain the power to change them.

Developing our Dual Awareness is also key. In neuroscience, exteroception, broadly defined, is our sensitivity to stimuli originating outside the body, and interoception is our sensitivity to stimuli originating inside the body.[11, 12] At the heart of Dual Awareness lies the integration of both exteroception and interoception. The more we practice observing what is going on in our minds and bodies and how this relates to the circumstances and environment around us, the better we can objectively understand what we are reacting to and *why*. This also enables us to detach from those thoughts and feelings and simply accept them or, even better, reframe them.

Most of the time, we are not even aware of our personal narratives and the predictions we are unconsciously making. Yet, they are constantly shaping our thoughts, our feelings, our emotions, and how we are experiencing our lives. A large piece of Deliberate Calm is *becoming aware* of our personal narratives and getting ourselves into a state where we can offer ourselves alternative options.

With Deliberate Calm, Reshma could have created an intention for how she wanted to show up and perform before the meeting. During the meeting, when she found herself shifting into protection, she could have paused and reframed. For instance, instead of thinking, *"I'm feeling stressed because this is a disaster,"* Reshma could have told herself, *"I am nervous, but I'm also excited because this meeting is important to me."* This simple shift could have made all the difference because, by framing the stress in a positive context, it could reduce the feelings of threat. The same thing happens when we are able to tap into our sense of purpose and connect it to the challenges we are facing.

Even holding on to the idea that Reshma *might* have been safe would have opened up space for learning because it would have led her to become curious instead of attaching to only one possible outcome. This in and of itself would have calmed down her nervous system enough for her to perform well even under stress.

Imagine what could have happened differently if Reshma had been aware of what was happening to her internally. She might have thought, *"I am telling myself a story about what is happening, but it might not be right. I don't have facts that say for sure that Monika doesn't like my presentation. I'm making an assumption."*

With that awareness, she may have chosen to pause and take a deep breath and consciously and intentionally adopt a mindset of curiosity and safety. Then she could have thought, *"Okay, I'm fine, but I still wonder what's going on right now."* She might have been calm enough to explore various options in her own mind with the openness and curiosity that best serve her. Then she could have decided to act.

"Monika," she might have said, "you look distracted to me right now, and I was assuming it was because you didn't like my presentation, and I was starting to feel really nervous. But maybe it's something else. I thought I would ask. Is this going okay for you? Should we do this some other time, or is there something I could do differently that you might find more engaging or useful?"

We'll never know for sure what Monika would have thought or said in response, but it's likely that she would have acknowledged to Reshma that she was distracted for personal reasons and suggested that they reschedule the presentation. When that day came, Reshma's brain would likely not have predicted that she was under threat because her feelings of safety would have become the new set point for this situation. She also could have reflected on what happened after the meeting and gained insight that would hopefully avoid the same downward spiraling pattern when she later saw Monika in the cafeteria.

While our brains may at times work against us by telling us stories that are fiction, they also have an amazing capacity to learn and grow. Learning happens when new connections are made between neurons. If the personal narratives that we repeatedly tell ourselves about our worth, our identity, and the world around us are like the well-worn grooves of a record playing over and over in our brains, then new stories, new interpretations, and new perspectives can etch in an infinite number of alternate options. This opens us up to a whole new world, where we are no longer limited by our standard tunes.

In this more open state, we are excited and positive, yet may still feel stressed. If those two things sound mutually exclusive, think about your state of mind when you were a child learning to ride a bike with your parent's hand holding on securely so that you wouldn't fall. Even after your parent let go, you weren't aware of it at first, so you were able to ride on feeling safe. You were still under some stress. Riding a bike was new and a little bit scary, but knowing that you were ultimately safe allowed you to learn and made that stress positive and even playful.

In this state of learning, the nervous system and the ventral vagus pathway, which primes the body for social engagement, are both active. In this state, we can connect with others, we can entertain multiple outcomes and options, we can experiment, we can learn, and we can remain engaged even when we are under stress. In this state, we can take more control of our performance and act as our own parent with one hand holding firmly on our metaphorical bicycle, giving ourselves the safety and freedom to soar.

WHAT IS YOUR STORY?

An important and difficult part of Deliberate Calm is becoming aware of the personal narratives that you are telling yourself. Of course, they don't seem like stories. They seem like the objective truth. But by offering yourself alternatives, you can begin to see that the truth isn't usually so black and white after all.

The next time you are feeling a little bit stressed, anxious, frustrated, angry, or agitated in general, pause and take a deep breath. Then ask yourself the following questions:

- What story am I telling myself about what is happening right now?
- What story am I telling myself about what has happened in the past that led up to this moment?
- What story am I telling myself about what might happen in the future as a result of this moment?

Now, take a moment to explore one alternative story. It doesn't have to be the opposite of the story you were previously telling yourself. It just has to be different. It might help to start by thinking, "Maybe instead, what's actually happening is . . ." Perhaps take a moment to write this new story down. Whatever comes up is okay. Don't judge yourself.

If you repeat this whenever you start to feel yourself shifting into protection, your personal narratives will begin having less and less of a hold on you, and you will be able to respond to new situations out of curiosity instead of reacting out of fear.

PART II

THE DELIBERATE CALM WAY

CHAPTER 4

WHAT LIES BENEATH

*No problem can be solved by the same
consciousness that created it.*
—ALBERT EINSTEIN

The executive team of a global energy company was in a remote location going through a two-day review of their top fifty people. One by one, the executive team went through all fifty of their most senior people, looking at their performance and leadership behavior with the goal of calibrating them against one another and as input for career development and succession decisions.

Near the end of the first day, two of the four leaders had already discussed their people and received input and feedback from their colleagues. Now it was Mary's turn. Mary was the head of a large European region for the company and had been working there for almost ten years. As soon as the team began their discussions of "her" people, the atmosphere changed. What had consistently been an open dialogue focused on objectively surfacing the strengths and development needs of their top fifty people suddenly turned a bit more tense.

One by one, Mary presented her people. "Drew has been with the company for two years," she began. "He is one of the stars of my team. Everyone loves him, and I think he has real leadership potential. We should definitely consider him for a promotion next year."

"Drew did a project for me last quarter," said Tony, one of Mary's colleagues on the executive committee. "He missed some key deadlines and then was slow in solving the issues. I think he needs to work on his ability to deliver and get better at making commitments he can stand behind."

"I wouldn't worry about that too much," Mary replied quickly. "I have seen him do this really well in other projects. Your observation is such an anomaly. Something else must have been going on." Tony, clearly annoyed, shook his head and looked out the window. Everyone else in the room was quiet. Mary simply moved on to her next person.

A similar dynamic played out again and again. Mary painted a very positive picture of most of the people on her team and their performance and did not seem open to any input. When her colleagues provided feedback and tried to calibrate their performance with the other candidates', she grew defensive, dismissed their observations and feedback, and insisted that her people should be rated in the top performance category. In Mary's opinion, about two-thirds of her people were in the "outperform" category compared with the rest of the top fifty people.

As this went on, the meeting grew more and more tense, and her colleagues became visibly frustrated by the fact that Mary was so openly pushing her own people. She wasn't really listening to what anyone else had to say, and apparently they were not able to have an objective, fact-based discussion about her people's performance. This made the last two hours of an already long day feel quite draining.

This behavior was not abnormal for Mary. She often jumped in to defend the people in her organization when they showed up in meetings or shared their work with the executive team. Some of them liked this because they felt supported. But it led to frustration on the part of other leaders in the organization who were eager to step up and take care of business themselves.

Over drinks that evening, the tension among the executive committee members eased up a bit as some of her colleagues lightly poked fun at Mary's behavior. Her colleague Kim said, "You have to tell us how you were able to attract all of the top performers from our top fifty to your department. What's your secret?" Mary looked at Kim, appearing a bit puzzled. Kim quickly continued, "I've got to give it to you, you really go to bat for your people. My team would love it if I fought for them the way you do. Not to mention my kids!"

Kim may or may not have been aware of it, but Mary did in fact act similarly protective with her teenage daughter, Tanya. For example, Tanya was the only one of her peers whose mother was still dropping her off and picking her up at parties to make sure she was safe. Mary's husband, Dave, was much more relaxed when it came to raising their daughter, and this disparity between them was a frequent source of tension in Mary and Dave's relationship and sometimes with Tanya, as well.

Mary's behavior as both a leader and a mother seemed to be having unintended consequences with her executive committee colleagues, her team members, and her family. It appeared that she was in a state of protection even though she was operating in the Familiar Zone, and her protection behaviors were stifling healthy dialogue, debate, and collaboration. But if she was in a safe and familiar environment, what was triggering Mary to feel threatened and shift into protection? In this case, Mary's triggers were internal, rooted in the layers deep below the waterline of her iceberg.

Yet Mary was not practiced in Dual Awareness, so she was not conscious of what zone she was in, what the situation called for, what had triggered her into protection, and whether or not her current behaviors best served her in this environment. The layers of her iceberg were just as unknown to her as they were to the people around her. But that was about to change.

LAYERS OF THE ICEBERG

As you read earlier, we find it helpful to think of the iceberg as structured with four interacting layers. These layers provide the ingredients for the self-reinforcing personal narratives that we unconsciously tell ourselves to make sense of the world and to guide our behavior to get our needs met. With awareness, we can become conscious of all four layers of the iceberg and how they reinforce one another in order to gain awareness, shift our patterns, and derive better results.

Thoughts and Feelings

A coach named Tomas was sitting in on the executive team meetings as a source of support. The next morning, he sat down with Mary at breakfast before the second day's session to reflect on what he had observed the day before. First, he asked Mary what she thought about the fact that, based on her assessments, 80 percent of her people appeared to be in the outperform category. She reflected on this, and in the quiet of the breakfast room she had to admit that it was indeed unlikely that she had such a disproportionate number of outperformers on her team.

After explaining the iceberg model to Mary, Tomas asked if she would be comfortable diving underneath the waterline of her iceberg with him to see what was down there, driving her behavior. She was very interested in personal growth and development, and she agreed right away.

Tomas and Mary had already pinpointed which behavior Mary wanted to move away from—promoting and defending her people without listening to feedback and criticism. Mary shared that this was not the first time she had received this feedback, but she had not been able to change it so far. Next, he asked her to consider what behavior she would like to move to, instead. How would she have preferred to show up in the calibration meeting with the executive team?

After some discussion, Mary said that she wanted to be a team player and get to a fair assessment of the top fifty people in the organization. According to her, this meant listening to her colleagues and getting different data points for all the people so they could objectively compare them to one another.

This was the behavior that Mary *wanted* to model. It was clear to Tomas that she had not been modeling it, at least not in the meeting he observed. Tomas asked if her behavior in the meeting was in line with her goals, and Mary quickly realized that it was not. "I jumped in to defend my people and found myself continuously pushing back on my colleagues' input."

Next, Tomas asked Mary what she had been feeling when Tony was providing feedback on Drew. Right away, she said, "I felt frustrated. And a little bit angry." Then he asked what she was thinking at the time. *"Drew is a good guy, he's being unfairly attacked, and I am not going to let this happen. Why doesn't Tony focus on the people in his own department? There is so much dysfunction among his team, and now he's making comments about our work?"*

These types of thoughts are commonly referred to as our "self-talk," or the tape in our heads that constantly plays in a loop. Often without realizing it, we repeat the same thoughts so often that, to a large extent, they determine our reality. We have thousands upon thousands of thoughts a day, and many of them are repetitive.

Our thoughts and feelings are highly personal. It is unlikely that two people in the same situation would ever be thinking or feeling the exact same things. To us, they feel not only reasonable but completely obvious. To a large extent, this is because our thoughts and feelings support and reinforce each other.

For example, there was no reason for Mary to question her negative thoughts about Tony's criticism of Drew, as her feelings of frustration and anger supported those thoughts. In her mind, *of course*, she was thinking about what Tony did wrong—after all, she had to be feeling angry and frustrated for a reason. At the same time, her negative self-talk justified her feelings of frustration and anger. *Of course* she was feeling angry and frustrated—just look at all the things that Tony was doing wrong!

Because of this self-reinforcing loop, it would never have occurred to Mary to feel or think or react any differently when Tony was providing input about Drew. If she was justifiably angry and frustrated and her team member was being unfairly attacked, then *of course* she would react defensively. Her feelings and her self-talk drove her behavior of fighting for and defending her team members.

Psychologist Susan David's work on emotional agility shows that it is often helpful to deepen our emotional awareness beyond superficial "umbrella" feelings like angry, happy, or sad, and to get more into the nuances of the specific emotions that lie beneath.[1] For instance, if someone is experiencing anxiety, the deeper emotion we experience might be confused, worried, afraid, vulnerable, or cautious, or some combination of these. Gaining mastery of Dual Awareness often means diving deeper into our emotional experience.

As for Mary, she could have been feeling and thinking any number of things in that moment. For instance, she could have felt curious and thought, *"What a great opportunity. Tony is really experienced in this area. Maybe he has some useful feedback for me."* Or she could have felt disappointed and thought, *"Drew really didn't do very well that time. What can he learn from this?"*

Either of these might have made sense given the circumstances. Why did Mary instead experience the feelings and thoughts that she did? Our feelings and thoughts are not objective, but they are not random, either. They come from the next level down in our icebergs.

Mindsets and Beliefs

Now that Mary was aware of both her actual and her desired behavior and the thoughts and feelings that supported them, Tomas had to go one level deeper in her iceberg and help her explore her mindsets and beliefs about leadership and protecting people. He could tell that Mary was operating from a potentially limiting mindset that was leading to her feelings, thoughts, and behavior and creating unintended consequences in situations like this. She was so focused on defending her team members that she wasn't able to listen to and work with her colleagues to objectively assess the performance of her people against the others. She had also lost the opportunity to fully explore what specifically Tony might have been concerned about and how to potentially work with Drew to address those concerns. This would have given him a better chance at getting the promotion. So, in focusing on promoting and defending her people, Mary was unwittingly holding them back.

Tomas asked Mary what she believed about leadership that led her to behave the way she did during the executive committee meeting. This took a bit more time and reflection, as is often the case. The third level of the iceberg, where we hold our default mindsets and our unconscious beliefs about how the world works, requires deeper inquiry to become visible, even to us. These mindsets serve as the lenses that we use to view ourselves and the world around us. They are the core building blocks of our personal narratives and are made of the underlying assumptions and private logic that color how we see and experience things.

We develop our mindsets over the course of our lives. Our childhoods leave a big imprint, combined with the cultures we grow up in and our life experiences. Together, these elements hardwire our beliefs about how we can get our needs met and avoid getting hurt. These beliefs encompass not just the current reality and its implications but also what has happened in the past and why, what we predict might happen in the future, and what our roles and responsibilities are. When we encounter a situation, our mindsets help us quickly interpret it, influence what we think and feel about it, and ultimately drive our behavior.

We cannot overstate the impact that our mindsets can have on our behavior and the results we generate in every area of our lives. Consider this: humans can receive sensory perception of over 11 million bits of information from the environment every second, but our minds can only process around 50 bits per second.[2] That is a tiny fraction of 1 percent of the information that is potentially available to us. And we consciously register, make sense of, and remember far less than that.

What determines which information we process versus what we ignore? Which information we focus on and interpret and remember versus which information we barely notice at all? When we thoughtfully process information versus when we take subconscious mental shortcuts, opening us up to biases? It turns out that our underlying mindsets sitting at layer three of our icebergs play an enormous role in shaping which information we pay attention to in the first place and how we interpret that information. In other words, our mindset is the lens through which we see the world, and it forms a filter that allows certain experiences and data in and leaves others out.

Our mindsets are essential in helping us simplify and shortcut decision-making in a complex world. We would not get very far in life trying to make sense of the 11 million bits of information that are being thrown at us each and every second. But because they offer an incomplete and subjective view of reality, our mindsets can easily lead to blind spots. These are things that we literally cannot see about ourselves, others, and our reality because our mindsets filter them out. Operating with blind spots and therefore unable to see the whole picture often leads to unintended consequences.

This is what happened to Mary. Her mindset had created a blind spot that was keeping her from being more open to the executive committee's feedback and less rigid in her defense of her people. To explore the mindset that had created this blind spot, Tomas asked Mary to reflect on how she thought about herself in her role as a leader in relation to her people, taking the discussion about Drew as an example. Mary thought about this for a while. They were getting into some underlying mindsets that she wasn't fully conscious of. Finally she said, "I guess I see myself as a good leader when I take care of my people and protect them. In my mind, doing right by them means that if they do their job, they will be taken care of, and it's my job as their leader to fight for them in every way possible."

As a result of this perspective, Mary looked at her people with an eye toward how she could take care of them, and she looked at herself as the one person who was responsible for making sure they did not get hurt. In this case, it was clear that while she believed that developing her people was important, she habitually prioritized protecting them instead.

"So," Tomas clarified, "you are their champion, and your main job is to keep the team safe." This was an interesting interpretation. By being the champion who made sure that her people were successful and did not fail, it almost sounded like *Mary* was the person who was accountable for Drew and the others and whether or not they were successful. She also defined successful leadership as helping her people avoid getting hurt.

Now her behavior made more sense, while before it had been somewhat baffling. Any leader who embraced that mindset would have reacted the way Mary did in the meeting when Drew's work was being questioned by an executive team member. Just imagine how different our lives would be if our entire icebergs were visible, not just to ourselves but also to the people around us.

Of course, we are not the only ones viewing reality through the limitations of our hidden icebergs. Everyone is, with each one shaped by our own individual experiences, cultures, needs, and fears. And many of us are living under the illusion that the way we see the world on any particular topic is the right one, and therefore objectively true. When we are in a state of protection, we are not able to change and learn with an open mind. As we interact with others while we are in this state, we should not be surprised that we encounter misunderstandings and conflict. These are often the results of two different icebergs bumping into each other, or two opposing worldviews colliding. This all happens invisibly, without either person able to see the iceberg on the other side.

If our waterlines freeze in a protective reaction when this happens, then we will harden our stance and react in ways that reinforce our existing views and beliefs. In this state, little exchange or growth can happen. If in those moments, however, we can accept and acknowledge our limited view, learn from the experiences of others, and try to see things through their lens, we will expand our view of the world and solve far more complex problems than we ever could on our own.

Mary's mindset was not good or bad, and in many cases it had served her well as a leader. People wanted to work for her, and she had a good reputation. But in this case, it had led her to alienate herself from the executive committee and had prevented her from getting a realistic view of her people's performance, development, and growth opportunities.

Tomas asked Mary to try to think of an alternative mindset that she could operate from in situations like this that would help her behave in the way she wanted: to listen to her colleagues and be a team player to get to a fair assessment of the top fifty people in the organization. "What would you need to believe in order to behave in that way?"

It took some time, but after a great deal of thought, Mary finally said, "To be an effective leader, I need to make sure that my people get an objective view of their performance, are exposed to growth challenges, and learn from their mistakes." Indeed, if Mary operated from this mindset, it would lead her to feel, think, and act very differently in the moment. She told Tomas that she would feel curious to see how her people managed their challenges and confident that they could handle it while remaining ready to offer coaching when needed. Her new self-talk would be, *This is their turn to shine. I wonder how they'll do. If they struggle or it doesn't work out, it will be a great opportunity for them to learn and grow.* And the behaviors that these feelings and thoughts would drive would be listening to feedback from colleagues, evaluating her people's performance as objectively as possible, and without overcoaching or micromanaging, providing them with challenges that would allow them to learn and grow.

By exhibiting these behaviors, Mary would send the message to her people that she believed they were capable of managing the challenges that came with their jobs and could still get her support when they needed it. Mary would become more of a growth leader, and the potential impact this could have on her team was huge.

Whether or not we are aware of it, we all operate from default mindsets that filter and color everything we experience. We hear, "History repeats itself," and now we can begin to understand why. Like Mary's, our default mindsets aren't necessarily good or bad, but when they exist entirely outside of our awareness, they can be limiting in certain situations.

In the Familiar Zone, the existing mindsets that worked well for us in the past usually continue to serve us as we address known challenges—unless, of course, we, like Mary, are triggered by something within our icebergs. In the Adaptive Zone, our default mindsets are often not effective at addressing the challenge at hand and can act as a big derailer of progress. First we must learn to manage our icebergs to stay out of the protection state when we are in the Familiar Zone. Then we can do the more difficult work of doing so in the Adaptive Zone, where transformation really happens.

All of us can and often do shift into a state of protection many times a day. It is impossible to prevent this, and there is nothing inherently wrong with reacting this way. It is normal and natural to feel threatened at times, even in a safe and familiar environment. The problem, however, is that we cannot adapt or learn in this state, and we give up our leadership when we react with default behaviors instead of choosing the most appropriate response given our current context. Instead, we have an opportunity to become aware of the moments when we shift into protection and *why* so that we are able to make a choice that helps shift us back out.

This is where Dual Awareness comes in. With Dual Awareness, Mary could have recognized that her feelings of anger and frustration in the meeting were signs that she was potentially in a state of protection with limited ability to have an open mind and true collaboration. She also would have recognized the underlying mindset and beliefs that she was operating from in this particular conversation. Then she would be at choice to adopt a different mindset and the thoughts, feelings, and behaviors that would go along with it. In other words, she could have switched out the lens through which she was seeing the world to take in a different view. When we do this, feelings of discomfort can become one of our gateways into a state of learning.

When we have time to go deep, we can gain a new arsenal of mindsets or lenses, and with them, more options about how to view the world and creatively respond to different life and leadership challenges. These new lenses each have their own filters and allow in an entirely new range of experiences, information, and interpretations of what is happening and the roles we might play in any given situation.

With these alternative mindsets, we are able to add formerly invisible nuance and complexity to our perception of reality. Previously invisible possibilities and outcomes reveal themselves. And we can see the blind spots that were previously unknown to us. Over time, as we practice operating from our new mindsets, we can rewire our neural connections so that our new mindsets and beliefs are embedded into our more fluid and adaptable icebergs. And we can gain increasing awareness of what is lurking beneath the surface at any given moment.

PROTECTION MINDSETS VERSUS LEARNING MINDSETS

While there is an infinite number of mindsets and variations thereof that we can operate from, there are specific mindsets that either keep us in the status quo or open our thought and behavior patterns to learning and innovation. While status quo mindsets may be useful when we are in the Familiar Zone, they often do not serve us in the Adaptive Zone. When the situation calls for it, it is possible to shift from a status quo mindset to a learning mindset.

As you read about these various mindsets, think about a challenge you recently faced. Which mindset or mindsets did you naturally gravitate toward at the time? Once you identify your default mindsets, you can ask yourself questions to open your mental lens to a new way of looking at things.

FIXED VERSUS GROWTH

Much has been written about fixed versus growth mindsets. When we are operating from a fixed mindset, we believe that our skills and intelligence are unchangeable. This means that if we can't do or aren't good at certain things, that will always be the case. When we are operating from a growth mindset, however, we believe that we can develop our intelligence and gain new skills over time.

If you find that you are operating from a fixed mindset, ask yourself:

- How can this challenge be an opportunity?
- What could be possible if I learn and develop from this experience?

EXPERT VERSUS CURIOUS

With an expert mindset, we believe that we should already have all the information and skills we need to tackle our current challenges and perform. This is a status quo mindset that can serve us well at times when we are in the Familiar Zone. But with a curious mindset, we are willing to ask questions, explore, and discover. We are eager to learn from trying something new in a state of learning.

If you find that you are operating from an expert mindset when it would better serve you to be in a learning mindset, ask yourself:

- What questions, new perspectives, or opportunities do I want to explore?

- If I approach this with fresh eyes, forgetting for now what I already know, what would I get curious about?
- What would be possible if I could embrace the struggles that come with learning something new?

REACTIVE VERSUS CREATIVE

When we are operating from a reactive mindset, we approach problems with existing, tested, well-practiced solutions. This can be a fitting mindset for certain Familiar Zone situations. With a creative mindset, however, we lead with purpose, empower ourselves and others to explore new possibilities, and experiment our way to innovative solutions.

If you find that you are operating with a reactive mindset in the Adaptive Zone, ask yourself:

- What is the bigger "why" that I am solving for?
- If this challenge were actually a hidden opportunity to create something different and better, what would I want? What could I imagine that would be important and meaningful?
- What is the smallest step that I can take toward getting to the end state I desire?

VICTIM VERSUS AGENT

With a victim mindset, we have an external locus of control. We believe that there are many factors outside our influence that determine our ability to thrive, grow, and get things done. In other words, we are victims of circumstance. With an agent mindset, we maintain an inner locus of control. We know that within reason, we have the ability to try new things, overcome challenges, and accomplish whatever we put our minds to.

If you find that you are operating from a victim mindset, ask yourself:

- What are the various ways I can influence the situation?
- What do I already have going for me? What capabilities, ideas, or resources could I access to successfully navigate this challenge?

SCARCITY VERSUS ABUNDANCE

When we operate from a scarcity mindset, we believe that resources are limited and challenges typically involve hard choices and trade-offs. With an abundance mindset, we see that resources are plentiful and do not need to be competed for. Challenges are potentially win-win situations looking to be discovered. This is an especially useful mindset to adopt when facing a negotiation.

If you find that you are operating from a scarcity mindset, ask yourself:

- What could be a win-win scenario in this situation?
- If I release some of the constraints on the situation, what might be a bigger opportunity?

CERTAINTY VERSUS EXPLORATION

With a certainty mindset, we want to be sure of the path before us. We would rather have things go according to plan than take a detour that might take us to an even better place in the end. With an exploration mindset, we are open to possibilities outside our original plan. We do not know what the future holds, so we believe that the best way to succeed is to plan ahead but remain flexible and curious as we go, keeping our eyes open for unforeseen opportunities.

If you find yourself operating from a certainty mindset, ask yourself:

- What is the smallest thing I can do to try out a different approach and learn fast?
- What are three other perspectives on potential solutions to this problem?

SAFEGUARD VERSUS OPPORTUNITY

With a safeguard mindset, our focus is on preventing something bad from happening. Mary is operating from a safeguard mindset when she jumps in to defend her team. With an opportunity mindset, we are looking for potential opportunities instead of possible pitfalls and believe that we can make something great happen.

If you find yourself operating from a safeguard mindset when it doesn't serve you, ask yourself:

- What if this is not a risk-avoidance scenario but an opportunity-capturing scenario?
- What is the most audaciously good thing that can come out of this?
- How might I be able to encourage that to happen?

Core Identity

After the second day of meetings, Tomas held a "storytelling dinner" with Mary and the rest of the executive team to try to foster connection between them and encourage them to open up and be vulnerable with one another. Each of them went around the table and shared stories about people or events that played an important role in shaping themselves and their lives. These are always inspiring and intimate dinners where team members get to know one another on a more personal level.

When it was Mary's turn, she told the team about her younger brother, Carl. Carl was her only sibling, and he was born with a mild disability. He attended the same local public school as Mary, where he was often bullied and picked on. When he entered the school, Mary was two grades ahead of him. She saw her brother being bullied, and this made her feel very angry. Right away, she started to interfere and jump in to defend Carl whenever she saw it happening. Mary got herself into quite a few fights and skirmishes as a result. But her parents never punished Mary for fighting. On the contrary, they were grateful that she was there to defend Carl and gave her a lot of positive reinforcement for coming to his aid.

Protecting Carl became second nature to Mary. She not only started to look out for him at the schoolyard but also tried to keep him out of harm's way in other parts of his life. Along the way, Mary created a personal narrative around protecting her brother. It appeared that this experience had shaped her purpose and values and had become frozen in the very foundational layer of her iceberg.

This bottom layer of our icebergs holds our values, needs (both met and unmet), hopes, dreams, and sense of purpose. These factors together form our core identity. For Mary, being Carl's protector became an important part of her core identity as a loving sister and daughter.

The human mind is so beautifully complex. As she told her story at dinner, it was the first time Mary connected the dots between this story from her early childhood and the behavior she exhibited as a leader defending her team members forty years later.

This bottom layer of the iceberg is the hardest to access and the most difficult to change. And while it's often helpful to gain awareness around the roots of our icebergs, it is not always necessary to do so in order to shift our mindsets and transform our cycle of feelings, thoughts, and behaviors. Like Mary's, our core identities often go back to our early childhood experiences. If these experiences were traumatic, then it is best to explore them with a licensed therapist. Otherwise, gaining awareness around our default mindsets and subconscious beliefs and making intentional shifts is often enough to make a transformational shift. In our work, we normally focus on the mindset and belief level with an aim to unlock clients' potential, increase their awareness and choice, and expand the pattern of results they generate.

After the retreat, Mary wanted to sit down with her team and tell them openly and vulnerably about the insight she had experienced around her childhood and how it had affected her protective leadership style. "I want to become more of a growth leader," Mary told them. "If you see me acting overprotective, please mention it to me. I'm not always aware that I'm doing it." As she spoke, several members of her team smiled at each other in recognition. It was as if they could not believe that Mary was finally acknowledging the behavior they had been talking about among themselves for years.

After that, things got off to a good start. Mary began allowing her team to take more risks and accept greater responsibility. Before board meetings, she didn't overprepare and coach them as much as she used to, and instead she let them rise to challenges on their own. It was gratifying for her to see that most of the time, they were able to succeed.

Of course, there were moments when Mary shifted into a state of protection and felt the urge to jump in to defend a team member's work or to prevent them from taking a risk. But with awareness, she was able to take a breath and remind herself that her new mindset was a better fit for her goals in this moment and better served her team's growth and development.

Over time, Mary's new opportunity mindset extended outside the office and to her family. One night, when her daughter, Tanya, asked Mary to drive her to a party, she responded, "Why don't you just ride your bike over instead?"

"It's late, though," Tanya said, accustomed to Mary's protectiveness. "I know you don't want me riding in the dark and coming home late by myself."

"I think you can handle it," Mary said with a smile. Slowly, a smile spread across Tanya's face, too. She was thrilled that her mother believed in her enough to let her take this small risk.

FROM-TO

This exercise will help you begin to gain some awareness around what is hidden in your iceberg and how it is affecting your current patterns of behavior and results. Then, you can start to form a new iceberg with a learning mindset that will drive more effective thoughts, feelings, and behaviors.

First, think about a business challenge you are currently facing. It is helpful if this is a problem that keeps coming up or an area in which you feel stuck, but it can also be a onetime issue with a boss or colleague, a difficult problem you are trying to solve, or a decision you are struggling to make. Once you have the challenge in mind, imagine yourself in that situation, dealing with it in the moment. Then ask yourself the following questions:

FROM:

- What behaviors am I exhibiting that are not working? What am I actually doing regarding this issue that is visible to others? (This is the behavior you want to move away from.)
- If I continue exhibiting these behaviors, what will likely be the end result?
- What feelings came up when I imagined myself in that situation?
- What thoughts came up? What was my uncensored self-talk?
- Which of my values are at play in this situation? Is there a conflict in priorities among any of these values?

- What do I believe about myself and my role that is leading to these thoughts and feelings?

TO:

- What is a more empowering belief that could also be true about myself and my role?
- Would it be helpful to prioritize a different one of my values in this situation to support this new belief?
- If I imagine myself back in this situation with a newly prioritized value and/or a different belief about myself and my role, what feelings and thoughts come up? How are these different from before?
- What behaviors would I naturally exhibit based on these thoughts and feelings?
- If I continued showing up in this new way, what would likely be the result?

Hopefully, this has helped you begin to uncover one or more blind spots that are holding you back from your desired results. The final step is to find moments to practice the new behavior that you wish to exhibit. The more you do this, the more you will be able to rewrite the personal narrative embedded in your iceberg and create a new pattern of results.

CHAPTER 5

PURPOSE

THE ROOT OF YOUR ICEBERG

If you want to build a ship, don't herd people
together to collect wood and assign them
tasks and work, but rather teach them to
long for the endless immensity of the sea.
—ANTOINE DE SAINT-EXUPÉRY

It was late in the evening, and Daniel, a senior executive at a nutritional foods company, sat in a stuffy conference room in Southern California as a consultant named Kimberly challenged his mindset about leadership. "Why do they need to agree with you?" Kimberly asked him. "Why do you need to know the answer?"

Inside, Daniel was feeling incredibly irritated. He was thinking, *Why can't she see my point?* He simply wanted to find a solution and solve his current problem. Why was that so difficult for her to understand?

Kimberly did understand where Daniel was coming from and saw that he was stuck. Daniel had built his whole career operating from a strong set of beliefs about how to succeed and what good leadership required. In the past, Daniel had been successful as an action-oriented problem solver. He delivered results by knowing how to come up with the right answer and then rallying others around that solution. But now this approach and the underlying mindsets that drove it were no longer working for him.

In fact, Daniel's mindsets around leadership and how to navigate challenging situations were limiting his ability to handle his current business crisis. Daniel wanted help, but he was mainly looking for tactics to get to an answer and to convince the other people in his organization to change their approaches. First, Daniel himself had to change.

Up to this point, Daniel's career had followed a consistent upward trajectory. He had joined a blue-chip global consumer goods company straight out of college. Daniel had been climbing the ladder to success for more than two decades. This ladder took him from marketing to sales to general management and from his birthplace in Europe to sunny California, where he had joined the executive team of a rapidly growing company that manufactured and sold vitamins, prepackaged meals and snacks, diet products, and nutritional supplements. Most of their success was in the United States, but they were beginning to take off internationally as well.

When he was first offered the role of chief marketing officer (CMO) of the company, Daniel wasn't sure that he wanted to take it. He didn't feel a personal connection to the company's products or mission, but it was a step up and ultimately too good an offer to refuse. Daniel tried to get excited about the business and knew that he would enjoy the creative and entrepreneurial aspects of the job. He was always up for the next big move, especially if it came with big challenges. That's where he shined.

And challenges there were, but Daniel had the skills he needed to solve them, and for a while he remained mostly in a high-stakes Familiar Zone in a state of high performance. The parent company had paid a premium for this company because of its tremendous growth potential. When Daniel joined as CMO, the team increased their marketing spend, pushed aggressively into international markets and adjacent customer segments, and invested in new manufacturing facilities and distribution networks to become less dependent on third-party suppliers. The company also hired a lot more people to handle the projected growth.

At first, this plan worked. Despite aggressive growth targets, they were exceeding them each and every quarter. The business experienced double-digit growth each year and rolled out in many new countries around the world. It was a success story, and leaders from the parent company started flying in to learn how they had so quickly achieved such remarkable growth.

Even though he was by far the youngest member of the executive team and the other executives had all been there before the acquisition, Daniel felt accepted and respected by his colleagues. They had fun and worked well together. In his personal life, Daniel was also in a good place. His family, including his wife and their three young children, had adapted well to the California lifestyle. Daniel was particularly enjoying the opportunities to be outdoors and play sports. Overall, life was good.

Then everything changed. One of the company's top competitors came out with a new set of products based on what they claimed were game-changing scientific breakthroughs, and their philosophy and products were garnering an almost cultlike following. The competitor was successfully executing an aggressive promotional campaign aimed directly at the business Daniel had been building. Consumers voted with their purchases, and within only a couple of months, Daniel saw his company's double-digit growth turn into double-digit decline. The bottom had suddenly dropped out of the business. Revenue not only continued to decline, but the speed of the decline kept picking up over time. Daniel had never seen or experienced anything like this before. Their competitor seemed to have created a movement that was catching fire across all their key market segments.

Daniel was now in a high-stakes Adaptive Zone context. His company was in uncharted waters, there was no clear answer, and the entire business was at stake. Unfortunately, as is so common in these situations, Daniel and the rest of the team shifted into a state of protection that started making everything worse. And this time, the solution was not as simple as mastering his internal triggers to shift into learning. In this context, there was a real, complex, and unknown problem to solve, too.

As the executive team struggled to digest the sudden and massive shift in consumer preferences, they could not agree on a way forward. Many people on the team were convinced that this was a passing fad, and the brighter the flame burned, all the more quickly it would burn itself out. But what if they were wrong? If this competitive threat was here to stay and they could not address it quickly, it could be catastrophic for the company, leading to layoffs and an inability to cover the fixed costs of their manufacturing investments.

When Adrienne, the CEO, faced big decisions like this, she relied on her team to reach a consensus about what to do. As weeks passed and the competitor continued to eat into their market share, many on the team started feeling an urgent need to act, but they were still at an impasse. They simply could not agree on what to do. Daniel was also feeling stuck and increasingly frustrated with his colleagues for their inability to make decisions and get aligned.

The first thing the team could not agree on was whether the competitive products represented a short-lived flash in the pan that

would quickly fade or if it was a long-term shift in customer preferences. Some people on the team insisted it was just a fad. "They're
making big claims and ridiculous promises, and when consumers see
that those guys can't deliver, our customers will all come flocking
back to us," insisted Rafael, the medical director. Rafael was also an
MD and co-inventor of the company's scientific approach. "Trends in
this space constantly come and go. This is no different. They'll fade
away a lot quicker if we just ignore them completely. We have much
better science behind our offerings, but let's not sink to their level and
dignify their pseudoscience with a direct response."

Others strongly disagreed. "We don't know that," said Daniel.
"Looking at their sales, consumers seem to believe in their science
and like their products. What if their products are good enough that
once they've switched, they stay and don't come back? We should be
developing a product line with similar products to address the consumer needs out there. This trend could last months or even years.
We can't just sit around doing nothing in the meantime."

"I agree," said Steven, the head of product development. "Why
don't we launch another set of products incorporating their new approach so our products can compete head-to-head with theirs?"

The sales leader, Ina, shook her head. "Well, I think you're both
wrong," she said. "If it's a fad, why would we invest in creating an
entire new line of offerings? But I agree that we shouldn't sit around
and do nothing. Let's go on offense and take our case directly to the
consumer and our large retail customers. My team can come up with
a targeted promotion campaign that will highlight our products' key
features, what differentiates us from others, and how what we offer is
superior."

Daniel felt like his head was spinning as he listened to the team
going around and around in circles. Any one of these approaches might

have made sense, but no one on the team was listening to the other points of view as they insisted that their own position was the only feasible option. And the more the team debated, the more stuck they seemed. While sales numbers kept dropping and the parent company demanded to know how the executive team was going to address it, emotions in the boardroom ran high.

This went on for weeks. Daniel grew increasingly frustrated with the team for not being more decisive, with himself for not being able to convince the team of what he thought was the right answer, and with his colleagues for continuing to argue. The only thing he felt sure of, although he couldn't prove it, was that they could not afford to do nothing. They needed to act. The worst possible course of action was to do nothing at all, which was effectively what they were doing by continuing to go around in circles debating the problem without reaching any alignment.

The only way Daniel knew to get the team unstuck was to revert to old methods that had worked for him in the past—to come up with the right answer himself and then convince the others with facts, logic, and a compelling narrative. But this was not a fit for his current Adaptive Zone context. And while Daniel was sure that doing nothing was the wrong answer, he didn't know what the right answer was. He feared that by the time the answer became clear, it would be too late. The longer they did nothing, the more stressed and anxious Daniel became and the more feverishly he tried to find the answer on his own, disengaging from the unfruitful team debates.

Meanwhile, continuous questions from the parent company were putting a lot of extra strain on the executive team. Yet, they remained stuck. The team members were really digging into their entrenched views. Every time a new piece of data came in, each team member used it to justify their own opinion. Their viewpoints became even more polarized, and their discussions grew longer, yet more contentious and less productive. Relationships between some of the team members soured as they tried to convince each other of their positions and then blamed each other for not moving forward when they still did not agree.

Daniel's feelings of frustration, uncertainty, looming failure, and lack of control were getting worse with each passing day, and the team was starting to unravel as this "passing fad" offered by their competitor continued to siphon away customers. At work, Daniel spent more and more time judging and criticizing others' positions and remarks. At home, he developed a short fuse and grew irritable and silent with his wife and children.

During this period, Daniel went skiing for a weekend and developed a severe throat infection. He was forced to stay in bed for a few days with a high fever. On the day that Daniel had planned to return to work, he woke up with severe muscle aches all over his body. He was tired and agitated, which was unlike him, and a few days later he started rapidly losing weight.

Doctors' visits and lab work revealed that Daniel had developed a runaway thyroid, the gland that regulates the body's metabolic rate. As a result, he was burning around eight thousand calories a day (over three times the normal amount)! When the doctor asked about what was going on in Daniel's life and heard about the tense business situation he was caught up in, he gave Daniel a choice: he could either take out Daniel's thyroid, which meant he would have to manage his metabolism with pills for the rest of his life, or he needed to address the stress, lifestyle, and behavioral factors (also known as the psychosomatic factors) likely causing his thyroid condition.

Daniel had failed to hear the whispers, and now his body was screaming.

RADICAL ACCOUNTABILITY

Daniel chose the latter, and that's how he ended up in that room with Kimberly, the consultant and coach working with him to address his current challenges. Instead of focusing on the simple decision of whether or not to change the company's products or marketing to increase sales, Kimberly focused on Daniel's leadership style and behavior with the executive team and the underlying mindset that was driving his behavior, along with his emotional responses to the current situation. Daniel already had a strong meditation practice and considered himself to be quite self-aware, but he knew that these health and business crises were linked and required him to go deeper.

Daniel's first breakthrough came from understanding his own default leadership behavior in challenging situations. His proven success model of finding a solution analytically, largely on his own, and then convincing others to join him on the path forward was not leading to the desired alignment of the team. Daniel had assumed that the misalignment was because of his team members. After all, this was his first time dealing with a crisis in this particular company and the first time in his career that his proven success model wasn't working. He figured that it must have been their fault and did not consciously investigate his own role in the crisis.

This is a challenge we often experience with successful leaders. They have a proven success model that has worked so well for them in the past that they have a hard time questioning it until they realize that they are in the Adaptive Zone and need to try something new. It is also common for all of us to blame others for our problems when we are in protection and operating from our default mindset and behavior patterns. We believe that the way we are seeing things is objectively true, so we do not look inward and examine other possibilities or the ways in which our own point of view might be skewed. This leads us to blame others or circumstances outside ourselves for our problems instead of taking ownership and finding ways we can change to create a better outcome.

Daniel's mindset about being a good leader had served him well in his career. But in this crisis situation, it prevented him from listening to others and their experiences. It also kept him from cocreating a shared solution and mobilizing larger and more diverse groups of people for change. The complexity of his current adaptive challenge had outgrown his mindset and the behaviors it drove.

By this point, Daniel knew that his old patterns weren't working, but he didn't have a new success model, and that made him feel very nervous. This is one reason why so many of us end up in a state of protection when we find ourselves in adaptive situations. It feels threatening to face the unknown without a clear path before us, and we cling to the comfort of what we have done in the past, even when it is no longer working.

Kimberly explained to Daniel that the first step toward finding a new success model was to develop deeper awareness about his current mindset and to discover *why* it was not effective in addressing his current challenge. What were the blind spots it was creating?

After a great deal of reflection, Daniel realized that his mindset about leadership was that good leaders solved problems, and others agreed and followed along with them. This clearly did not work for him in this situation, as the challenge he was facing now did not have a clear solution. In fact, there might not be one right answer to this challenge, and even if there were, the facts to prove it could come far too late. In addition, there was the added challenge that everyone on the team was entrenched in their own ideas. They needed to explore actions together as a team in the midst of uncertainty. As this uncertain future unfolded, everyone needed to have their voices heard. Only then could they come to a collective set of decisions, experiments, course corrections, and redirects as they took action and learned together.

Daniel realized that he had been prioritizing knowing the answer above getting to an aligned vision and set of actions with the whole team.

Daniel's next breakthrough was regarding accountability. In a state of protection, he had been waiting for Adrienne and the rest of the team to change and blaming them for the lack of progress. Once Daniel gained the awareness that his leadership behavior was falling short of what was needed to address the challenge, he realized that he was equally part of the problem. Regardless of what anyone else was or wasn't doing, Daniel could adapt his mindset and his leadership behavior to better address the current crisis.

Once he embraced the idea that he did not need to know the answer to be a good leader but rather needed to rally the team to collaborate on a journey of discovery, Daniel felt a huge sense of relief and freedom. He didn't have to wait for other people or for external circumstances to change. He did not need to wait for Adrienne to decide or for the team to align or for all the right data to emerge. Of course, he had no control over these things anyway. Now he could refocus on what he *could* control and change in order to improve things—himself. While he was disappointed and frustrated about this business crisis, all he could do was manage his own response to it. This felt incredibly empowering and opened up the space for Daniel to explore new mindsets that would allow him to play a different role in resolving the crisis.

After building awareness and acceptance, the next step was for Daniel to make the choice to change. After a great deal of reflection and answering Kimberly's probing questions, Daniel developed an alternative mindset that he was willing to try out. His mindset changed from, "To be a good leader (in this challenge), I have to know the answer and people need to follow me," to, "To be a good leader (in this challenge), I need to collaborate, listen to all the different perspectives, and support people to come to a collective decision."

Daniel and Kimberly then discussed what behaviors would become possible if he operated from this new mindset and made a plan for Daniel to practice those behaviors. It would not come naturally at first, so he needed to consciously pick "practice occasions" where the new behavior and mindsets would be relevant. The first thing Daniel did was to identify the people who most strongly opposed his point of view—namely, the people who thought they should wait it out and basically do nothing. He listened to them more deeply and asked questions that got to the underlying beliefs and assumptions behind their opinions. He then tried to understand those who did want to do something and why they were proposing very different courses of action.

Once he had a clearer sense of the different perspectives, Daniel brought the various opposing views into the room together and worked on helping the team to really hear each other before debating solutions. He helped facilitate a number of "what if" scenarios to pressure-test the various ideas and assumptions behind the different positions. And he encouraged the others to do the same, inviting colleagues to get curious and ask questions to gain a deeper understanding and broader perspective. This led to a much more creative process of solution finding, where people could air their emotions, thoughts, and deeper beliefs without being interrupted.

For Daniel, this was quite refreshing. Instead of feeling on the hook all the time to come up with the answer, he was able to create space for dialogue and look for commonalities between other people's opinions and ideas. He noticed that he was becoming less rigid in his opinions and could listen to other people's viewpoints without immediately judging whether they were right or wrong or being preoccupied with forming his own reactions. He also saw that as he became more open and interested in other people's points of view, their discussions flowed without as many sharp edges. The team was more open to coming together and experimenting with different solutions to their current market challenge.

Feeling more at ease, Daniel started to become more helpful to the others and to gain more influence in resolving the current conflict. Interestingly enough, he also felt a physical effect on his thyroid condition. Some of his energy was returning.

Eventually, the company's decline in revenue stabilized, their cost base was adapted, and the team started to look at adaptations in their product range to address the consumer needs that their competitor had tapped into. Daniel was incredibly energized by his ability to facilitate the collective leadership of others to make this progress. All of this was unlocked by gaining awareness of his default leadership mindset and making a conscious pivot. He dove into additional work with Kimberly, deepened his meditation and other awareness practices, and continued uncovering blind spots, growing further in self-awareness and personal mastery.

This work led Daniel to expand his insight about accountability outside of work. Now Daniel saw that he had an opportunity to take radical accountability for everything that happened in his life. This breakthrough energized Daniel and forced him to look at his entire life with greater honesty and awareness. If he alone was accountable for creating his life's experience, then he also had the power to change it. This knowledge led him to start asking himself if this was really the life he wanted. And if not, what was?

Daniel enjoyed many things about his current life. He loved his home and his community, his family, and the respect and challenges that came with his job. But he had to admit that deep down he did not feel truly fulfilled. His connection to his current role was based on his ambition, not on a deep sense of meaning or purpose. He found meaning as a father and husband and friend, but as someone who devoted so much of his time and energy to work, he was beginning to realize that he could not be truly fulfilled if his work wasn't in some way connected to a larger purpose.

Looking back, Daniel could see that as he had been busy climbing the ladder to success, he had slowly but surely lost interest in what was waiting for him on the next rung. It had been well over a year since he had voluntarily picked up a marketing book, and studying competitors' commercials was not as much fun as it used to be. As someone who was in charge of a large advertising budget, these were clear signs that Daniel had just been going through the motions.

After spending a lot of time reflecting on this, Daniel realized that while there was a clear connection between his health and work crises, there was a third crisis bubbling up behind the scenes, and there was a dynamic interplay among all three. Ambition is finite while purpose is not. And since Daniel's connection to his career had been based primarily on ambition, the energy it had given him all of these years was finally running out.

WHERE YOUR PASSION MEETS THE NEEDS OF THE WORLD

Everyone benefits from living with a sense of purpose. As part of the foundational layer of our icebergs, our purpose in life creates a large piece of our identities and drives everything above it. Like Daniel, many of us find this type of meaning in multiple roles and areas of our lives. Many people are fulfilled by living out their purpose outside work. But for those of us who aspire to high levels of performance, connecting our work to a deeper sense of meaning helps us perform better, gain energy, and more easily shift into a state of learning when we find ourselves in the Adaptive Zone.

When we are connected to a deeper sense of purpose, we are healthier, we are more productive, we are more resilient, and we are more tolerant in the face of change and uncertainty. People who say they are "living their purpose" at work report levels of well-being that are *five times* higher than those who say they are not.[1] The boost in health and well-being that comes from living with purpose can have a dramatic impact on our entire lives—and even how long we live.

One study that looked at seven thousand Americans between the ages of fifty-one and sixty-one over four years found that people without a strong life purpose were twice as likely to die over the course of the study as those who did.[2] Specifically, they were more likely to die from cardiovascular causes, even after accounting for income, gender, race, and education level. In the study, the impact of purpose on mortality was even greater than lifestyle factors like drinking, smoking, and exercising. Many other studies have confirmed the role of purpose in creating positive health outcomes and a reduced risk of mortality as we age.[3]

Perhaps no one has written more poignantly about the importance of purpose than psychiatrist Viktor Frankl. His book *Man's Search for Meaning* chronicles his experiences as a prisoner in four Nazi concentration camps during World War II.[4] After losing his parents, his brother, and his pregnant wife in the camps, observing how other prisoners coped, and later treating many of his fellow prisoners after they were released, Frankl came to believe that maintaining a sense of meaning even in the darkest times plays a pivotal role in how we experience trauma and even in how likely we are to survive. He found that the prisoners who were living for a specific purpose had a better chance of survival than those who were not, regardless of their specific circumstances. After the war, Frankl went on to develop his own method, called logotherapy, founded on the principle that finding meaning in life is our most powerful driving force as humans.

In addition to the physical, mental, and emotional benefits to connecting to a sense of purpose, it is also a meaning-making opportunity.

We already know the impact that our mindsets can have on our ability to lead and perform within the Adaptive Zone. Likewise, connecting to a sense of purpose allows us to rewrite our personal narratives about what is happening to us and *why*. It shifts our mindsets by offering us meaning that makes stress and challenges worthwhile and expands our tolerance for change. In other words, it helps us frame adaptive situations more positively.

When we are able to tell ourselves that we are doing something difficult because it is serving a bigger and more important "why," we anchor ourselves in a positive context and narrative that creates an inner sense of courage and safety. Even if the activity we are doing in this moment is not going well, or not going well according to our expectations, we can see it as a bump in the road that will help get us to our ultimate destination. We might feel stressed, nervous, frustrated, angry, or any number of difficult emotions, but because our brains get the message that we are feeling those things in the context of a far-reaching journey toward a larger purpose, we can see that our negative emotions are connected to achieving what we want most and not because we are under threat. Therefore, we are able to better stay in learning and gain the energy we need to keep going during hard times.

When framed within this broader perspective, even extremely effortful work feels more rewarding and less challenging. This method of "feeding" ourselves a positive message, especially when facing difficulty, is an emotional regulation tactic that keeps us from being swept away by emotion when facing challenges at any level. In the face of change or turbulence, our purpose can act as an anchor that keeps us rooted to who we are and what we stand for. No matter what is going on around us, we are able to remain steady and constant as we look out at that dot on the horizon and remember where we are headed.

Without that dot on the horizon to aim for, we are so much more likely to shift into protection. We don't know what we really want, so we act to protect what we already have. This leads us to become reactive, looking for problems to solve instead of opportunities to innovate. This is especially important when we are in the high-stakes Adaptive Zone. Without a sense of purpose in this context, we are like a ship at sea in a storm with no destination and can only react to the next wave that is hitting us instead of proactively striving forward.

This means that when we are anchored to our purpose, we are also more intentional about getting outside our Familiar Zone to grow and learn and evolve, as well as showing up and performing within the Adaptive Zone. Without a larger purpose, there is little reason to learn new things in the first place. After all, it's certainly easier to stay in the Familiar Zone and coast than it is to push ourselves into the Adaptive Zone. But this only leads to complacency, and we end up without the tools we need to thrive when changing circumstances force us into the Adaptive Zone or worse: vulnerable to burnout or other negative physical impacts.

Part of what kept Daniel stuck in his business crisis was his lack of awareness, but another problem was that he was chasing a generic idea of success that wasn't rooted in a meaningful sense of purpose. In a challenging new situation, he had no compass to guide him. Along with awareness, the mental, spiritual, and emotional anchoring that a strong sense of purpose provides helps us navigate adaptive situations when there is no clear answer and/or our habitual responses no longer work and we need to learn something new.

So, what *is* our purpose and how do we find it? We define purpose as the intersection of where our passion meets the needs of the world. We are not all fortunate enough to make a living by creating things we are passionate about, but there are still many ways for us to connect our lives and our roles to a deeper sense of purpose. We can derive meaning from our organizations' cultures, values, and leadership, or from the feeling that we are adding value. Ultimately, there are many ways we can feel that our work is aligned with our talents and our values, but this isn't normally something that happens *to* us. Finding and connecting to our purpose takes intention and practice. We can start by asking ourselves: *What am I passionate about, and how can I link that to the work I do?*

Like Daniel, many of us confuse ambition for purpose. We want to be successful, period, and this can be enough to motivate us for a time. But many leaders get to the level of success that would certainly satisfy them if that were truly what mattered, only to find themselves feeling unfulfilled. As American Trappist monk, poet, activist, and scholar Thomas Merton says, "People may spend their whole lives climbing the ladder of success only to find, once they reach the top, that the ladder is leaning against the wrong wall." Indeed, as Daniel saw the light at the end of the tunnel of his health and team crises with new insights about himself, he began to wonder if he had been climbing a ladder against the wrong wall.

Over the months that followed, Daniel was able to operate from his new leadership mindset more and more. He gained flexibility in the office and felt less stressed, more encouraged, and better able to relate to others and find shared solutions. And he was thrilled to see that he experienced more physical relief from his hyperthyroid condition. His mood also started to pick up now that he wasn't so exhausted all the time. This increased his courage and ability to address issues head-on. Within a year, his health completely revived without any medicine.

Soon after, Daniel was in a group session when the facilitator asked the group to reflect on their big dreams. Daniel thought about the transformation he was experiencing since learning to shift his default leadership mindset and wondered what could happen if he found a way to enable other top teams to resolve conflict and tap into their collective leadership potential, especially in times of crisis when this is especially hard to do. It would have been so helpful for his team if they had gotten these tools at the start of their crisis!

This idea was incredibly exciting to Daniel. He started by signing up to get trained as a group facilitator to help people discover their blind spots. He read everything he could find about the work he wanted to do. And he reached out to people in the field to begin making connections. Right away, he noticed that he was far more excited about this reading than he was about the marketing books he'd set aside. Daniel spent many weekends on retreats, learning more about this work. After he returned home from one of them, his wife mentioned, "When you do your training weekends, you come back with so much more energy than when you come home from work."

Daniel could no longer deny what he really wanted in life. "But it would mean taking a huge salary cut," he told his wife. "Up to fifty percent. And I'd basically be starting over without any of the security or perks that I have now."

"We can figure that all out," his wife said. "You should be doing what you're passionate about."

His wife's support combined with the confidence Daniel had gained from finding his purpose and his accountability insights ultimately gave him the courage to take the risk and leave his highly prized position for a new role in an entirely new field. Now he knew that if it didn't work out, he had the awareness and personal accountability tools to change course again. And this time, he would become aware of it sooner and spend far less time climbing a ladder that was placed on the wrong wall.

PURPOSE AS A PRACTICE

Finding our purpose is not a onetime thing. It is a lifelong practice of connecting to the things that matter most and reminding ourselves of *why* they matter to us in the first place. This is a critical part of Dual Awareness, as our purpose sits at the bottom of our icebergs and often evolves as we gain experience and wisdom, learn, and grow. Our internal awareness is not only about our state in the moment but also who we are and what we stand for and how it changes over time. This awareness can anchor us in a very different way, and we need to revisit our purpose regularly to either reanchor ourselves and/or allow it to evolve.

Particularly when we are facing Adaptive Zone moments, continually reconnecting to our purpose fuels us with the inner resources and sense of safety that we need to shift into learning. We can do this at an institutional level, a team level, and an individual level. There is a lot of value in connecting our personal purpose to our company's institutional purpose, even if it's not a direct link. For example, if our purpose is to support our families, our role can help us fulfill that purpose. This is often enough to find meaning in the work we do. Similarly, simply viewing challenges as opportunities to learn infuses those challenges with purpose and helps us shift into learning during difficult times.

Daniel learned this shortly after starting at his new job. He had been a senior leader for many years. Now, he had taken a step down to follow his passion. To get onboarded within the new organization, he was working with colleagues who were at least ten years younger than him. He spent his days completing the types of tasks that he hadn't done in years, such as creating slides and writing meeting reports. On top of that, Daniel's colleagues often gave him difficult feedback, usually around the fact that his presentations weren't sharp enough or weren't following the company's ways of doing things.

Daniel was frustrated by how much time he was spending completing these mundane tasks and talking about how his work wasn't in the right format when he really wanted to focus on the bigger picture of helping top teams transform. To him, it felt like a waste of time. He also felt belittled by the younger team members who weren't treating him with the respect that he felt he deserved.

Daniel's self-talk was saying that he knew better and had far more experience than the rest of the team. Who were they to tell him how things should work? He had taken a big step down in order to live his dream of changing the world through corporate boardrooms, and now he was stuck "cleaning the toilets," as he thought of it. It hardly seemed worth it. At the same time, he was judging his younger colleagues as ignorant kids.

Daniel was clearly in the Adaptive Zone. In a state of protection, he was creating tension with his new colleagues while defending his old ways of doing things. Of course, this only kept him from learning the company's methods and from productively collaborating. By the end of his first week on the job, Daniel already felt like it was never going to work. He was beginning to regret his decision.

Who knows how long this would have gone on if Daniel hadn't gained so much awareness before taking on his new role? That weekend, he went for a long walk and asked himself what was really going on. By getting clear and practicing awareness, he was able to become conscious of his feelings and thoughts and the mindsets that were driving them. He thought about his goals and why he had taken this job at this particular firm to begin with, and he realized that in order to fulfill his dream, he had to learn the rules of this new game he was playing.

In order to do this, Daniel had to shift his mindset. If he learned the ropes as quickly as possible, he could more quickly move on to the work he wanted to do, and that would make this difficult period worth it. The work he was doing now was necessary in order to live his dream. There was a reason he had decided to take the job at this company. No one had forced him. He had chosen it himself, and he had done so for a reason. Now it was up to him to adapt to this new environment in order to start living his purpose.

This was a critical moment of insight. Daniel decided to consciously try to look at the situation differently and get himself trained as quickly as possible by being open to feedback, listening to his colleagues, and working hard to understand how he could be most effective in this new environment. The story that he was telling himself changed from, "Who do they think they are trying to tell me what to do?" to, "I am grateful that they are teaching me what I need to know so I can live my dream." With this shift in mindset, Daniel's brain received the signal that he was safe and that there was a good reason for the stress he was experiencing. All of this helped him shift out of protection and into learning.

In this state, Daniel became more collaborative. He proactively asked his colleagues for support and feedback, especially when he was doing things that didn't fit with their model. This helped ease the tension in the group and motivated his colleagues to open up and share with him. As we have seen before, when two frozen icebergs bump into each other, the result is often friction and discord. But when we melt our icebergs, they can meld together as effortlessly as the collaborations that stem from people working together in this state.

Within a few weeks, Daniel was learning the ropes and getting along much better with his colleagues, but it still wasn't easy. He felt frustrated and impatient from time to time and caught himself slipping into his old patterns. When this happened, Daniel excused himself, went to the restroom, and closed his eyes. He imagined himself in six months doing the work he was so passionate about and told himself that this would all be worth it. Then he reminded himself that it had been *his choice* to take this new job and that he was *choosing* to stay so he could live his purpose through work. By consciously adopting an agent mindset rather than a victim mindset, Daniel kept himself in a state of learning where he could efficiently keep moving toward his dream.

From his leadership and health crises that forced the realization that his work was not truly fulfilling to creating a practice of reconnecting to his purpose to get through difficult times more quickly, Daniel underwent a huge transformation. He realized that this wasn't the first and wouldn't be the last time that he would run into his blind spots or feel unfulfilled. Circumstances would continue to change, and he would continue to find himself in the Adaptive Zone. But now he knew that he was accountable for whatever happened to him and how he chose to respond. And he had the awareness and the tools he needed to connect to his purpose, avoid being swept away by emotion, and even anticipate when he might be challenged and set an intention to stay in an open, learning state.

Sure enough, six months later Daniel found himself living his dream as he started to work with executive teams in challenging circumstances. After everything he'd gone through to get there, doing work that was so meaningful to him felt incredibly rewarding. Daniel also recognized that while he may have spent years mistaking ambition for purpose, these two things were not mutually exclusive. In fact, the more his work was aligned with his true purpose, the more energized he was to deliver success. The difference was that now he was doing it without a sense that something was missing. While his specific roles and circumstances and goals would continue to evolve over time, the big thing remained constant—a life and career of true purpose and meaning.

CONNECTING TO YOUR PURPOSE

Discovering and connecting to your purpose is a lifelong practice, not something that you can ever fully complete. But these questions should help you begin to reflect on what matters most to you and where you can find a sense of true purpose and meaning in your life. After answering these questions, look for patterns and overlap between your answers for greater insight into the things that drive you on the deepest, most personal level.

- What did you enjoy most when you were a child? Why did you enjoy it?
- What are three to five core qualities you have always had?
- Think back to one or two of the most challenging times in your life. Then ask yourself:
  - What did I learn from this?
  - Who did I become as a result?
- Looking back over your life, what were one or two moments when you were truly fulfilled and able to show up as your best self?
- What do you stand for? What are your top values?
- What would you like to leave behind?
  - Looking ahead, what is the biggest possibility for you? What big questions are you currently facing?

CHAPTER 6

RECOVER LIKE AN ATHLETE

Our humanity rests upon a series of
learned behaviors, woven together into
patterns that are infinitely fragile.
—MARGARET MEAD

Alex is a high-energy, creative, and charismatic "people person" who works in marketing and customer service for a large airline. He loves nothing more than making others happy. Among friends and colleagues alike, Alex is known as throwing the best parties—magical events from the smallest details to the grandest, most elaborate gestures. Every party feels like a signature special event not to be missed. This is partly because of Alex's vision and creativity and partly because he pays such close attention to what people like and executes all the details flawlessly. He loves putting the same talents to use at the airline, creating special experiences for customers.

Of course, being so detail oriented can come with a downside. Alex is a self-described perfectionist who likes to plan and control the minutia. He simply wants everything to go perfectly, and when he's involved, it usually does.

As a result, Alex was recently promoted, landing his dream job at the company, a new position called vice president of customer experience, reporting directly to the chief marketing officer. He is in charge of launching one of the most critical and high-profile initiatives at the company to turn around declining customer satisfaction. The airline's net promoter score (NPS), a measure of how likely customers are to choose and recommend the company and its services, has been heading downhill for the last several years. An NPS is calculated by taking the percentage of people who feel very positively about a company ("promoters") and subtracting the percentage who feel negatively ("detractors"), yielding a score that is anywhere from positive one hundred to negative one hundred.

The average NPS in the airline industry is currently around thirty. Alex's company has had the lowest NPS in the industry for a while, and in the last quarter it dipped below zero to negative two. The airline's CEO and executive committee have responded in part by creating Alex's new role, with the primary goals of transforming customer experience, reducing customer complaints, and significantly improving satisfaction and customer loyalty. The CEO told Alex that he wants to go from "worst to first" in NPS.

Alex is frustrated by the customer issues plaguing the company, but he is over the moon about this new opportunity. Not only is it Alex's dream position but he also has the opportunity to play a hand in building his own team. Because the customer experience transformation is such a high priority, Alex has been given significant resources. "Whatever you need," his boss, Rachel, keeps telling him. He was also able to handpick talent from across the company to put on his team and has incredible people now working for him. This includes a woman named Joanne, who has been a leader in the company's marketing department for years and prior to that worked extensively in airline operations. With Joanne as his number two running the day-to-day operations and responding to various tactical issues, Alex's plan is to focus on the transformational initiatives to improve NPS.

At home, Alex brings as much passion and energy to his family and community as he does to work. He seems to have a motor that just won't quit. Alex and his husband, Gabe, have seven-year-old twins named Leo and Abby and are very involved in their church and school community. Alex is also the president of the local board of education.

Alex's first steps in his new role are to ensure that his organization is executing on the day-to-day, that his new team is working well together, and that they have adjusted to him as their new leader. At the same time, he begins taking several flights on the airline, keeping his identity to himself as much as possible, to live the experience as customers do and see firsthand where improvements are needed. He notices a number of issues and crafts twelve targeted initiatives to deliver the transformation. These initiatives span a broad range of changes, including boarding protocols and checked luggage policies, flight attendant training, changes in the call center such as automated call routing and new customer service scripts, the improvement of in-flight meals and entertainment, pricing changes for ancillary services, and the updating of the airline's website and customer apps to enhance user experience. The company runs their NPS number monthly, and Alex's ambitious goal is to get the NPS from negative to positive within a month, and up to fifty within a year.

However, Alex quickly hits a number of roadblocks. The IT department says they won't be able to do anything for at least six months; the flight attendants' union is balking at the training; procurement and legal are locked into contracts for meals and entertainment for the next eighteen months; and it seems that nearly everyone in the company has to agree to any changes in policies or procedures relating to ground operations at the airports. The first challenge Alex takes on is the IT improvement. Increasingly, the customer's first experience with the airline is online or via its app, and right now it is way too clunky and counterintuitive. Alex handles this personally and is quickly able to secure additional resources, bring in outside vendors to shore up the team, and convince IT to start making the changes now. "If I want something done right around here," he tells Joanne, "I better do it myself."

The next challenge Alex tackles is flight attendant training. He believes this is at the core of the current issue, but Joanne tells him that she has spoken to the head of HR, and the union is not willing to roll out the new training. "Why wouldn't they want to do it?" Alex asks in disbelief. "They interact with the customers more than anyone, and it's supposed to make them better. I would think the union would be demanding better training, not digging in their heels against it!"

Joanne shrugs sympathetically. "I'm with you," she says. "I'm just telling you what HR said."

Alex shakes his head and picks up the phone. "I bet they didn't position it right," he says to Joanne. "Of course, they won't want to do more work if they don't understand why they're doing it." He sighs. "I'll talk to the head of the union directly. I know how to sell it." Alex spends the rest of that week going back and forth with HR and union leadership. They finally agree to the new training, but with some substantive changes. Alex and his team get back to work designing the training, frustrated that they have to eliminate some of the most important changes, at least for now.

The next week, the IT department shows Alex their mock-ups of the new mobile check-in page, and he is disappointed by their lack of creativity and inattention to detail. "Has a customer actually tried this? There's so much information, I can't even see where to check in. Also, if I'm a platinum loyalty member, why isn't it recognizing me?" he says as he scrolls up and down the page. "And the options around checked bags are so tiny, you can hardly see them. We're trying to make this easier for people, not harder."

Alex sighs. "We'll come up with a detailed list of feedback so you can take another stab." Thankfully, Alex's team is working together well, but he is frustrated by the fact that they have to keep picking up the slack for other departments. Even more upsetting, at the end of the first month, their NPS has gone from negative two to negative five. It is still going in the wrong direction, and Alex is devastated.

Soon after, Gabe's mother, who lives alone across the country, falls and breaks her hip. She has no one else to take care of her, and Alex and Gabe agree that Gabe should fly out and stay with her for a month or two while she recovers. Before he leaves, Gabe expresses his concern for Alex. "You have a lot going on already, and I feel terrible leaving you with the kids," he says. "Make sure to take care of yourself, okay?" Gabe is more than familiar with Alex's habit of taking on too much, believing that he is a superhero who can do it all, but Alex simply waves away Gabe's concern. "Don't worry about me," he tells Gabe. "Go take care of your mom. I'll be fine."

Alex dives into single parenting with his trademark energy. He wakes up early to make breakfasts, pack lunches, and get the kids to school. Alex can't attend church or board of education meetings because he has to be at home for the kids, but he knows it's only temporary. Without Gabe at home, the kids also have to attend the school's aftercare program. They are tired and more difficult than usual at the end of their long days, and by the time he gets them to bed, Alex is often exhausted himself.

IF YOU WANT THINGS TO GO DIFFERENTLY, YOU HAVE TO LEAD DIFFERENTLY

Now Alex is in a high-stakes Adaptive Zone context both at work and at home. But he fails to realize it and keeps pushing forward with the same tactics that have worked for him in the past. Unfortunately, things for Alex are about to get even worse. The next week, Joanne tells Alex that she is leaving to become the chief customer experience officer at a competing airline. Alex is desperate for her to stay and makes a generous counteroffer, but he cannot compete with the role she is being offered, and he has to admit that she will do a great job in this position. The worst part is that Joanne has accumulated a lot of vacation time, and she is going to take it now. This means that she is essentially leaving without any notice at all.

"I'm still around to help do a handover with my replacement or if you have any questions, but otherwise I will be taking a long-needed vacation," she tells him. "I haven't really taken one in over a year." Alex can't help but feel a little bitter. *Must be nice for her. I haven't had a real vacation in over a year, either,* he thinks to himself.

With Joanne gone, the demands on Alex's time grow. He had not fully realized how much Joanne was running the day-to-day of the organization and holding the whole team together while he focused on the transformation initiatives. Now he's trying to do Joanne's job as he looks for a replacement. Meanwhile, the initiatives he's launched all seem to be hitting roadblocks. He is still waiting for final approval on the new flight attendant training, the second iteration of the online check-in still isn't up to snuff, and the ten other initiatives are all struggling as well, each one vying for his time and attention. Alex starts staying up later and later at night to work on everything.

Soon after, Alex hires a woman named Vanessa to fill Joanne's role. She has a lot of potential but was an external hire and needs a lot of onboarding, so Alex can't start delegating to her quite yet. He feels like the weight of the world is resting on his shoulders. By the time he is done working at night, Alex is physically exhausted, but his mind just keeps spinning, thinking about all the things he wasn't able to get to that day. Despite how tired he is, he has a difficult time falling asleep. His mind just keeps racing, and he can't seem to settle it down.

The stakes get even higher when an article comes out ranking the best and worst airlines to fly internationally, and Alex's company is ranked as the second worst. (The only worse airline is a state-owned enterprise that has a monopoly in its home country and is notoriously mismanaged.) Alex's dream job seems to be turning into a nightmare. He obsessively makes long to-do lists for himself each night, waking up frequently to add notes and comments. Feeling completely out of control and exhausted, Alex starts taking an Ambien with a glass of scotch each night to help calm his nerves and get to sleep. This quickly becomes a nightly habit, often with two glasses of scotch when the first one doesn't work.

Then Alex gets a call from Gabe, whose mother isn't healing as quickly as expected. The one- or two-month trip is now looking like it will be three months or more. Later that same afternoon, Alex gets an email from their son Leo's teacher, asking him to come in for a parent-teacher meeting. Alex shows up at the school first thing the next morning, worried that something is seriously wrong. But the teacher says that, although Leo had always previously completed his homework on time, he hasn't been doing it over the last few weeks. "Leo also seems a bit tired during the day," the teacher says gently. "I'm wondering if there's something going on at home?"

"What's going on at home?" Alex repeats evenly, thinking, *You have got to be kidding me*. "What's going on at home is that I don't have time to do homework with a seven-year-old! Why does he even have homework at this age?" He looks at his watch with irritation. He is missing an important meeting to be here, and this feels like a huge waste of time. The teacher stares back at Alex with wide eyes, but he is so worked up that he barely notices. "Have a good day," he says as calmly as he can as he leaves the classroom.

As soon as Alex gets in his car, he slams his fist down on the steering wheel in total frustration. He can't seem to make any progress at work, customer satisfaction keeps slipping, he's lost his trusted second-in-command, he is stuck single parenting for months on end, now his son is having a hard time in school, and instead of the teacher dealing with it, she's wasting his time and judging his parenting. *What's next?*

Alex feels a slight burning in his chest that has become very familiar over the past few weeks. He already chugged several cups of black coffee that morning, but he can't remember the last time he ate a real meal. He reaches into the glove compartment for a roll of antacids and notices that he's down to the last one. Alex pops it in his mouth, makes a mental note to buy more, and drives to work.

As soon as he gets there, the head of HR comes to Alex's office to tell him that the union leaders are requesting more changes to the new flight attendant training. "Then why even bother?" he snaps. "I'm burning myself out trying to create something that will help them be better at their jobs, but they obviously don't care. Either they're more interested in delivering terrible customer service than they are in learning to do their jobs better, or you're not doing your job in convincing them. So just forget it!"

The head of HR leaves without a word, and Alex sits down at his desk with his head in his hands. *Why do these things keep happening to me?* He's not proud of his behavior, but he also believes that it is mostly justified based on the situation. He feels that familiar burning in his chest again and pulls open the desk drawer, where he keeps another roll of antacids. This one is empty. Alex slams the desk drawer shut loudly enough for it to be heard down the hall.

A few days later, Alex sits down with his boss, Rachel, the head of marketing for the airline. "Well, the NPS held steady at negative five this month," she says. The disappointment is clearly visible on Alex's face. "Hey, it's not so bad—it's been on a downward trajectory for a long time, and it finally bottomed out. I have faith that you'll turn it around," she says, "but we'd love to have you start working with an executive coach."

A coach? Alex thinks to himself. *I don't need a coach. And I certainly don't have time for a coach!* "Thank you," Alex tells his boss, "but that won't be necessary."

"We have a few great people who are eager to work with you," she responds, "whenever you're ready to get started."

That weekend, Alex wants to relax and enjoy spending time with the kids. He decides to take them to the beach, but he has trouble letting go of his stress from work. On the way to the beach, he is replaying his conversations with the head of HR and his boss in his head, and he gets so distracted that before he realizes it, he has taken a wrong turn and gotten lost.

"Dad, how much longer? I'm hungry," Abby whines from the back seat, snapping Alex back into reality. "When are we gonna be there?"

"Hang on a second, hon," Alex says, fumbling with his phone to pull up directions and try to figure out where they are.

Alex's phone isn't getting any cell service at the moment. The light he is stopped at turns green, and he has no idea which way to go. "But I'm hungry," Abby whines again as the car behind them honks impatiently. Alex's frustration boils over, directed at Abby. "ENOUGH," he yells at her. "That's. Enough. I am doing my best, and nothing is ever good enough for you."

Predictably, Abby begins sobbing uncontrollably in the back seat.

Alex pulls over to get his bearings and buys the kids a snack. Abby calms down, and eventually they make it to the beach. But the fun day Alex had imagined doesn't feel like so much fun now. Pretty soon, the kids ask how long they have to stay there and if they can just go home.

That night, Alex's usual Ambien doesn't do the trick. He just can't seem to stop his thoughts from spiraling. He has another scotch while he stays up and cleans the kitchen, reflecting on the past few days. As he's now cleaning an already pretty clean kitchen, Alex realizes that with everything feeling so out of control, he is clinging to the few things he can control with all he's got.

Between the suggestion from his boss that he start working with a coach and his blowup at Abby, Alex recognizes that something has to change. Despite his best efforts, things are not going the way he had hoped or planned. He feels like he is not delivering in any area of his life. By the time the kitchen is spotless, Alex has decided that he might as well show that he's willing to try everything by working with the coach. After a third glass of scotch, he is finally able to drift off into a restless sleep.

During his first meeting with his new coach, named Steve, Alex is feeling skeptical, but he is hopeful that Steve will have some useful tips for how to get others on board with his plans rather than slowing things down at every turn. But Steve doesn't want to talk about other people. He wants to talk about *Alex's* performance and what's getting in *Alex's* way. With Alex's permission, he has already interviewed some people from his organization to get their perspectives.

"Your team respects you, and they really care about what you think of them," he tells Alex now. "They hate letting you down. But there's a perception that people can't push back against your ideas and that it's hard to tell you the truth when it's not what you want to hear."

Alex swallows and takes it in. "You have high standards, and there's nothing wrong with that," Steve continues. "It's like you're a parent who wants everyone on your team to get an A+ on every assignment. And when they get an A+, so to speak, all is well. But when they don't, they're afraid to bring you their report card. So they've started not telling you everything. Part of the reason you might feel so out of control is that you don't even have all the information because your team is afraid of your reaction."

Alex nods. He knows the report card is a metaphor, but it reminds him of how he had felt about showing his parents his grades as a kid. "At the end of the day," Steve says, "if you want things to go differently, you have to start leading differently."

Steve asks Alex if he agrees with the observation that Alex tends to be all over the details. "Well, not *all* the details. Just the important ones. But I do think details are important, so that's mostly a fair observation."

"And why is that?" Steve asks.

"Because that's how you make sure things are executed properly," Alex says. "You get into the details."

Steve comments that this is Alex's belief. It might or might not be true in a given situation. Regardless, the fact that Alex believes this guides his pattern of leadership. "Leaders with this kind of mindset tend to act controlling because they believe that they know better than others," Steve says. "If they could, they would do most things themselves. I'm sensing that you tell others what to do, especially when you're strained for time, because it's faster than having people on your team find their own answer or coaching them toward it." Steve leaves a long pause as this observation sinks in.

Alex also feels a biting sting as he listens, knowing deep down that there is a lot of truth in what Steve is saying.

"Trust me, Alex," Steve continues, "as a recovering perfectionist myself, I know what it feels like. Leaders like this also tend to believe that this is what makes them great leaders: knowing what to do, taking action, getting it right, and directing people with precision. This pattern can lead to people working harder and harder. If they are successful, they will be rewarded with more and bigger endeavors, and at some point they reach their personal leadership capacity to do it all. And because these kinds of leaders tend to be very controlling, they often miss things because they're not getting the benefit of diverse ideas, thoughts, observations, and perspectives from an empowered team. When things get tough, they tighten their control and perfectionism even more. At some point, overwhelm is inevitable, which can lead to burnout."

Alex has to admit that to a great extent this does ring true. This is how he operates when he and Gabe throw their parties and how he has been running the transformation initiatives. He came up with all the ideas himself and then farmed out the execution to his team. And when the IT and HR departments didn't deliver on his vision, he got very involved, at times taking their jobs onto his own shoulders, believing, *If you want it done right, do it yourself.*

Steve and Alex discuss this for a few more minutes before Steve changes the subject. "By the way," he says. "You look tired. And some people have commented that you've lost weight, even just over the past few weeks. Are you taking care of yourself?"

"Of course," Alex says without hesitation. "I'm fine." But Steve doesn't let it go that quickly.

"How much sleep are you getting?"

"Well, sleep's been tough," Alex admits. "But I've been trying to be in bed by midnight so I can get up before the kids at five."

Steve hesitates. "That's only five hours a night," he says. "And what about food?"

"Food? What about it?"

"Yeah, are you eating well? You'd be surprised by how much nutrition can affect your performance at work."

"I'm eating fine. I've been too busy to worry too much about my personal meal plan, but I grab a bite when I get hungry," Alex replies. "I always grab something at some point during the day—fast food or a sandwich from the deli. After I've put the kids to bed, I'm too tired to cook dinner all over again, so I end up just eating their leftovers."

Steve nods. "Exercise? Time to yourself? Anything else you're doing to recharge your battery?"

Alex looks at Steve with a half-smile. "I'd say my battery charge is pretty low right now."

PERSONAL ENERGY RESERVES

At any given point in time, we all have a finite capacity of resources, including our physiological energy, our mental and emotional energy, and our cognitive or attentional energy. There is also an interplay among these types of energy; each one can reinforce or undermine the others. It can be helpful to think of this as a multifaceted "battery" of sorts that stores our energy and personal resources. This battery power plays a huge role in whether or not we are able to access a state of learning, particularly when it matters most.

In one experiment, people trying to learn and perform a complex air traffic controller simulation found that learning occurred faster with lower levels of motivation. That is, higher motivation created higher stress and slower learning. However, taking short pauses during the exercise allowed highly motivated performers to outlearn both their low motivation and "no break" counterparts. The short breaks were chances to replenish their cognitive resources so they could more quickly learn the challenging task.[1]

Similarly, another study found that young violin prodigies out-learned and over time outperformed their almost-as-good counterparts not because of their discipline, rigor, or the many hours of intense, deliberate practice in which they engaged every day, but because they took more frequent breaks, including naps, during the day, to recharge their batteries.[2]

In our current story, Alex is clearly in an Adaptive Zone environment in multiple areas of his life. He needs to adapt to new conditions, unlearn old habits, and learn new skills in order to lead and parent in the midst of challenging circumstances. He is attempting to do so on the fly without replenishing his battery and the personal resources he needs to power his learning. In a state of protection, he loses his awareness and becomes like a proverbial frog in a pot of water. He does not feel the water heating up around him and is unaware that he has moved into the Adaptive Zone.

In fact, Alex is unaware of both his inner state and his external context. With all the small changes adding up, he does not realize that he cannot manage his current challenges with his existing mindsets and behaviors. He keeps reacting to new situations with his old patterns of behavior, pulling the same levers harder and harder. Then he doesn't understand why things aren't going as he wants or plans.

If Alex had a fully charged battery, he would have a greater ability to be resilient and, perhaps more important, to take stock with Dual Awareness. He would realize sooner that his context requires something new from him and that doing the same thing, no matter how well he does it, will yield similar disappointing results. Instead, he needs to pivot, abandon some of the old methods that served him in the past, and shift into a state of learning. With this increased awareness, he could have also recognized sooner when his battery power began to run low, that he was contributing to his downward spiral by not taking care of himself, and that this impacted how he experienced the world around him.

Dedicating adequate time to recharging our batteries sets us up to successfully lead and learn and ensures that we have the necessary emotional resilience and flexibility to handle life's challenges. To recharge our batteries, we need to carve out time in the low-stakes Familiar Zone for recreation, practice, and especially intentional acts of recovery along four dimensions: physical (sleep, nutrition, and exercise), mental and emotional (mindfulness, emotional flexibility, regulating moods, having a sense of hope and optimism, creating emotional safety and balance, processing and resolving emotional challenges and "baggage" over time), social (interpersonal connections and a sense of community and belonging), and spiritual (connecting to a deeper and more expansive sense of purpose, meaning, and values).

Even without any of these forms of recovery, Alex is able to function for a while by tapping into his personal energy reserves. At a certain point, those, too, become exhausted, and he can no longer keep things in perspective or see them objectively. Increasingly, he cannot see the signs that what he is doing isn't working and defaults even more to the habitual behaviors rooted in his iceberg.

Like Alex, if we allow ourselves to reach this point of depletion without sufficient recovery, it can seriously undermine our health, our well-being, and our performance. Some of us are good about getting adequate recovery until life gets hectic. Then, when we need them the most, the very activities that bring us peace and balance are the first ones we give up in order to gain more time for whatever crisis we're facing. Look at how quickly Alex let go of the church activities that were key to his emotional recovery and the sleep and healthy food that were critical to his physical recovery.

But we have found that most of us don't really think about our recovery much when things are going well. We sleep as much as we can. We eat well when we can. We attempt some type of self-care when we find some free time for ourselves. But most of us don't sufficiently plan for recovery and don't build it into our routines across all four dimensions, often because we don't think we need it. After all, when we are performing well and feeling just fine, why put seemingly unnecessary recovery practices in place?

Then something happens. Work gets hectic or a wrench is thrown into our personal lives, or, as Alex experienced, several different things happen at one time. Suddenly, we desperately need recovery precisely when we have the least amount of time or energy to devote to it. The problem is, by the time we really need our recovery practices, it's often too late. We are already in the downward spiral of depleted energy inhibiting our ability to learn and adapt to challenges, leading to even more depleted energy.

The best way to handle challenges is by investing in our own well-being before, after, and in the midst of a challenge or crisis. To put it simply, we have to be intentional about recharging our batteries *before* they become depleted. Just like athletes who consistently invest in their own physical, mental, and emotional health, we all must be fully charged in order to face challenges. Athletes don't just recover from injury and physical strain. They manage their nutrition, sleep, energy, and physical recovery from training and workouts. To be at our best, we all need to take care of ourselves holistically instead of waiting to recover until it's too late.

One big difference, however, is that athletes know when they will be most challenged to be at their very best. Leaders are often challenged in ways and at times that are surprising and occasionally prolonged, making it all the more crucial to establish effective recovery routines as part of our day-to-day. This way, we have the reserves we need when life throws us a curveball.

Some leaders believe that attending to their own well-being is selfish, but the opposite is true. When we are thriving, we are much better at solving problems, being creative, demonstrating compassion, demonstrating resilience, and helping others through challenging times. The more the world gets VUCA—volatile, uncertain, complex, and ambiguous—the easier it is to shortcut our recovery time, yet the more important it is to have those resources ready for when things get even more difficult.

DOLING OUT OUR BODY BUDGET

Even in the best of times, recovery is critical to our well-being, our performance, and our ability to access a state of learning and practice Deliberate Calm. In fact, it goes both ways. *We need adequate recovery and charged batteries to practice Deliberate Calm, and practicing Deliberate Calm helps us recover better and keeps us from draining our batteries too quickly.*

Let's take a closer look at why this is true. Recall the prediction process we discussed earlier that plays a large role in creating our emotions. The more frequently we predict that we are in danger or feel a high degree of pressure to perform, the more likely our brains are to continue making similar predictions. In other words, *the more frequently we feel threatened or under pressure, the more easily threatened we will feel.* Once we get caught in this reactive cycle, our bodies may begin operating from a place of anxiety and hypervigilance, constantly reacting to every internal and external stimulus as a threat.

It is our internal response to our external circumstances that determines whether or not we shift into a state of protection, so it is essential to pay attention to our internal environment. When our physical resources are depleted because we don't sleep enough, don't eat well, or exercise too hard without recovery, our bodies become stressed. This makes us more vulnerable to the external stressors that can tip us over the edge into protection.

We can't always control those external stressors, but to a great extent we can control what happens to us internally. In fact, whether we are aware of it or not, one of the most important levers we can pull to avoid shifting into protection is to take care of our own physical well-being. This is the foundation of our mental and emotional resilience.

Imagine that our brains are worrywarts, constantly asking, *"Am I safe or under threat? What do I need to do to stay safe?"* Our worrywart brains function to keep us alive. That is their primary focus. And when they get the answer *"You are under threat,"* whether it is a physical threat, a threat to our goal attainment, a threat to identity, or a threat to our emotional safety, we tend to react from a state of protection. And we are especially likely to react this way when we are tired, hungry, or operating in "low battery mode."

If we are aware enough to notice in these moments that we are shifting into the protection state, we can take steps to respond effectively. It's helpful to pause and use simple breathing, visual, and vocal techniques. This reduces our feelings of being under threat and frees up the resources that were previously being used to protect us so that we can use them instead to learn something new, connect with others, or adopt a new way of seeing things.

When our batteries are charged, we have the resources to better identify our own challenges and shortcomings. In one experiment, subjects with low "cognitive load" were able to self-identify and correct their own gender biases, while those with a high cognitive load and therefore limited resources were not able to do so and demonstrated significantly higher biases. These people were not inherently more biased. They simply lacked the cognitive resources at the time to be self-aware.[3]

A simple way to make sure we have the resources we need to stay in learning is to take care of ourselves physically so our brains do not misinterpret an internal stress signal to mean that we are under threat. We all know how much more likely we are to get carried away by our emotions when we are "hangry" or tired. For instance, a 2013 study found that poor-quality sleep led to worse fights among romantic couples, potentially putting the entire relationship at risk, regardless of other factors (i.e., stress, anxiety, depression, or overall relationship satisfaction).[4]

Throughout this book, we have seen several examples of leaders who assumed that their stomachaches, chest pains, and other physical symptoms were physical reactions to their external stress. Just look at Alex and his heartburn. Alex is stressed, he has been eating poorly, and he starts experiencing frequent heartburn. But his brain doesn't know any of this.

Alex's brain, which has been busy asking, *"Am I safe or under threat?"* simply gets the message that his chest hurts. To his brain, this is a sign that he is, in fact, possibly under threat, and it quickly starts up a stress response. Once he feels the impact of that physiological stress response, Alex tells himself a story to explain what is happening: *I am stressed, and it's causing heartburn. If the people around me would only step up, I wouldn't have to deal with this heartburn.* Of course, this story is not objectively true. Alex could also feel his stress response and tell himself, *There's that heartburn again; I should really stop drinking coffee on an empty stomach.* He could tell himself any number of things.

We will never know for certain what was actually causing Alex's heartburn. It was likely a combination of his stress and his poor eating habits. The more important point is that if Alex had been taking care of himself and practicing Dual Awareness, he would have been able to better interpret the messages being sent between his body and his brain and use that information to improve his brain's prediction process.

Lisa Feldman Barrett uses the helpful metaphor of a "body budget" to explain how the brain budgets the energy in our bodies. Read that again. The body budget represents not only the *amount* of stored energy in our bodies; it also determines *how* we spend it. In other words, if our batteries store energy, they also decide where we direct, allocate, and channel that energy both internally, in terms of what we think about and focus on, and externally, in terms of what we say and do. This includes how we interpret situations, the emotions we construct based on our prediction process, and our mindsets and beliefs about what is important and *why*.

From a purely budgetary perspective, getting adequate recovery helps save energy. When we are digesting a heavy meal, it takes up energy. When we are tired, it takes up energy. When we feel lethargic from sitting on Zoom meetings all day, it takes up energy. Even some of our coping mechanisms that help us sleep, such as drinking alcohol or binge-watching TV, take up energy. When we drink alcohol before bed, it increases our heart rate and causes our heart rate variability, a measure of physical resilience, to plummet during the night. This leads to poor-quality sleep and therefore less energy.

In order to function optimally, our brains require 20 percent of our total body budget.[5] When our body budget is running low, our resources are more focused on our survival, not on our cognitive performance. This means that, figuratively speaking, when our battery charge is at less than 100 percent, we do not have enough energy to fully power our brains. This affects our moods, colors our thoughts and perceptions, and makes us more likely to predict that we are under threat and therefore shift into a state of protection. It's no wonder, then, why we communicate poorly, have difficulty making the right decisions, and have trouble accessing a state of learning when our batteries aren't fully charged.

Clearly, this is what happens to Alex. His body budget is running low, which makes him far more likely to shift into a state of protection, whether it is at work, with his kids, or with his son's teacher. While he still may have felt frustrated or angry in any one of those situations no matter how well rested and recovered he was, he likely would not have been as easily carried away by his emotions. He would have had access to additional resources to think more clearly and make a better choice. Even the fact that he gets lost on the way to the beach is likely in part due to the fact that his brain was so muddled from a lack of energy.

To complicate matters, however, it's important to note that not everything that drains our batteries is negative. Quite the contrary. Operating in a state of learning, for example, is positive, but it requires a great deal of engagement, which can be draining.[6]

Whether we are working a muscle at the gym or taxing our brains by learning something new, real growth happens not when we are actively pushing ourselves but when we are deeply relaxed. Children grow when they are asleep because that is when they experience an increase in the release of growth hormone. Athletes create microscopic tears in their muscles when they exercise, and it is during rest that their bodies heal those muscles, allowing them to get stronger and grow. And when we learn new things, the corresponding neural connections in our brains are strengthened when we sleep, forming memories. This means that we need to recover from what we experience as good stress as well as from "bad" stress.

Two underlying nervous systems work together in our bodies when we are in different zones. When we are in the Familiar Zone, the parasympathetic nervous system (PNS), which regulates bodily functions like digestion and recovery, and the sympathetic nervous system (SNS), which prepares us to respond to threats both mentally and physically, are in balance. When we are in a deeply relaxed state, the PNS is more dominant. When we move into the Adaptive Zone or a high-stakes Familiar Zone situation, the SNS becomes dominant. Both systems are essential to our survival, and to practice Deliberate Calm, we should aim to keep them overall in balance. This does not mean that we always need to avoid stress. As a matter of fact, stress is essential to learn, grow, and develop. This simply means that we should aim to find time to recover after we have experienced any form of stress to allow for learning and growth to happen.

Sleep researcher Nathaniel Kleitman, who discovered rapid eye movement (REM) sleep, hypothesized that we have a basic rest-activity cycle of 80 to 120 minutes when we are both asleep and awake.[7] When we are awake, our brain waves move faster during the first half of the cycle, causing us to feel more energized and focused. During the last twenty minutes or so of the cycle, our brain waves slow down, and we begin to feel tired. Other experts, such as Andrew Huberman, agree that an ideal "learning" session should last about ninety minutes, as that is how long the brain can maintain a high degree of focus.[8]

The exact schedules and routines and modes of recovery that work best for each of us are highly individualized. There is no one path to recovery. It takes experimentation and trial and error to find out what works best for each of us. But for those of us who aspire to high levels of performance, it is essential to plan our days for adequate recovery and with a healthy balance between time spent in the Familiar Zone and time spent in the Adaptive Zone.

TRACKING YOUR RECOVERY

It can be difficult to know when your battery power is beginning to run low. Of course, it is best to practice Dual Awareness so you begin to notice right away when you need additional recovery. It's even better to have a consistent recovery practice in place so your battery remains charged most of the time. But in the real world, we all slip up and become drained from time to time. Luckily, there are both low-tech and high-tech ways to track your recovery so you can take action when necessary and quickly recharge.

TAKE A DAILY QUIZ

Andrew Hamilton, a sports science writer and researcher, asks athletes to take a six-question quiz each morning by rating statements such as "I slept really well last night," "I feel vigorous and energetic," and "I have very little muscle soreness," on a scale from 1 (strongly disagree) to 5 (strongly agree) and then adding up the total. When an athlete's score dips below 20, he recommends taking a recovery day or switching to light "taper" workouts until the athlete's battery is sufficiently recharged.

It is helpful to think similarly about our own conditioning, although with equal emphasis on physical, mental, emotional, social, and spiritual recovery. We expanded on Hamilton's quiz to help you assess and gain awareness around your level of recovery. Each morning, rate the following questions from 1 (strongly disagree) to 5 (strongly agree), and then add up your total score.

1. I slept very well last night.
2. I have clear, purposeful intentions for the day.
3. I am looking forward to the day's activities.
4. I am optimistic about my future.
5. I feel vigorous and energetic.
6. My diet is healthy and well balanced.
7. I am experiencing very little fatigue or burnout.
8. I can focus on the things that matter most.
9. I feel connected to the important people in my life.

If your score is below 30, it means that you are not fully recovering along all dimensions and you should plan additional recovery time.

GET ANALOG FEEDBACK

Pay attention to intentional or unintentional feedback you receive from the people around you. If they consistently inquire about your well-being, especially during or after tense meetings, they may sense that something is "off." Even better, solicit open feedback from any of the following people:

- Your colleagues
- Your team members
- A coach or mentor
- Your family members
- Your close friends and/or partner

GET HIGH-TECH FEEDBACK

Wearable technologies can give you great insight into your personal recovery pattern. You can track your heart rate, blood oxygen levels, sleeping patterns, movement patterns, and so on. Some of them include a special algorithm to give insight into your stress levels.

Specifically, many wearables track your heart rate variability (HRV), the variation in the time interval between heartbeats, which is a measure of resilience. While everyone has their own baseline, in general, the higher your HRV, the more resilient you are, the better your heart is able to adjust and accelerate or calm down when needed. Low HRV is a predictor of reduced resilience, burnout, and cardiovascular disease.[9] Your HRV is influenced by many factors, including stress, lack of sleep, fitness levels, nutrition, age, and genetics. Tracking yours over a period of time is a good way to discover how well you are recovering. If your HRV reduces over time, it is a sign that your resilience is going down and that you need to integrate additional recovery time into your schedule.

SLOW AND STEADY

When we left Alex, he was beginning to realize that his battery power was sorely depleted and causing him to cling to his perfectionist, controlling habits, even though they clearly weren't working anymore. At this point, Alex has to face the fact that something has to change, and it has to be something he can actually control. He can't make Gabe come home sooner. He can't force Joanne to come back and work for him. And he can't add more hours to the day to get everything done. But he can delegate more, he can stop trying to do everything himself, and he can seek out help to get some time back for himself.

Alex is terribly disappointed. He really thought that he could do it all by himself and do it well, but he clearly cannot. He has to accept the reality that he's burned out and needs real recovery. This means there are things that he will not be able to do as planned. If he keeps going this way, he'll fail at something important, or perhaps several things. After giving it a lot of thought, he realizes that he would rather choose to do a few important things well than to keep doing everything poorly.

To make this change, Alex also has to confront his iceberg and his beliefs that if he wants something done right, he has to do it himself, and if he can't, then he is a failure. This is ultimately why he becomes so controlling and perfectionistic when the stakes are high. He tells Steve that he doesn't like to admit defeat.

"It's not a defeat to admit that you're not Superman," Steve says. "By refusing to face your limits, you're holding yourself and your people back." Steve pauses for a moment and then asks, "What would be possible if you no longer believed that you had to do it all yourself in order for things to be done correctly?"

Alex thinks this over. "I would be more compassionate with my people and with myself," he says. "I could take more advantage of the people around me and empower them to contribute creatively instead of just executing on my vision." Alex thinks for another moment. "I guess that would help *all* of us from getting burned out," he realizes.

With this insight, Alex is motivated to take an honest look at his life and make some changes. The first thing he does is hire a nanny to stay with his family until Gabe is home. Then he thinks about his role on the board of ed. Alex really enjoys serving on the board, but the responsibilities of being president are just too much. He makes the difficult decision to step down as president and stay on the board.

This gives Alex more time to sneak in a quick workout, eat a real dinner, and have more time to himself each evening. As a high performer with young kids, it's been years since Alex had any real time for himself, and he has to reflect on what he even enjoys doing when he isn't going all the time. Simply having a few moments each evening to sip some tea on the back deck and reflect on the day feels like a vacation.

At Steve's urging, Alex also tries to prioritize sleep, but simply having more time to sleep in the evenings isn't enough. After his tea, Alex catches up on email and then stays up tossing and turning no matter what time he goes to bed. After a while, he tells his team that he won't be checking his email after eight o'clock at night. He is hoping that this will not only help him sleep but will help the rest of the team recover, too.

Liberated from his phone, Alex develops a nightly routine. After his tea, he thinks about three things he is grateful for and why he is grateful for them. Then he gets ready for bed and reads a novel before falling asleep. After a few weeks of this, he is able to sleep without his nightly Ambien.

At work, Alex decides to sequence the NPS initiatives. For now, he will focus on the two biggest and most impactful pieces—the flight attendant training and the online check-in update. They will launch the next two a month later, and two more each month after that. Alex is disappointed that he can't do it all right away, especially because this means he won't be able to meet his goal of getting the NPS to fifty within a year. But he also realizes that this will help his team focus and avoid getting burned out themselves. Perhaps, he thinks, this is how he should have planned it from the beginning.

After discussing this plan with his team and telling them that he wants their ideas and feedback for the remaining initiatives, Alex sits down one-on-one with both the head of HR and the product development lead from the IT department and tells them how much he is counting on them to help him launch these two new initiatives. He explains how important they are to the bigger picture of customer experience and says that he is going to leave the rollout to them. They are clear on the vision, and from here on they need to handle it with their teams. This will allow Alex to focus on working with his team to get the remaining initiatives right.

Alex is recovering more and performing better at work and at home, but he is still frustrated. He wishes he could move more quickly on his initiatives and make a bigger impact. But at the end of the next month, he gets some good news. The NPS is above zero for the first time in months. It's only at a two. That's far lower than the fifty he wanted. But Alex recognizes that it wasn't going up at all when he was trying to do everything. At least now things are moving in the right direction, albeit slowly. And with more recovery, Alex is able to find fulfillment in his work again and enjoy spending time with his kids.

After tucking Leo and Abby into bed that night, Alex reads them a story. "Slow and steady wins the race," he reads from the story of the tortoise and the hare. Then he closes the book of fables and kisses each of them on the forehead. Alex realizes this is a good reminder for himself. By cutting back and facing the real consequences of slowing down, Alex has created a more sustainable performance. Perhaps this way they will win the NPS "race," after all.

CREATE YOUR RECOVERY PLAN

The most important part of planning your own recovery is to understand what activities and routines give you energy and which ones drain you. We all need adequate sleep, exercise, and nutrition, but other elements of recovery are highly personal. For instance, introverts may find going out with friends highly draining, while the same activity may be energizing for extroverts. Observe yourself for a week and then make a note of how energizing or draining your daily activities are. Then you can put a plan in place to maximize your charge.

To get started, think about how energizing or draining you find the following activities:

- Commuting
- Attending group meetings
- Attending one-on-one meetings
- Attending Zoom meetings
- Doing highly focused individual work
- Going out to lunch with colleagues (list individually)
- Spending time with a group of friends
- Spending time with specific friends (list individually)
- Spending time alone

Once you have an idea of what charges your battery and what depletes its charge, think about how you can better organize your days and weeks to maximize your battery power.

CHAPTER 7

DEVELOPING DUAL AWARENESS

Real change, enduring change,
happens one step at a time.
—RUTH BADER GINSBURG

Simone simply cannot believe what she is hearing. She looks at Jonathan, her product design lead, and shakes her head in disappointment. The health care company they work for is undergoing a digital transformation that involves creating new software to change how their company engages with and supports both health care providers and patients. Simone is a senior vice president in charge of the department that is developing the new software, applications, and features and the department that is responsible for embedding these products into the business. It's critical that customers start using these new products at scale to meet market demands, grow the business, and give the company access to valuable patient and health care data.

This is crucial for the overall strategic direction of the company as they move more into digital and analytics-enabled solutions.

For months, there has been tension, disagreement, and strong emotions between the two departments that Simone leads, and she is beyond frustrated. She is doing everything she can to support her people, often staying up late to complete work when one of them seems overwhelmed. But no matter what she does, they still can't seem to get it right, and they keep falling further and further behind schedule. Now Jonathan is telling Simone that his team was not able to include one of the most important features to be added in the latest iteration of the software. Worst of all, he is telling her this on the very day that they are presenting the updated version to the rest of the team, when it is too late for her to do anything about it.

"Why am I just hearing about this now?" Simone asks, slightly raising her voice. "I would have happily stepped in to help make this happen, but now it's too late, and we're set up to fail in this meeting." She keeps going, seemingly without taking a breath, as her voice grows louder. "If we can't get this new software off the ground, they could just decide to kill the whole thing. We could all lose our jobs."

Simone hates being blindsided like this, and her team knows it. Why do they keep letting her down and bringing problems to her at the last possible moment? No matter what she does, circumstances keep conspiring against her. Or maybe the team just isn't up to this task and she needs to find new leaders.

Jonathan sighs as he gathers his belongings and leaves Simone's office. He knows that he should have told her about the missing feature sooner. Instead, he has kept focusing on the many other improvements that his team was able to make, including accelerating several features that test users found extremely compelling. In his view, there are a number of areas where they over-delivered, and this outweighs the one area where they under-delivered. But he never had this conversation with Simone because, in truth, he had been dreading her reaction.

Whenever the team is struggling with a setback or obstacle, Simone gets agitated and ends up making the situation worse. He and his team hate to disappoint her, and they feel like they are constantly doing so when things don't go perfectly according to plan. During a major transformation like this, things rarely go perfectly according to plan. Setbacks are inevitable, but whenever they do raise an issue, Simone is disappointed and jumps right to the worst-case scenario. This leaves the team feeling demoralized. As a result, Jonathan finds himself trying to solve issues on his own, even when raising them with Simone sooner would give her an opportunity to help and perhaps give them all a better chance of success.

From Simone's point of view, she is doing everything right. She is showing her team how much she cares, she is constantly offering to help, and she is asking tough questions to get to the root of problems and get results. Yet, Jonathan feels that Simone is contributing to many of the team's problems, if not directly causing them. While she blames the team for failing to surface issues sooner, Jonathan feels that she exacerbates many of the problems that do come to her by expressing her own strong reactions.

AWARENESS LEVEL 1: UNAWARE—NOT AWARE OF INTERNAL STATE OR EXTERNAL ZONE

Simone is operating at the first of five levels of awareness that we travel through as we go from lacking awareness to practicing Dual Awareness. At Level 1, Simone functions largely on autopilot. She looks at the world through her own lens and assumes that she is seeing the objective reality and that, for the most part, she is responding appropriately. She is largely unaware of her own hidden iceberg and

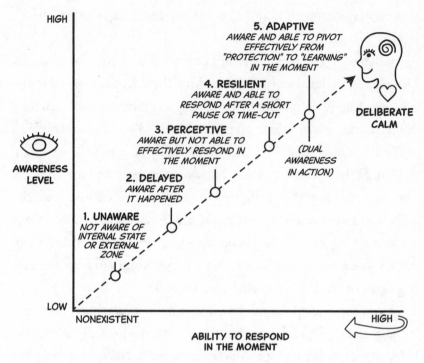

FIGURE 7.1: Five Levels of Awareness

patterns. And she is blind to the impact that her behavior has on herself and others.

Simone genuinely wants to help her team when they encounter setbacks and challenges, but she fails to recognize how her behavior is making it less likely for them to ask her for help. Simone attributes this to their own behavioral and leadership shortcomings, failing to see that in many ways it is actually a response to *her* behavior and leadership style. This is why the same challenges keep coming up for her across multiple teams and situations.

In this state, our reactions and emotions and behaviors, to the extent that we are aware of them, are completely logical based on the situation as we see it. We assume that the causes of our problems are external to us. We often don't stop to look at how we may be contributing to the problems we face or what may be going on inside us that is causing us to react the way we do. We also fail to see how many options we really have in terms of how we might interpret a situation, feel and think about that situation, and respond.

Interestingly, at this level of awareness, we often view other people in the exact opposite way. When we observe others' behavior, we see it as a reflection of their personality, their competence, their choices, or their character, even as we often attribute our own actions to our situation and circumstances. We judge ourselves on our intention yet we judge others on their behavior. In social psychology, this is called the fundamental attribution error.

When we look at the actions of others, we often see the person front and center and are less aware of their context. Therefore, we attribute their actions more to the person than to their situation. However, when we look at the world and make choices about how we should act, the circumstances we are reacting to are primary. Therefore, we attribute the causes of our own behavior more to the contextual factors leading us to behave in ways we believe are appropriate and logical. When we make this error, we are more likely to make excuses for our own behavior and let ourselves off the hook while judging and blaming others for their behavior.

The truth, however, lies somewhere in between. Each person's actions are the result of a complex interaction between that person and their situation. The situation is constantly affecting the person, but the person is also constantly shaping their own situation. To our conscious mind, we perceive our situation as objective, but someone else might perceive and respond to the same situation completely differently. Because so much of our cognitive and emotional processing happens subconsciously, we aren't aware of how much we are shaping the very situations we find ourselves in.

As we develop our Dual Awareness, we are able to slow down

and better observe the situation we are in, our internal reactions, and our related behavior. As we become more aware of this dynamic in ourselves, we also gain empathy for other people's behavior. This has an additional influence on our own awareness. When we intentionally act with empathy and open our minds to other people's points of view, we can gain insight into our own behavior and how it impacts others, increasing our self-awareness.

———

Later that afternoon before the meeting to present the new version of the product to the team, Simone receives a text from Jonathan. "Hey, Simone," it reads, "for this meeting, if you have a lot of criticism, it would be great if you could hold off and tell me after. Then I'll share it with the team when they're in a better place."

Simone rereads the text, feeling a bit perplexed. Jonathan's request seems reasonable enough, but she has a nagging feeling that maybe there is more behind it than meets the eye. Perhaps, she realizes, there is some feedback in there for her about how she interacts with the team and gives constructive criticism.

She simply responds, "Okay," but after the meeting, Simone asks Jonathan to come back to her office. "Before I give you my feedback on the presentation," she says, "I'm wondering what is going on with the team that would make them so fragile that we have to do this offline? Or maybe there is a way I can deliver my criticism differently, so I don't have to share everything negative with you and then have you relay it to them separately."

Jonathan recognizes that this is his chance to say some things he has been holding back for a while, but he is also feeling a bit nervous about how Simone will react. He proceeds cautiously. "Maybe you can try not to show your frustration so much on your face," he says hesitantly, "and try to maintain a calm tone. My team doesn't like to disappoint you, and when you look frustrated it can be really hard for them to open up."

"I stay calm, don't I?" Simone asks. "I mean, I'm not yelling and screaming. We're just talking."

"Maybe you don't notice," Jonathan replies, "but when you get frustrated you start talking faster. You may not yell, but your voice goes up a notch, and you start clenching your teeth a little, and it puts the team on edge."

This is news to Simone. "Okay," she says, taking a deep sigh and nodding her head as she takes his words in. "What else?"

"Well," Jonathan says slowly, "when you mention all the terrible things that might happen if we don't succeed, that can be really tough. The stakes already feel high. The team already feels accountable and hates to disappoint you. You don't need to spell out all the worst-case scenarios."

"Like when?"

"At the last team meeting about the new technology, you said that if it fails, basically the whole company might fall apart," Jonathan says quietly. "One of my people was crying after that. She was worried about losing her job."

"Oh." Simone is quiet for a moment. "I did not realize that. Thank you, Jonathan," she says. "I'll give this some more thought."

Simone has trouble sleeping that night as thoughts swirl in her mind about what Jonathan said. At first, she wonders if Jonathan and his team are just being overly sensitive. Why are they reacting so strongly to a facial expression? But she has to admit to herself that his words did touch her and must have some truth to them. She wonders if it's possible that she is actually contributing to her team's problems.

The next day, Simone sits down with the five senior leaders on her team to discuss the latest iteration of the new software. Tempers flare as the people who need to incorporate the product into the business are angry that their feedback has once again been ignored. Maya, one of the leaders responsible for embedding the software into the business and getting access to critical data, stands up during the meeting. "You just aren't listening," she says to Jonathan. "You have not incorporated our feedback again! We can't use this!"

"But we did incorporate your feedback, all of it!" Jonathan says. "It's not perfect, but it works. Every must-have feature you prioritized is in there. Even though we said we could only include two or three new features in this release, we included all six. And they all work. What you're asking for is totally unrealistic."

"Again, you are not hearing me," says Maya, sitting back down looking exasperated. "If our users have to click through *that* many screens, and the way to get to the report they want is *that* counterintuitive, and then once they finally get there, the report is *that* hard to read, then what's the point? It needs to be one click, easy, and intuitive."

Simone has been trying to let them work it out, but she cannot watch this back-and-forth any longer. "That's enough," she interjects. "Quit blaming each other and take some accountability to solve this together. If this was the most important thing, Maya, then why were we trying to do six 'must-have' features instead of just nailing this one and getting it right? And Jonathan, honestly, doing six things poorly is the worst of all worlds. You know there's already a huge barrier to getting users to agree to this new technology and integrate it into their service model, and now we're starting to lose the few users we've already converted. Maya, you and your team need to stop creating unrealistic wish lists of every possible thing and focus on the few critical things. If this report was that important, you should be working with Jonathan's team to mock up exactly what you need instead of just throwing it over the fence. And Jonathan, honestly, I agree with Maya. You're not listening. Obviously, this is way too clunky, and the report itself is so non-visually appealing and so hard to read, what is even the point? And now we're at the brink. If we lose two customers for every new one we gain, we might as well just pack up our stuff and go home. Start working together and figure it out!"

With that, Simone gets up and storms out, with her heart beating quickly. She tells herself that this was exactly the kind of tough love they needed. But after Simone is back in her office, she closes the door and sits down with a sinking feeling. She wonders, *Was this the sort of behavior that Jonathan was talking about?* She wishes she could take back what she'd said, or at least go back and say it in a calmer tone. She's also wondering how often she actually does this. Simone is keenly aware of the fact that Jonathan just gave her that feedback yesterday, and she's shown the exact behavior he mentioned the very next day. Perhaps she is doing this more often than she had imagined . . .

AWARENESS LEVEL 2: DELAYED—AWARE AFTER IT HAPPENS

For Simone, Jonathan's feedback has begun to bridge the gap between Level 1 of awareness and Level 2, where we become aware after the fact that we have acted from a state of protection with habitual and often ineffective behaviors, and then wish we had said or done something differently.

It can be difficult to receive negative feedback, but feedback plus reflection can help us become aware of unhelpful behavior patterns that might otherwise escape our attention. As they say, feedback is a gift, and, as Simone experiences, the feedback that hurts the most is often the greatest gift of all. When the feedback we receive hits on something that we consciously or unconsciously know is true, we often feel an uncomfortable sting. If we pay attention, this discomfort is a sign that we have an opportunity to learn.

Feedback can come in many different forms. We typically tend to think of feedback as something that is given explicitly from one person to another, but there are many other ways we can seek feedback to gain insight about ourselves and the impact our behavior has on others. For instance, we can get passive forms of feedback by carefully observing others' reactions, by asking questions about how people feel as a result of something we have said or done, or by tracking the results we are getting or not getting relative to our intentions.

Receiving feedback, however, does not mean that we have to agree with or act on it. Think of feedback as a gift. If your aunt gives you an unattractive sweater as a holiday gift, you can accept it and thank her for it, but that doesn't mean you have to wear it. That sweater may be a reflection of her taste and not really say anything about you. The person giving feedback is operating from their own invisible iceberg, so their perception is not objective, either. No one's is. But their feedback still might hold important information if we are open to hearing it. Even if we decide that a piece of feedback has been deeply skewed by the other person's lens on reality, it can still be helpful to know that this other person (and potentially others) sees things this way. Therefore, there is really no such thing as unhelpful feedback, even if it is entirely inaccurate.

In 1955, psychologists Joseph Luft and Harrington Ingham developed a tool called the Johari Window[1] to help people understand their relationships with themselves and others. The Johari Window consists of four quadrants: things about us that are known to others but not known to us (blind spots); things about us that are not known to others or to us (unknown or undiscovered information); things about us that are known to us but not known to others (façade or private information); and things about us that are known to us and known to others (arena or shared understanding).

The bigger the shared understanding quadrant is between us and another person, the more effective that relationship has the potential to be. When we listen to feedback from others, we grow the shared understanding quadrant by shrinking the blind spot quadrant. And when we share openly about ourselves with others, we grow the shared understanding quadrant by shrinking the private or façade quadrant. The unknown or undiscovered quadrant is where our hidden icebergs lie. It requires deep reflection and inner work to shrink the unknown or undiscovered quadrant and then share this information with others in order to move it into the shared understanding quadrant.

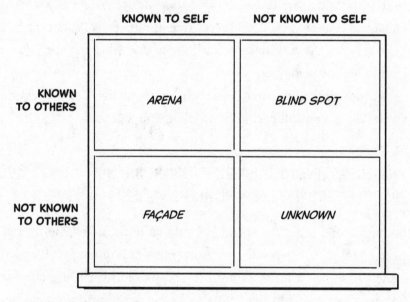

FIGURE 7.2: Johari Window

By pulling on the string of Jonathan's feedback, Simone has grown the shared understanding space between the two of them and has become aware of one of her blind spots. Back in her office, she reflects on the meeting and realizes that she had felt disappointed and frustrated and had shown those feelings openly. She had spoken quickly and loudly, and her closing comment about packing up could be seen as shutting the whole operation down, catastrophizing a worst-case scenario. This was all very much in line with the feedback from Jonathan.

Simone considers other ways she might have responded instead. She could have calmly asked questions to try to help surface the collaboration and prioritization issues. She could have talked about the higher purpose of the effort around helping health care providers and improving patient outcomes and left out the part about potentially closing shop. She might have talked about creative solutions in the near term to improve the report that some of the users really wanted and asked how she could help accelerate it. She really wishes she had done some of those things. Instead, she worries that she might have made a bad situation even worse.

Although she isn't aware of it in the moment, this Level 2 delayed awareness is a crucial part of Simone's learning process.

AWARENESS LEVEL 3: PERCEPTIVE—AWARE BUT NOT ABLE TO EFFECTIVELY RESPOND IN THE MOMENT

Soon, Simone begins to notice her own patterns of behavior in real time. When she receives disappointing news or is unhappy with what someone on her team is telling her, she starts to catch herself. She becomes aware of warning signals like her jaw tensing up and her heart beating more quickly. She starts noticing that her self-talk is blaming other people and downward spirals into worst-case scenarios. *Oh, no,* she starts to realize. *I'm showing my frustration on my face, aren't I? I can see the team reacting to my expression and to the tone of my voice. They're tuning out, and it looks like they're shrinking into themselves because they're worried about what I'm going to say next.*

This is Simone at Awareness Level 3. She is observing herself in the moment and becoming conscious of the circumstances that trigger her to shift into a state of protection, along with the habitual feelings, thoughts, and behaviors that she exhibits in this state. She is also learning to recognize the cues that she is starting to shift into protection. These cues can come from our bodies, from our minds, and/or from observing our own behavior.

Cues from the body that we are shifting into protection can include tension building up in our shoulders, necks, or stomachs, trembling, sweaty palms, clenching our jaws, breathing from our chest as opposed to our belly, an increased heart rate, and shallow breathing. Cues from the mind that we are shifting into protection often include negative thoughts, particularly about other people, and defending our own truth. And cues from our own behavior that we are shifting into protection might include a change in our tone of voice, yelling, shutting down, and avoidance. As we practice observing ourselves from a distance, we can learn to recognize that we are shifting into protection more and more quickly.

Like many of us, Simone gets a bit stuck at this level of awareness. It can be intensely uncomfortable to watch ourselves act in a way that we know is likely not helpful and feel unable to shift. This creates cognitive dissonance, or the perception of inconsistent or contradictory information.[2] We are naturally inclined to reduce cognitive dissonance. One path is to shift our behavior, but it's easier to blame or deny or self-justify, which keeps us from feeling discomfort but essentially and ironically shifts us right back to protection. If we can instead sit with this discomfort, it is the gateway to greater awareness.

At this level, there are times when Simone is able to dampen her response—she yells less loudly than she otherwise would have, for example—but in general, she is still in a state of protection and does not know how to pivot to learning. She is trying to intervene at the behavioral level, but her beliefs and mindsets are still driving her old patterns. In order to create real change, she must look at what is frozen beneath the waterline of her iceberg. This is why our resolutions so often fail. We make a behavioral change commitment without looking at the drivers of this behavior. With time, Simone starts to wonder, *What is going on with me that is causing me to get so frustrated that I am no longer helping my team?*

Simone has a close mentor within the company named Marcia, and she asks her to meet for lunch. Over their meal, Simone fills Marcia in on what has been going on with her and with the team, including the behavior she has recently become aware of. "I try to lead them and coach them," Simone tells Marcia, "but sometimes I shut them down without meaning to. I just get so frustrated. It's like I can't help myself when I feel that we're falling behind."

Marcia asks, "What behaviors exactly do you want to change?"

After some thought, Simone says, "I don't want to raise my voice. I don't want to catastrophize, and I don't want to show my emotions so openly, especially my disappointment and frustration."

"Okay," Marcia says. "Well, what would you rather do instead?"

Simone considers this for a moment. "Ask more questions. Stay calm and positive. And motivate the team without scaring them." Simone thinks for a moment longer. "I don't mean for it to happen, but when things don't go well, I think my team feels like I'm angry and disappointed in them."

"What are you feeling in those moments with your team?" Marcia asks her. "Are you actually feeling angry and disappointed?"

"Yes," Simone says without hesitation.

"With your team?"

"Well, yes, no, not entirely," Simone says carefully. Then she takes a long pause and lets out a big sigh. "To be honest, I used to be frustrated with my team members' behaviors, but in this case I was really angry with myself. I feel like if I was a good enough leader, I should be able to lead the team to find the answers and collaborate better so there wouldn't be so many surprises and setbacks. Deep down, when this is happening, I feel like a failure, and then I start feeling pretty emotional about that and wanting to fix it. But I don't know how, so my frustration and anxiety levels just go through the roof." Simone pauses, and then says, "I guess I've been holding on to the idea that I'm personally accountable for everything that happens within my team, so I blame myself when things don't go well."

Simone has identified her default mindset: *To be an effective leader, my team needs to be successful and deliver on their promises.* When she is operating from this mindset and something negative or surprising happens, Simone reacts emotionally because her self-worth feels threatened and the stakes seem enormous.

To be clear, the question is not whether a mindset is right or wrong. The question is whether or not the mindset is serving us. Is it leading to behavior that gets the results we want? Her mindset about leadership has at times served Simone well. It has helped her to step up and proactively take ownership in many difficult situations. But now that Simone is a senior leader facing more adaptive challenges, she is removed from the day-to-day details and needs to deliver results through her team. Her role and her circumstances have outgrown her mindset.

Marcia and Simone discuss what other mindsets might serve Simone better in this situation. Finally, Simone says, *"As a leader, my job is to create an open learning environment that is collaborative so my team can surface shortfalls or deviations quickly and work together to solve challenges and deliver results. My role is to coach and guide them, remove obstacles, help them get at root causes, and also replace leaders who are not up to the task, not to take ownership or base my worth as a leader on their ability to deliver."*

Marcia and Simone then talk about what might happen if Simone operated from this mindset. It's important to visualize ourselves exhibiting the behaviors we want to emulate, as it creates new neural connections in our brains.[3] "I could push the team hard but calmly," Simone says, "by asking questions in a way that feels aspirational, meaning I have high expectations and a sense of curiosity and compassion but no personal judgment. So, hopefully the team will feel challenged without taking it personally or getting defensive."

AWARENESS LEVEL 4: RESILIENT—AWARE AND ABLE TO RESPOND AFTER A SHORT PAUSE OR TIME-OUT

Simone is committed to doing whatever she can to exhibit her desired leadership behavior and stop contributing to the tension on her team. At times, she succeeds, but she often still gets upset when facing a challenge or setback and finds herself getting carried away by her emotions and reverting to her protection behaviors.

After this happens a few times, Simone develops a "trick": she observes herself in meetings, and instead of reacting when she catches herself getting emotional, she takes a "time-out." Then she goes to the restroom or suggests that the team take a bathroom break. Once she is alone, she takes a few deep breaths, splashes some cold water on her face, and takes stock of what is happening inside and around her. She asks herself how she is feeling and why she is feeling that way, and then she allows those emotions to pass through her. She is surprised to see that when she does this, her emotions generally fade very quickly.

Once she has calmed down, Simone works on coaching herself through a reframing of the situation at hand. Instead of thinking about who she can blame or what her team's current problem says about her as a leader, she starts to ask herself what she can learn from this and how she can best coach her team through this challenge in order to come to a positive resolution.

These small breaks help Simone redirect and choose the best response instead of acting from a place of emotion. The more she succeeds and is able to respond calmly to surprises and challenges, the more the tension among her team members starts easing up just a bit. There is more conversation during meetings and less silence, holding back, and accusations. And with practice, Simone is able to work through her reframing process more quickly.

There are still times, though, when Simone reacts out of emotion even after her "time-out." When she reflects on these moments afterward, she realizes that this tends to happen when she takes action without fully accepting the situation for what it is. We teach a technique called Awareness, Pause, Reframe, and a big part of the awareness piece is developing not only awareness of the self but also awareness and acceptance of the context and the situation. This is how we develop Dual Awareness.

As leaders, we often want to move forward and get to solutions as quickly as possible, but during times of stress it is essential to *pause in order to move faster*. Slow down to speed up. A real-time pause allows us to decouple from the immediate challenge and the protection state we may enter as a result, engage the parts of our brains that are in charge of executive functioning, and explore new options and ways of responding. The more we do this, the better we are able to interrupt the well-grooved habits that are activated under stress and create space to try on a new lens that allows us to see and respond to the world differently.

This is a dynamic process that is not always linear. When we begin developing awareness, we rarely go straight from one level to the next and often fall back a level or even two as our context and circumstances change. It is as if we are playing the children's board game Chutes and Ladders. We climb up a ladder with practice and hard work, and then we slide back down the chute as we face a new adaptive challenge that activates our hidden iceberg in unforeseen ways. We do this again and again, but even when we slide all the way down, we are not starting over completely. Each time we start traveling up a new ladder, we can do so more quickly.

PHYSICAL AND COGNITIVE INTERVENTIONS

Pausing before reacting is an important step toward Deliberate Calm, but what we do during that pause is equally important. First, we can utilize techniques that interrupt the body's stress response. Then, once we are in a place of physiological calm, we can use reframing techniques. Through this cycle, we can pivot from protection to learning even when facing the most complex challenges.

PHYSICAL TECHNIQUES

These quick and easy interventions can help calm us down in the moment so we can choose the best response. As we gain awareness, we will be able to stop the stress response sooner and sooner, until we reach the point where our bodies do not have a chance to respond at all before we have already reframed the situation and chosen the best response. Until we get to that point, or when circumstances inevitably catch us off guard, implementing one or more of these techniques can dampen the stress response and prepare the body for learning.

Focus on the Exhale

We all know that taking deep breaths can help calm us down, but it is actually the exhalation that reduces stress in the body. Deep breaths with longer inhalations than exhalations increase the heart rate, inducing a state of stress. Some athletes use this technique to amp themselves up before a game. Deep breaths with longer exhalations than inhalations, however, decrease the heart rate and a state of physical stress.

Stanford neuroscientist Andrew Huberman recommends the "physiological sigh" to quickly calm the nervous system. To do this, take two quick inhales through the nose (inhale, pause, inhale again), and then a long exhale through the mouth. Do this two or three times in a row to quickly calm the body at the first sign of stress.[4]

Zoom Out

When we are in a state of protection, we develop tunnel vision. We focus on what is comfortable and familiar in order to stay safe, and we become blind to new information and possibilities that exist outside our line of vision. This works as a metaphor, but it is also literally true. Zooming out and opening our peripheral vision to take in a panoramic view of the room we are in calms down our physiological stress response.

To practice this, look straight ahead and sit back in your chair so that you can see the whole room. Then focus on taking in the bigger picture, as far to your left and right as you can see. Huberman recommends spending two to ten minutes a day practicing this panoramic vision to remain in a place of calm. You can also do this to calm down quickly during stressful moments.

Move

When we are in a state of stress, our bodies are primed to fight or flee. Instead of resisting this and sitting still, we can release some of that stress by moving our bodies. Even taking a brisk five-to-ten-minute walk can help. Huberman explains that when we do this, our bodies believe that we are taking forward action toward solving our problems and reward us by releasing dopamine. Plus, as we walk, our eyes naturally move from side to side, and we take in a panoramic view of our surroundings. These two things together help us think more calmly and rationally when we are stressed.

Calm Your Voice

Speaking calmly can create a calming effect for yourself and for those around you.[5] There are various ways to make your voice more "calm." For instance, speak more slowly, take more pauses between words and sentences, lower the volume of your voice, and even lower the pitch of your voice slightly. Even when no one else is around, speaking out loud using a calm voice can have a calming effect for ourselves. Vocal techniques such as singing, humming, chanting, or gargling can reduce the body's stress response. As the American philosopher, historian, and psychologist William James said, "I don't sing because I'm happy. I'm happy because I sing."

Breathe Deep

Slow, deep belly breathing calms the body by getting more oxygen into the blood, relaxing muscle tension, slowing our heart rate, and lowering blood pressure. It also helps us find a natural, calm, and lower pitch in our voice. When we are stressed, we often begin breathing from our chests. In these moments, practice dropping your breath to the belly. Ideally, combine this with your focus on the exhalation, as mentioned above.

REFRAMING TECHNIQUES

The way we frame our circumstances can greatly limit or expand our options. When we are driven by emotion, we are generally unaware of how we are framing our situation and believe we are seeing things objectively. Of course, this is not the case. Pausing first and intervening in our physiological stress response helps us gain awareness of how we are mentally framing the situation and, if necessary, look at the situation from a different perspective. Following are a few simple reframing techniques that can help open our minds to a state of learning.

View Challenges as Opportunities

In a state of protection, we tend to frame things negatively and see challenges or surprises as problems. But even framing something as a problem limits our choices in how we respond. Some things are objectively problems, but many can also be viewed as opportunities. This simple reframing is powerful and may open up a whole new set of possibilities.

Seek First to Understand[6]

We often get stressed because of our assumptions about what other people are thinking or feeling. But we only really know our own frame of reference. Pausing what is going on for us helps us stay open so we can try to understand what is going on with the other person or people with whom we are communicating. The "reality" that applies to us does not always apply to others. They have their own contexts and hidden icebergs causing them to act in certain ways, and their thoughts and feelings may be very different from our own or from what we assume. Simply asking for more context about what is going on with someone else can grow the shared understanding between us. This can help us calm down, open our minds to different realities, and prevent our icebergs from bumping up against each other's, creating unnecessary friction.

Get Curious

Asking questions to ourselves or others causes us to slow down, reflect, and engage the executive functioning parts of our brains.[7] It also keeps us from reacting in the same ways as always and forces us to see new possibilities. As leaders, we fail to adapt when we see ourselves as experts who must have the right answers instead of as curious learners who must ask the right questions. When we shed our expert status, we can flexibly navigate uncertain situations by collecting information in new and productive ways.

A few examples of open-ended questions are:

- What other possibilities are we not seeing?
- What other questions should we consider?
- Who can we/I ask for help?
- What is the most important thing to focus on right now?

Connect to Why

When we feel strong, even negative emotions, it is generally because underneath those feelings is a deep sense of caring about the issue or situation at hand. If we did not care about something, we wouldn't feel a lot of emotion around it. During stressful moments, it is helpful to ask ourselves, "Why is this important to me?" This often brings us back to our purpose, and connecting with that deeper sense of meaning allows us to tell ourselves a different story about what is happening to us and why.

Pause

Many of us feel pressured to respond to situations right away, but when we are stressed or emotional, this does not always lead to the best possible outcome. Instead of checking out or avoiding taking necessary action, it can be liberating to decide with intention not to act in the moment. As they say, the not doing is the doing. Of course, some situations do require immediate action, but many do not. When we feel the need to intervene and take control of the situation, we find it helpful to ask ourselves three questions to determine the best way to respond:

1. Does this absolutely need to be said or done?
   This takes our attention away from what we want to do and reframes it around what the situation requires.

2. Does it need to be said or done by me?

   Take a moment to look at the situation strategically. This, too, takes us out of our own emotional response. Some things land differently depending on who says or does them, leading to an entirely different end result. Perhaps this action is better taken by someone else.

3. Does it need to be said or done right now?

   Often, there is no downside and perhaps a big upside to delaying our reaction until we and the people around us are all operating from a place of calm. If it can wait, let it sit for a bit and create time and space for a little more perspective.

AWARENESS LEVEL 5: ADAPTIVE—AWARE AND ABLE TO PIVOT EFFECTIVELY FROM PROTECTION TO LEARNING IN THE MOMENT (DUAL AWARENESS IN ACTION)

Over time, Simone has fewer and fewer moments when she needs to pause, calm down, and reframe the situation. And when she does, she is able to move through this cycle quickly. But it still happens more often than she'd like. So, she begins a new practice of looking ahead at her day in the morning and trying to pinpoint the moments when she is likely to be challenged. As she identifies those moments, she is able to reframe them in advance from a calm physiological state before ever feeling threatened. When the moment arrives later on, she is ready and armed to face it with her chosen mindset and behaviors. It is almost as if she is bypassing her body's stress response by taking a time-out *before* the stressful moment instead of in the middle of it. And this goes a long way toward helping her reach Awareness Level Five.

At this level, Simone is able to shift to the learning state without taking a time-out. She is not only aware of herself and her circumstances in the moment, but she can respond effectively as well. Simone thinks of this as being able to "catch the arrow" as it is flying toward her. Without pausing, without panicking, and without missing a beat, she can sense herself becoming stressed in the very early stages, reframe the situation, and respond before her body elicits a full-blown stress response.

Oh, she thinks when her team comes to her with bad news, *I can feel my emotions starting to heat up. My heart is racing. I have to remember that this isn't about me and whether or not I'm a good leader. This is about the team. It's normal for plans to deviate, and the accountability needs to stay with them.*

Over time, Simone no longer needs to reframe. Her new mindset is simply how she identifies as a leader. She is now able to act in ways that create a safer environment for her team to share setbacks and challenges. Her response isn't to feel frustrated or to take the entire burden onto herself but rather to get into a constructive problem-solving mode while keeping accountability with the team. After multiple positive experiences with this new mindset, she is building another groove in her iceberg, this time of habits that serve her well in the adaptive challenge she is facing.

Of course, there are times when she ends up sliding down another chute. When Simone finds out that Jonathan's team has missed a deadline and didn't even tell her about it, she needs to take a few moments to breathe deeply and remind herself of how she wants to show up as a leader. *They don't always tell me about problems because I have a history of reacting badly, so I'd better not do that,* she reminds herself. She manages to stay calm as she asks Jonathan and his team about what happened. But it's bad. The missed deadline puts the company in a real bind, and it could have serious consequences.

In the past, when Jonathan's team didn't deliver, Simone blamed herself. But now she can clearly see that despite her efforts to help him grow and develop, Jonathan's talents are better suited for another role. It's very difficult for Simone to replace Jonathan, and a part of her still feels like a failure for not being able to get him to where he needed to be. But she is aware of the reality of the situation, she is aware of her feelings and thoughts about the situation, she is aware of where these feelings and thoughts are coming from, and she is able to make what she truly believes is the best decision for her team and for the people her company is trying to serve.

Replacing Jonathan is an important action that Simone would not have been able to make when she was unaware and operating from her iceberg patterns. Collaboration immediately begins to improve between the two departments she leads, and meetings don't have the negative emotional charge that they used to. They're still facing challenges, and the new product has not yet been finalized or incorporated into the business, but they're in a much better position than they were before, and the team seems confident that they will ultimately rise to the challenge.

Simone incorporates more and more techniques into her daily life to continue practicing Dual Awareness. She can see that it has all been worth it when she receives a small piece of feedback from Jonathan's replacement, Lisa. After she has been onboarded and is in the flow of her new role, Lisa tells Simone how much she appreciates her approach. "Thanks for pushing me," Lisa says to Simone at the end of one of their one-on-ones. "When my old boss questioned me, I always felt like a failure. But you just make me feel like you really care."

"I do," Simone says, smiling as she takes in the small win. "Thanks, Lisa." And she gets back to work.

WHAT IS YOUR LEVEL OF AWARENESS?

At the end of the day, reflecting on the moments when you shifted into protection can help you begin to understand your current level of awareness. As we continue through the book and especially the four-week protocol later on, you will continue to increase your awareness and hopefully move through the levels until you are regularly practicing Dual Awareness and experiencing fewer and fewer moments when you shift into protection. Start by asking yourself the following questions at the end of the day:

1. How many stressful or triggering moments did you experience today?
2. On average, which awareness level did you find yourself in during these moments?
   a. Level 1: Unaware (Not aware of internal state or external zone)
   b. Level 2: Delayed (Aware after it happened)
   c. Level 3: Perceptive (Aware but not able to effectively respond in the moment)
   d. Level 4: Resilient (Aware and able to respond after a short pause or time-out)
   e. Level 5: Adaptive (Aware and able to pivot effectively from protection to learning in the moment—Dual Awareness in action)
3. Which moment was the most stressful today?
4. What do you think made it so stressful for you? Was it something someone said, something you thought, a sound, or something you saw?
5. Around roughly what time today did this most stressful moment happen?
6. What level of awareness (refer to question 2) did you experience during this most stressful moment?

7. What thoughts did you have during this moment?

8. What emotions did you experience during this moment?

9. What physical sensations did you feel during this moment?

10. What was your overall response to the situation? Did you move toward or away from your goals?

PART III

THE DELIBERATE CALM PRACTICE

CHAPTER 8

WHEN ICEBERGS COLLIDE
INTERPERSONAL DYNAMICS

You cannot shake hands with a clenched fist.

—INDIRA GANDHI

I t's not just one supplier," says Latha, a leader in the company's distribution and logistics organization. "This is a much deeper and more systemic problem."

Giovanna, the team leader, sighs. Once again, she is finding herself irritated with her team and with Latha in particular, who seems to be ignoring the fact that Giovanna, not Latha, was asked to lead this initiative.

"I agree," Giovanna replies to Latha with a raised voice. "But as I just said, I'd like to wrestle at least one problem to the ground so we can make some progress. This supplier seems to be the biggest source of our issues, so let's start there."

"*Seems* to be the biggest source of our issues, but is it really?"

challenges Latha, who is used to focusing on the big picture, not this kind of micro-problem. "And if the root cause is how we select and work with our partners more broadly, then trying to fix one supplier won't really solve the problem."

"Actually, I could argue that they're one of our best suppliers," Mark, the procurement lead, chimes in.

At this point, Giovanna is becoming exhausted. "And by what measure could you possibly argue that?"

"Well," says Mark, "they can meet all our specifications, always deliver on time, and have the lowest cost."

"The lowest unit price isn't necessarily the lowest total cost when you factor in the quality problems on the back end," says Roberto, the director of product quality.

Chad, the director of product manufacturing, shakes his head. "Latha's right," he says. "'Seems to be' isn't good enough. Where is the data?"

Silently, Giovanna is fuming. If her team can't even agree on what to talk about or what the problem is, how are they ever going to find a solution?

Giovanna, Latha, Mark, Chad, and Roberto are each functional leaders at a global business-to-business technology company that makes industrial electronics used by large manufacturers. Their company produces state-of-the-art sensors and connectivity devices that help the most advanced manufacturing facilities run smoothly, powering everything from predictive maintenance to AI-driven operations optimization. They charge a premium for it, and, until recently, customers were happy to pay extra for a better product.

As customer demand began to outstrip the company's supply, they responded by increasing production and raising prices to an even higher premium while continuing on their fast growth trajectory. Unfortunately, this led to a run of defective products. A number of their customers didn't receive their products on time, and those who did are starting to complain that they aren't working properly. Now the company is facing customer complaints, lost business, and even a lawsuit.

The executive committee asked Giovanna, the associate vice president of key accounts in the commercial organization, to lead this cross-functional team to come up with solutions to the company's supply chain and product quality problems. After several meetings, not only are they making very little progress, but there is so much friction between Latha and Giovanna that it seems like they will never be able to work together to solve anything. A successful leader who normally shows grit, resilience, and optimism in the face of challenges, Giovanna is starting to feel frustrated and despondent. No matter what she does, she cannot seem to get any traction.

"Team!" exclaims Giovanna. "We've been through all of this already. This is a crisis, and we have made zero progress. We just keep chasing our tails. Where is your sense of urgency? We have to start somewhere, and the supplier that seems to be contributing the most to the quality issues is as good a place as any. And since you all can't seem to agree, as the team leader I'm making the call. Let's start with this supplier, identify the problem, and fix it!"

Mark promptly gets up and starts walking out. "Sorry, but I just looked at the time. We've run over, and I have another meeting I need to get to."

The rest of the team files out, and Giovanna sits alone in the conference room feeling defeated. She doesn't understand why her leadership seems to be suddenly failing her, exactly when she needs it most. On top of their lack of progress, it feels like Latha is being passive-aggressive and undermining her at every turn, and she doesn't understand why. Latha has a reputation of being very collaborative, but to Giovanna she seems to be exactly the opposite.

Giovanna wonders if she should go back to the executive committee and ask for Latha to be replaced on the team, but she is worried about how that will reflect on her leadership ability and affect her future with the company. At the same time, she knows that if this team fails to solve these problems, it will reflect just as badly on her, if not worse. It feels to her like an impossible situation, and she is at a loss about what to do.

WHAT GOT US HERE WON'T GET US THERE

Up until now, Giovanna has had a great track record of leading high-performing teams. Her approach is decisive and action oriented. She starts by clearly defining and structuring the problem that needs to be solved, which gets everyone on the same page and provides the focus the team needs to get moving. Then she structures a set of tasks to tackle the problem and doles out a clear set of work streams to each team member, defining specific objectives so they know exactly what is expected of them. Giovanna has a reputation for setting a high bar, but also for helping to motivate and empower people to deliver on the high expectations she sets.

In this case, Giovanna's tried-and-true leadership approach isn't working. She's even struggling with the very first step—defining the problem. For starters, there are multiple problems here, not just one, and not only are they murky, multifaceted, and complex, but the biggest issues lie outside her area of knowledge and expertise.

Unfortunately, Giovanna is unaware that her current challenge is adaptive and calls for a new response. She is in unfamiliar territory and the stakes are high, but she is approaching it with her usual leadership style. It's not that she's not doing her job well enough; it's that this particular situation requires a completely new approach. As we know from the adaptability paradox, it is exactly in these situations when we are trying to solve a complex adaptive challenge and the stakes are high and our old way of doing things isn't working that we so often panic and revert to those same ineffective solutions.

Giovanna's team is under a tremendous amount of pressure. The problems they are trying to solve are incredibly complex, and they keep evolving. None of them have dealt with anything like this before, and there are a lot of unknowns that amplify the uncertainty. When we face stress and pressure like this, especially in the midst of high uncertainty and complexity, the parts of our brains that we need to innovate and creatively problem solve tend to take a back seat while our body's stress response takes over. This can create a "do loop" where the more stressed we are, the more we react with default patterns of thinking and acting, while the content of the problem requires a new response. And when the problems persist, we face even more stress and are even more reactive and less creative.

The issues Giovanna is now facing are not only with her own adaptability, her own iceberg, and her own behaviors when she slips into a state of protection. Giovanna's iceberg is also colliding with Latha's, often in ways that neither of them is aware of, further contributing to those protective reactions. To solve their current challenges, the entire team need to leverage their collective skills, ingenuity, and resources. This requires them to get into a *virtuous* cycle where they are listening to and helping each other. In other words, in order to work together to solve their adaptive challenge, they need to shift into a state of learning individually and on an interpersonal level. If they keep doing the same things they've been doing, they will undoubtedly keep getting the same frustrating results.

The team is now in their second week of working together, and they've made little to no progress. They're working hard, but they are not collaborating or communicating or finding new ways to work effectively. Siloed and disconnected, they are stuck doing things in the same old ways as always, even though they know those methods are no longer working.

Each member of this team is an individual high performer with a successful track record, and they cannot fathom why this team has become so dysfunctional so quickly. They aren't communicating well, so they can't get to an understanding of where the other team members are coming from. And since none of them have experienced this before, they all assume that the fault lies with the other team members and they have started to implicitly blame each other for their lack of progress.

Giovanna is feeling more and more hopeless with each ineffective, conflict-ridden meeting. On top of leading this team, she is working hard to retain some of their biggest accounts that have been signaling they might cancel their contracts and switch to competitors.

After a few weeks without any progress, Giovanna finally goes to Frank, the executive sponsor and global head of operations and supply chain for the company. Instead of singling out Latha, she says, "I think we should shake up the team. They all know a lot, but we just aren't jelling. They can't seem to work together."

Frank thinks for a moment. "We picked each of these people because they have the skills and experience we need," he tells Giovanna. "I'll reach out to our organizational effectiveness group to see if they can provide some team-building assistance to get the project on track."

"Wait, what?" Giovanna is somewhat alarmed. They're already facing so much time pressure. They don't have time for a big off-site with trust falls and ice breakers. But Frank assures Giovanna that this will be different.

"A team dynamics expert from the organizational effectiveness group is just going to sit in on your meetings, offer a few suggestions, and see if she can help you get unstuck," he tells her. Feeling desperate and clueless about how to make any headway with this team, Giovanna has no choice but to agree.

A woman named Elizabeth from the organizational effectiveness team shows up to sit in on the next team meeting. The team tackles a lot of topics but once again makes little progress. The tension among the group is obvious, and when the meeting quickly devolves into unproductive arguments, Elizabeth asks to interject. "I know that time is a constraint right now," she says, "but if you'll humor me, I'd love for us to get out of this stuffy room and move our bodies, just for a little bit. We can continue our conversation while we walk. Think of it as a working break."

It's a brisk but sunny day. Elizabeth leads the team to a nearby park and asks them to pair up and talk about their beliefs around success and what each of them sees as critical to their own success in this effort. Elizabeth pairs up with Giovanna. When they get back to the office a little while later, Elizabeth asks them to go around and share what they discussed with the rest of the team.

"I have to get all the materials we need at the lowest possible cost," Mark says simply.

"I need to be able to implement long-term, predictable plans, so that we can reliably deliver products to customers, on time and on budget," Chad says.

"We need on-time delivery of our materials and products, no stock outs, while maintaining low inventory and working capital," says Latha. "With more predictable plans and more reliable operations and better service from partners, we can make just-in-time delivery work."

"I just need to eliminate defects," says Roberto. "With a bigger budget and more robust quality processes, we can minimize variability and get to a zero-defect rate. I just need to get others on board to prioritize quality."

"For me it's simple," Giovanna says. "To be successful, we need to grow our sales volume and deliver for our customers, so they remain loyal and we can continue to grow. And I need to lead this team to solve the problems that are getting in the way of that. If we could just each do our jobs and communicate better, it shouldn't be this hard."

Elizabeth nods. "These are the success models that have worked for you in the past," she says. "And it seems like they've served you all really well. But how is the challenge you're facing different this time? What is this situation asking of you that is above and beyond what you just described?"

"Well, the market is much less predictable, that's for sure," Chad says. "Maybe we need to find ways to deliver even when plans change."

"And with the current strain on the distribution system—sometimes there's more to the story than just cost," Mark admits.

Latha is quiet for a while, and then she says, "Maybe just-in-time delivery and minimizing working capital costs and inventories isn't the most important thing to focus on right now."

"Even without the full budget that I need long-term," Roberto adds, "I guess I need to focus more on navigating the immediate quality crisis."

Giovanna thinks for a minute. "Maybe the problem is harder than I've been willing to admit, and each person just doing their individual job isn't enough," she finally says. "It won't work for each individual to do their thing separately. I thought that if each team member just did what I told them to do, I could integrate everything and figure it out. But I think we all need to go beyond our formal roles and tackle this thing more holistically as a team. We all need to adapt our success models, and we need to adapt them in as-yet-unknown ways. This is new territory, for sure."

With her questions, Elizabeth is helping the team gain external awareness that they are in the Adaptive Zone. They are also starting to realize that without known answers for their current problem, they've been doubling down on the success models that were effective when they were in the Familiar Zone, facing a more predictable market. Before this, their jobs were all difficult and stressful at times, but they had the skills they needed to work hard and succeed. Now that they're in the Adaptive Zone, they need an entirely new approach. "This reminds me of one of my favorite quotes from Marshall Goldsmith's book, *What Got You Here Won't Get You There*," Elizabeth tells the team: "'Now we can let go of what got you here and figure out how to get where you need to go.'"

USING CONFLICT TO DRIVE LEARNING

We often think of conflict as inherently negative or harmful. For many of us, conflict feels threatening and shifts us into a state of protection. But this doesn't have to be the case. Like stress, conflict can be either negative or positive, depending on how we interpret and handle it. When handled well, with an open mind instead of judgment, defensiveness, or blame, conflict can in fact be a major catalyst for learning.

After all, when two people see things the exact same way, we don't really learn anything new from each other. But when two people disagree and openly share our different ideas and views, we can learn something new and come to see things from a broader perspective. This can help each of us adapt and grow and help us solve complex challenges together. That is, if, and only if, we are able to avoid feeling threatened and stay in an open state of learning.

When two people are operating in a state of protection, on the other hand, our behavior above the waterline is from a state of protection. We are two "closed" minds talking but not communicating, only interested in getting our own point across. Not only is this ineffective, but it can lead each of us to shift even deeper into protection. Since something is at stake for both of us, we often feel threatened by the other person's protection behaviors, which only serves to strengthen those very behaviors in each of us. When this happens, we must not only gain awareness around our own icebergs but also try to help the very person with whom we are in conflict to gain awareness around theirs.

This is no easy task, but practicing Dual Awareness can help us achieve it. If we can observe ourselves from that skylight and notice when the person with whom we are in conflict is in a state of protection and how their protection behaviors are affecting us, we gain the power to change the dynamic. To help someone else get out of protection, we must first shift into learning ourselves. We can demonstrate calm visibly by slowing down, using a calm voice, and so on, and then ask questions to promote learning and/or focus on a common goal. It is a matter of synchronizing both people toward a state of calm instead of throwing oil on a fire by reacting to someone else's emotions from our own state of protection.

Without Dual Awareness, we run the risk of being triggered in a state of protection, judging and blaming others, and beginning to form negative opinions about them. Then we perceive what they say and do in light of those opinions. One of the most powerful yet subtle cognitive biases that we all have is confirmation bias—the tendency to seek, find, and interpret new information in ways that confirm what we already believe. This is greatly amplified when we are in a state of protection. And when we constantly look for confirming evidence of our opinion through the very lens that created it, there is no doubt that we are going to find it.

This also ties into the fundamental attribution error, which we discussed earlier, that causes us to judge others based on their actions, which are visible to us, while we judge ourselves based on our context and intentions. When we judge someone else's behavior without knowledge of their intentions or context through the lens of our preconceived notions about them, it affects our own behavior. We begin to act as if our opinion about the other person is true. Then the other person sees us behaving this way, which likely confirms the opinion they have already formed about us, without any knowledge of *our* intentions or context. This becomes a vicious cycle and leaves little room for learning or collaboration.

Interestingly, there are biological factors behind this confirmation bias. When we receive validation of our preexisting ideas, our brains reward us by releasing dopamine,[1] and neural networks form, solidifying those beliefs into place.[2] It feels good to find confirmation that we are right. In his book *On Being Certain: Believing You Are Right Even When You're Not*, neuroscientist Robert Burton[3] explains, "Once firmly established, a neural network that links a thought to a feeling of correctness is not easily undone." This is because "an idea known to be wrong continues to feel correct."

These biological processes allow us to rationalize. Studies show that people with strong affiliations, such as partisan voters, recruit the prefrontal cortex to filter inconsistent information to fit with previously established beliefs and ignore inconsistencies.[4] Believing it has received validation, the brain then releases dopamine as a reward.

We should never judge ourselves for the ways we act when we are in protection. It requires awareness, willingness, and hard work to break free from our wiring and open our minds to new ideas. Compassion, toward both ourselves and others, is a necessary part of the process.

On top of our biases, another obstacle to learning from conflict is a lack of clarity between types of communication: requests, recognitions, critiques, feedback, and all-important learning conversations. A request is simply an ask regarding the future. For example, "Please show up to our next meeting on time." It can be said in a way that is completely separate from anything that has or hasn't happened in the past. A recognition celebrates something that we judge to be good. For example, "Well done" or "Good job." A critique admonishes something we judge to be not good. For example, "That was a terrible presentation."

Recognitions and critiques are not feedback, and none of these forms of communication do much to create meaningful learning. Real feedback, however, can create real learning in two ways: Evaluative feedback is concrete. It describes a goal or a standard and compares someone's behavior or performance to that standard with details about the ways in which the standard was or was not met. Developmental feedback describes a behavior or action without judgment and then states the impact of that behavior. Ideally, this is done using "I statements," such as, "When you were late, I felt disrespected," instead of "When you were late, you were acting disrespectful." The person giving developmental feedback then offers a specific suggestion for the future to either amplify the positive impact or minimize the negative impact of their actions.

When we are in the Familiar Zone, requests, recognitions, critiques, and feedback are typically sufficient for effective communication. But when we get into the Adaptive Zone, they do not jointly evolve our approaches to address an adaptive challenge. Particularly when we have to work together with no known answer and the stakes are high, we need to engage in *learning conversations*, in which two icebergs collide *constructively*. This is a form of creative and productive conflict that often leads to unique insight and innovation.

It is difficult to have learning conversations when our hidden icebergs are colliding in a state of protection. It is possible, however, to interrupt and repair this dynamic through various tactics to improve communication, build trust, and increase shared understanding. Even if we do not agree, when we are open to what is going on with the other person under the surface and can explore it without judgment, conflict no longer feels like a threat, and we can leverage our differences through a creative collision of icebergs in a state of learning.

GETTING UNDER THE SURFACE—EXPLORING OUR ICEBERGS TOGETHER

Later that week, Elizabeth invites the team to a dinner to help foster trust and intimacy. She calls it an "Origin Stories Dinner." The team found Elizabeth's last intervention helpful and is curious to see what's next. Even though they have not made much progress yet on their challenges, they are starting to see how working in their own silos with each of their overly narrow objectives might be getting in the way, so they go into the dinner with open minds.

After they've gathered, Elizabeth explains that this dinner might be a little bit different from anything they've experienced before. She invites the team to reintroduce themselves to each other with a story that consists of three parts. The first part of the story should be about where they came from, starting with a parent or a grandparent and the impact that person had on them. The second part of the story should be about a formative experience from any point in their life that shaped who they are as a person and a leader. This could either be related to the first part of the story or completely separate. The third part of the story should be about one of their traits that often shows up as a leadership strength but perhaps sometimes as a weakness, as well as how that trait connects to the first and/or the second part of the story.

Latha surprises the team by volunteering to go first. She begins by talking about her mother, who was an artist and refugee. There was a lot of emotion in Latha's home growing up, and at a young age it often felt scary. She remembers a lot of creativity and compassion, but it was also somewhat volatile, with Latha's parents getting a divorce when she was twelve. Latha learned to carefully manage her own emotions, often suppressing instead of freely expressing them.

For part two of her story, Latha tells the group about the childhood trips that she took with her parents to India before their divorce. Latha's parents were both spiritual seekers who brought their family to an ashram every year. Experiencing such a different lifestyle from the one she and her family enjoyed in Connecticut had a lasting impact on how Latha viewed herself and the world. The ashram, too, was a place of passion, faith, expression, and reflection.

Finally, for part three Latha talks about her trait of objectivity. She still meditates regularly, rarely lets her emotions cloud her judgment, and generally tends to be thoughtful, reflective, curious, and good at elevating her perspective to see problems and opportunities from many different angles. This often shows up as a strength. She tends to be a broad, strategic thinker, which is especially helpful when looking at complex supply chain networks. Latha's ability to remain calm in emotional situations, to be strategic, and to integrate different ideas and perspectives has served her well.

However, at times people describe Latha as aloof, say that she fails to build deeper relationships, or believe that she lacks empathy and compassion in emotional situations. She tends to focus on the big picture, which is mostly good, but her day-to-day interactions can come across as transactional. She acknowledges that perhaps at times this has prevented her from building deeper relationships in her personal and professional life.

Earlier, we spoke of the Johari Window, a tool to help people understand their relationships with themselves and with others. As each team member goes around the table and shares their own story, they are growing the shared understanding quadrant of each window, not only by shrinking the private or façade quadrants but also by shrinking the unknown or undiscovered quadrant. In other words, they are gaining a far greater understanding not only of each other's behaviors and where they stem from but also of their own hidden icebergs. None of them have ever really been pushed to connect the dots between their formative experiences and their leadership traits, or to think about how those traits can show up as weaknesses or strengths, depending on the situation.

When we grow the shared understanding between us and another person, the relationship naturally becomes more effective. Instead of blaming each other and looking for evidence of our own prejudgments, we start to see each other more fully as complete, complex, three-dimensional humans whose behavior in a given situation might reflect something much more complex than what we see on the surface. This often starts to promote more understanding, trust, empathy, and intimacy as we feel more comfortable sharing deeper elements of who we are.

THE LADDER OF INFERENCE

Chris Argyris, a towering thought leader in organizational development and organizational learning, has written extensively about action science,[5] a method for generating usable knowledge and insights and taking action to apply them in a way that not only improves results but also helps drive further learning and insight. Over the years, Argyris and his colleagues (including Donald Schon and Robert Putnam) have introduced several important methods to help create learning in action in teams and organizations through healthy dialogue and learning-oriented collaboration.

Argyris uses the helpful metaphor of a ladder, which he calls the ladder of inference, to describe how we each interpret information and interactions differently. Each rung of the ladder represents a step we take as we read into our interactions with others. In some ways, it is the inverse of our iceberg model. The farther we go down the ladder, the more rooted we are in objective truth and shared reality. The more we work up the ladder, the more we move from the objective truth to our choices, behaviors, and actions.

Moving up the ladder to action also means layering interpretations and meaning onto objective reality. This, of course, leads us to focus on some pieces of data and information and to filter out others, to interpret (or misinterpret) that data, and to draw different conclusions based on our orientations, goals, and biases. All this can lead to significant interpersonal conflict as our positions, beliefs, preferences, and choices diverge the farther up the ladder we go. When we understand what lies on each rung of each other's ladder of inference, we can interrupt this dynamic and come closer to the objective truth. This helps us shift out of protection and into learning, where real dialogue and understanding are possible and we can discover new possibilities, options, and ways of looking at things.

At the very bottom of the ladder lie all possible data and facts—objective reality as it is or was or could be without any interpretation or meaning beyond the facts themselves. Working our way up, the first rung of the ladder is our factual raw *observations*, that is, all of that data in the world that we observe or have access to, even if we didn't notice it, if we choose to ignore it, or if we forget about it. These are often not the things we remember. Most of us keep the stories we tell ourselves about that data fresh in our minds, not the raw facts that existed before we created meaning out of them.

For example, after the storytelling dinner, Giovanna and Latha are getting along a little bit better, but Giovanna still often feels that Latha is undermining and does not fully respect her. Giovanna reaches out and asks Latha to grab coffee the next morning. Giovanna shows up exactly at 9:00, but Latha doesn't arrive until 9:12. When Latha arrives, Giovanna says, "I was wondering if you were going to show up. I almost left."

"Of course I showed up," says Latha. "I said I would be here." She then quickly moves on to a new subject. Their meeting isn't particularly productive, in part because Giovanna is stewing over the fact that Latha was late. Later, Giovanna mentions to Elizabeth that Latha must not have thought their coffee meeting was important. Perhaps Latha's relationship with Giovanna isn't that important, either, she thinks, since Latha showed up twelve minutes late and didn't even apologize.

Later, Elizabeth helps Giovanna work down and up her ladder of inference. At the bottom of the ladder, we can see that Latha showed up at 9:12. This is an objective fact. However, the idea that Latha showed up twelve minutes late is an assessment, not a fact. The word "late" is a judgment that layers on an interpretation and an assumption that they were meant to meet at precisely 9:00 a.m. and not a minute later. Furthermore, Giovanna assumes that Latha was aware of the fact that she showed up late but didn't really care and then draws the conclusion that Latha didn't apologize because she doesn't think their meeting, or Giovanna herself, is important. But at the very bottom of the ladder, the only objective fact is that Giovanna showed up at 8:59 a.m. and Latha showed up at 9:12.

The second rung of the ladder is *selective data*. As we mentioned earlier, there is far too much data in the world for us to perceive or hold all of it in our minds. This rung of the ladder is based on which data we pay attention to and select and which data we either don't have access to, don't notice, or choose to ignore (consciously or unconsciously). Each of us pays attention to certain pieces of data more than others, often based on our mindsets, preconceived opinions, and beliefs. This is the confirmation bias that leads us to find evidence of the data we are looking for.

When Latha and Giovanna were planning their meeting, Latha had said, "Let's meet at around nine or so on Wednesday morning." Giovanna selected and remembered "nine" but not some of the other words, like "around" and "or so," which Latha had intended to mean that the meeting time was approximate.

The third rung of the ladder is the *meaning* we make out of the data we have selected. After Giovanna selected the data that Latha said "9:00 a.m." and Latha showed up at 9:12, Giovanna created the meaning that Latha was late.

The fourth rung on the ladder is the *assumptions* that we layer onto the meaning we've made of the data we've selected from our raw observations. This elaborates on our interpretations of what is happening. Here, Giovanna interprets not only that Latha is late but also that Latha knows very well that she is late and that her failure to acknowledge or apologize for her lateness means she doesn't care. Giovanna also holds the assumption that people are obligated to show up on time, particularly to meetings that are important. Failure to be prompt is unprofessional and often a sign of disrespect.

The fifth rung of the ladder is the resulting *conclusions* that we draw based on everything that lies farther down on the ladder. Giovanna is not entirely sure about whether or not Latha is rude or unprofessional in general, but she has drawn the conclusion that Latha doesn't care that she was late because she does not value their relationship.

The sixth rung of the ladder is the positions and *beliefs* we adopt as a result of our interpretations and conclusions. Based on this experience and her conclusions about it, along with some other interpretations and conclusions drawn from other observations, Giovanna adopts the view that Latha does not respect Giovanna and this is why Latha has been undermining Giovanna's authority and influence on the team. Giovanna now believes that she has to either earn Latha's respect and/or assert her authority with Latha in order to be an effective team leader and get Latha back "in line." The only other alternative is for Latha to be removed from the team. Otherwise, Giovanna cannot be successful.

These conclusions and beliefs will very quickly start to show up in Giovanna's choices, behaviors, and *actions* (the top of the iceberg, if you will). These visible behaviors will then serve as another set of data for Latha to interpret, make meaning out of, and draw conclusions from, all filtered through her own assumptions and beliefs. Latha's actions, in turn, will reflect their selected and interpreted data and her own conclusions and beliefs, providing more data for Giovanna. And on and on the cycle will go. All this can start from something as minor as being twelve minutes late for coffee! Think about how often this happens at every level in our professional and personal lives and how much unnecessary conflict could be avoided if we increased our shared understanding.

This type of conflict is an example of icebergs colliding in a way that does not create learning. The mindsets lying underneath the waterline of our icebergs are driving us as we move up the ladder of inference. The data we pay attention to, the meaning we create, the interpretations we add, the assumptions we make, and the conclusions we draw all stem from our mindsets and lead to actions that often serve to reinforce our original beliefs and positions.

Problems occur when everything except our actual behaviors is invisible, both to ourselves and to others. One of the most effective ways to navigate conflict and create a more expansive understanding of a situation is to work up and down the ladder of influence to parse out the various conclusions, beliefs, interpretations, and observations that each person is making. Then we can start to form a more complete picture of our own contributions to the current situation.

INQUIRY AND ADVOCACY

One way to gain insight into someone else's iceberg is to create a learning dialogue with a healthy mix of effective *advocacy* and *inquiry*, or the positions we take versus the questions we ask. When we are in protection, we tend to see the conflict as a battle that we want to win. We don't want to give any ammunition to our "opponent" in the conflict, whether that is a colleague, a family member, or a teammate. This leads us to keep our real thoughts and feelings to ourselves, avoid sharing what we are really thinking and feeling, filter out things that feel risky, and not be fully transparent about the *why* behind our positions and conclusions.

On the other hand, advocacy can create learning when we articulate very clearly and transparently what we believe and what actions we propose to take and *why*. Here, it helps to understand that conflict can be a source of learning and even innovation and creativity rather than a threat. As we each explain the *why* behind our beliefs, positions, choices, and proposed actions, we work down the ladder of inference, illuminating the observations that have informed our opinions as well as the attitudes, assumptions, meanings, and interpretations that we have layered on to form our conclusions. We open up our icebergs, and even if we still don't agree, we can come to a much better understanding of the various dynamics at play that are leading us to view things differently. Leaders who practice effective advocacy clearly voice their opinions and proposed solutions with vulnerability and authenticity as they explain the deeper why along their ladder of inference *and* their hidden iceberg.

Equally important to learning dialogue is effective inquiry—asking curious, nonjudgmental questions that help clarify the other person's viewpoints, choices, and actions. Through a series of probing, open-ended questions, effective inquiry helps work down someone else's ladder of inference so we can truly understand where they are coming from and *why*.

This might seem easy, but when someone else articulates a point of view that we strongly disagree with, it can be difficult to suspend judgment and simply ask curious questions, listening for understanding without arguing, judging, attacking their logic, or defending our own position—especially if we are in a state of protection. But asking open-ended questions is a great way to shift ourselves and the person we are in dialogue with into a state of learning. We can always switch back into advocacy mode later and restate where we are coming from. Our position does not need to be influenced by the other person if we have truly listened and still disagree, but it is important to be clear about when we are moving from questioning someone to articulating our own perspective without invalidating their experienced truth.

Latha and Giovanna are able to start repairing their relationship by putting a couple of their beliefs on the table and exploring them together in learning rather than protection. Giovanna shares that she thinks Latha does not respect her and has been undermining her efforts as the team leader. Latha shares that she believes someone with experience in supply chain should be leading this effort, not Giovanna, who came up through the company in the commercial organization. Latha believes this is why Giovanna is rushing to action before really understanding the problem.

Through their discussions, Giovanna and Latha never fully agree on whether or not some of the other's specific actions and behaviors were "right," but they do come to a better understanding of the *why* behind them. Giovanna learns that Latha feels it is incredibly important to be a team player and has great respect for Giovanna as a person and a leader in general. Latha believes their relationship is very important, even if she still thinks this initiative should be led by someone in supply chain rather than commercial.

Giovanna also learns that a number of specific interactions (including Latha showing up "late" for their coffee meeting) were misunderstandings, not signals of disrespect or a belief that Giovanna isn't important. While Giovanna still thinks that some of Latha's actions did have the impact of undermining her, she understands that that was not Latha's intention.

Latha, on the other hand, learns that Giovanna actually did have some experience in supply chain at her prior employer, that Giovanna's tendency to take action was a leadership style and a sense of urgency based on feeling a need to report some kind of progress as a signal to try to retain customers, and, in fact, Giovanna does believe that this is a problem that requires them to understand its complexities and root causes. After hearing about Giovanna's recent discussions with customers, Latha starts to come around to Giovanna's view that being able to report some progress, even if somewhat superficial, might be critical in the near term to maintain customer relationships.

Using these tools, Giovanna and Latha are able to practice staying in learning amid conflict and make their colliding icebergs more productive, and they experience a number of interpersonal unlocks. Now, in order to fully address the adaptive problems that they are facing, they must find a way to expand this learning throughout the rest of the team.

FROM CONFLICT TO LEARNING

This exercise from *Action Science* can help you gain understanding of your own ladder of inference as well as of someone you are in conflict with. It also illuminates the key differences between what you or another person may be thinking or feeling and how your actions and behavior might be interpreted by someone else.

To start, think of a conflict you recently had with another person. On a piece of paper, create three columns. In the first column, write down exactly what each of you said and did as objectively as possible. You won't remember every single word, but do your best. In the second column, next to each action or statement you made, write down what you were thinking and feeling in that moment but did not say. In the third column, look at each statement or action from the other person and try to put yourself in their shoes. What might they have been thinking or feeling but not said when they said or did this?

Now look back at all three columns. Can you see how what you were thinking and feeling was disconnected from what you actually said and did? How might the other person have interpreted these things? And how similar or different are the possible things that the other person could have been thinking or feeling from the assumptions you made in the moment? What would be possible in your personal and professional relationships if you saw things differently, without layering on assumptions, meanings, and beliefs?

To take this a step farther and gain even more self-awareness, work your way up the ladder of inference to understand why you were thinking and feeling what you did at each step during this conflict. The better you understand your own ladder of inference, the more effectively you can use advocacy to create learning dialogue.

CHAPTER 9

DELIBERATE CALM TEAMS

We are caught in an inescapable network of
mutuality, tied in a single garment of destiny.
Whatever affects one directly affects all indirectly.
—MARTIN LUTHER KING JR.

Mark, now they're asking us to pick up the components that we need from their warehouse if we want the supplies sooner," says Chad in frustration and disbelief. "Why did we go with this vendor if they can't even get the product to us?"

Mark turns his body slightly away from Chad and looks down at his laptop. "Well, whatever your team specified is in the contract," Mark replies. "I'm not a mind reader. If you want something specific, it's got to be written into the contract."

"Delivery to our manufacturing plant is standard for these kinds of materials," Chad tells Mark. "How on earth can I make product when the raw materials aren't there? I feel like I can't count on anything. Latha seems to be constantly changing our forecasts, Roberto can't tell me anything without more data, and everything feels like chaos right now."

"Hey, leave me out of this," Latha says. "Your problems with this vendor and getting the materials have nothing to do with me or our forecasts."

"Come on, people," Giovanna intercedes. "Mark, Chad is right. If you don't know what Manufacturing needs and expects in terms of product delivery from a supplier, you need to ask and not assume. And let's stop trying to point blame and start working to fix the problem."

Roberto sighs in frustration. "But we still don't understand the problem. I'm sorry I keep asking for more data, but without it, I can't really help. We are chasing symptoms, and it's like that Whac-A-Mole game, we solve one thing and a new problem just pops up the next day."

Giovanna looks at her watch and wrings her hands. They are almost out of time and haven't made much progress, again.

After all the work they have done, Giovanna and Latha are getting along better. The team members in general are communicating a bit more effectively, and there is more trust, but they are still struggling to align and make real progress on the company's supply chain and product quality problems.

Elizabeth, who has been quietly observing the meeting, speaks up. "Since we only have a few more minutes left today, I wonder if we can quickly shift gears." She looks at Giovanna, who nods her head in approval. "I think it would be helpful to take a step back and align on a team-level goal that you all feel equally, fully committed to, beyond your individual goals."

"I thought our goal was to fix these problems," Latha says, "to make sure customers get what we agreed to get them, on time, without quality problems."

"That's absolutely right," Elizabeth says. "But how will we know the problems have been fixed in a way that we're all happy with? And what would success really look like for this team, for our organization, and for our customers and business partners if we were fully successful, including but not limited to an absence of problems?"

The team thinks about this for a moment. "We'd have enough volume so we can grow," Chad offers.

"And our sales commitments and manufacturing volumes would align," adds Latha. "We make everything we sell and sell everything we make."

Elizabeth nods and starts writing down on a flip chart. "Okay, what else?"

"We would have high quality of supply, and our products would have zero defects," adds Roberto.

"Our customers would be happy with our products and would really see how we offer something better than our competitors," Giovanna adds.

"We'd have solid relationships with trusted suppliers, true partners with us, so we could sustain the high-quality volumes over time with confidence and do it at reasonable prices," says Mark.

"And we'd have good transparency and processes in place," Roberto says, "so we could identify and resolve any issues and deviations much quicker, ideally heading problems off before a customer is ever impacted."

"One more thing," Latha adds. "I think we would build robust networks that are efficient, but also with enough flexibility that we still get product to customers when there are issues or disruptions in the supply chain."

"These are great," Elizabeth says. "Is it fair to say that achieving only some of these elements but failing miserably at others would not

be good enough? And that we are all committed to the entire defini-
tion of success, including all these elements?"

The team nods in agreement.

"Yes, this is a nice summary of our goal as a team," says Giovanna.
"It's nice to write it all down, but I think we already knew this, right?"

After a brief pause, Mark says, "I don't know. Honestly, I've
been focusing on getting the lowest possible unit price, and I kind of
assumed that everything else was other people's responsibility. This
does make me think about my job differently and what we need to
solve for. Like finding reliable partners who will really collaborate
with us and building more resilient networks with some flexibility so
we can more easily weather problems. I think I can really help with
those things, but I never thought about them as in-scope for me."

When we are working in teams, we often don't take the time to
come to this kind of alignment. The goal seems obvious—to solve
the urgent, pressing problem each team member faces. But when we
are facing adaptive challenges, simply trying to solve an individual
part of the problem is not enough. We need to take it a step further and redefine success on an individual, team, and organizational
level.

Making a joint commitment to a larger goal provides insights in
interdependencies and a new sense of purpose for the team and can
help us get to new levels of collaboration as we shift our focus to op-
timizing the whole instead of maximizing the individual parts of our
work. Complex problems require us to engage with them together in a
new way and learn together to discover new solutions and achieve our
shared aspirations. Yet, when we need to collaborate in new ways to
solve complex problems, teams and team members too often operate
in a self-reinforcing state of protection that keeps them from adapting
and holds them back.

DELIBERATE CALM AND LEARNING TEAMS

We already know why it is so important for us to be able to access a state of learning when facing adaptive challenges. But true learning and growth do not happen in a bubble. In the Adaptive Zone, being an individual learner or even in a group of individual learners is not always sufficient. Today's world requires collaborative learning in order for teams and entire organizations to adapt quickly and succeed.

This means that to solve adaptive challenges, teams need to shift into learning as a unit. We are talking about opening up and connecting not only one or two individual icebergs but several individual icebergs in addition to the team iceberg, which often goes unacknowledged and unseen but influences the team culture as well as every aspect of how the team interacts and collaborates.

When we ask the most senior teams how much of their time they spent in learning and how much in protection, the average answer is that they spend 60 to 70 percent of their time in protection. When they are facing high-stakes adaptive challenges, this percentage increases even further. When the team at the top needs to solve the most difficult dilemmas the organization is facing, they mostly do this from a state of protection! With so much lying underneath the surface and knowing that we human beings are wired to go in protection when the uncertainty increases, this should come as no surprise.

Because we stop listening and truly communicating in this state, our wisdom drops below the sum of our parts. Remember that in protection, we are not leveraging the full thinking power of our brains. As the challenge we face becomes more paramount, this decrease in wisdom, creativity, and innovation can become more and more pronounced and pervasive. Ironically, the more important the topic is and the higher the stakes are for failing to collaborate creatively, the more likely we are to shift into a state of protection as a team, often rendering us even less capable of solving the current challenge.

Now, we are facing the adaptability paradox on a team level: *the more complex the challenge, the more we require our teams' collective experience, skills, wisdom, and creativity, and the less available they are to us.* This makes it even more important for us to learn how to shift ourselves and our teams into learning. When we are able to shift into learning as a group, we unleash an exponential amount of collective brain power that we can harness to create innovation and transformation.

Just as learning to operate in the Adaptive Zone individually is more important now than ever, so is shifting into learning as a team. As the world moves from hierarchical to diverse team-based models, the composition of teams and how they work together is becoming increasingly important to organizations' overall learning and performance. Teams are becoming more cross-functional and diverse across many dimensions—expertise, abilities, beliefs, education, language, geography, ethnicity, and so on. Team members are often not even physically in the same place as they work together on complex challenges with an overwhelming amount of information.

This diversity can be a tremendous asset to learning, but only if handled properly.[1] Homogenous teams often have less friction than diverse ones. There are fewer polarizing points of view, and the sense of familiarity among the team feels safe. But it is also less likely to lead to creativity or innovation and more likely to create joint perception, the tendency for people working on teams to align with the group on emotions and attitudes.[2] This leads to a team iceberg made up of joint beliefs about how to be successful and drives the team's typical way of working and collaborating.

As in individuals, the team iceberg may serve the team well in the Familiar Zone, where they operate as a well-oiled machine as they solve sometimes challenging and perhaps high-stakes yet familiar problems. But when a team is in the Adaptive Zone and needs to learn new things, starting with what it is that they need to learn in the first place, having a homogenous team with aligned points of view and a well-established way of doing things is no longer an asset.

On a more diverse team, we do not have the sense of security that comes from joint perception and are more likely to shift into protection when we are confronted with diverse attitudes and points of view.[3] However, when we are able to navigate and welcome this diversity, shift into learning as a team, and inquire into all points of view in the room, we are able to surface the assumptions and joint perceptions that may be holding us back, along with fresh ideas. In a way, this opens up the different icebergs of the team members around a challenge and gives us insight into not only what people think but also why they think that way.

The most successful organizations not only have diverse teams but they tap into the richness of that diversity to innovate and solve the toughest adaptive challenges. This is what it means to be a "learning team," which strengthens both our personal and collective resilience and adaptability. When we work together on a learning team with curiosity and true collaboration, our whole becomes greater than the sum of its parts.

PSYCHOLOGICAL SAFETY—THE FOUNDATION OF LEARNING TEAMS

When Amy Edmondson, an American scholar of leadership, teams, and organizational learning, was a PhD student, she conducted research on health care teams to try to understand and predict team performance. She measured teams' "error rate," based on the number of small or large errors reported by each team. She assumed that teams with higher error rates would have poorer patient outcomes and was surprised to find that there was a significant correlation in the opposite direction. The teams that reported more errors had significantly *better* patient outcomes.[4]

Edmondson found that all the teams experienced errors. It was the teams' likelihood of reporting them and ultimately learning from them that was correlated with better patient outcomes. The teams that did not surface, report, discuss, and learn from errors performed worse over time compared to teams that did.

What allowed some teams to surface and learn from their errors while others did not? "Psychological safety" is a term popularized by Edmondson to describe a shared belief that a team is a safe place for interpersonal risk taking. Psychological safety is a precursor to adaptive, innovative team performance. When we feel comfortable asking for help, sharing suggestions informally, or challenging the status quo without fear of negative consequences, our teams are more likely to innovate quickly, unlock the benefits of diversity, and adapt well to change.

In order to succeed, teams collaborating in the Adaptive Zone first and foremost require a team environment characterized by psychological safety. In 2012, Google embarked on an initiative with the code name Project Aristotle to study hundreds of teams and find out what led some to succeed more than others. They found that the number one predictor of team performance was psychological safety.[5]

The key word here is "safety." On teams lacking psychological safety, we feel at risk of being blamed or shamed for our mistakes and sense that it is risky to disagree or admit failures. Of course, this implicit feeling of being under threat leads us to shift into protection and revert to reactive behaviors. In a psychologically safe environment, however, we know that our identities and relationships are safe and secure if we make a mistake and open up about it. This feeling of safety allows us to shift into learning both individually and as a whole, even when under stress and pressure.

In this state of learning, we can develop a new relationship with failure. Of course, we do not *want* to make mistakes or fail, and we must be held accountable for finding solutions. But when we are trying to innovate in a dynamic, uncertain environment in which we need to learn and master entirely new skills, errors and missteps are inevitable. In fact, if we do not encounter hiccups in an adaptive environment, it often means that we haven't set our sights high enough. Or perhaps we haven't fully accepted that we are in the Adaptive Zone to begin with. When we go big and bold, failure and related adaptation almost always comes with the territory. It is a natural part of being outside our Familiar Zone. By learning from those failures in a psychologically safe environment, we can continuously adapt and improve in a dynamic environment.

Most of us got to where we are because we are good at one kind of learning: single loop learning, which involves solving hard problems with known methods and approaches. In the Adaptive Zone, however, the situation calls for us to learn in a different way. As we see with our current team, at first we don't even know *what* we need to learn. After all, we don't know what we don't know. This is precisely when we are most likely to get very uncomfortable and want to revert to something that feels safe and familiar. We tend to shift into protection and react by relying on known methods that simply won't work in this new situation. And the more they don't work, the more we tend to pull the same old ineffectual levels harder and harder.

This is the worst possible course of action. Yet we do it anyway, often because we don't want to let go of old success formulas or slow down enough to look deeper into our failures and use them to learn and adapt and rise to our next level of solutions, ideas, and performance.

There is, however, a second form of learning, called double loop learning or adaptive learning. Chris Argyris uses a thermostat to illustrate single versus double loop learning. A thermostat set to sixty-eight degrees that turns the heat on anytime the room drops below sixty-eight degrees is engaging in single loop learning. A thermostat engaging in double loop learning would explore the best and most economical way to heat the room, asking, "*Why* am I set to sixty-eight degrees?"[6]

With double loop learning, we explore and discover new methods and solutions by modifying our goals and decision-making rules in light of our experience. The only way to create a new reality is to move into the unknown and change our orientation, and failure will almost certainly be a part of the journey. *This means that we can only engage in double loop learning in a psychologically safe environment, where we make learning from experience (and therefore mistakes) part of the adaptive solution-finding process.* We integrate this learning when we are able to fail without facing disastrous consequences and keep going. If we fail and are punished or demeaned for it, we learn that we should avoid taking risks that might make us look bad or cause others to think less of us, so we play it safe and limit our potential to learn and grow. When we embrace the idea that there is something better out there that is yet to be discovered instead of feeling threatened by the unknown and inevitable failure, real transformation is possible.

HOW TO FOSTER PSYCHOLOGICAL SAFETY

Leaders play an important role in fostering psychological safety within their teams.[7] In fact, as leaders our emotions often have a multiplier effect on our teams and organizations. When a leader is impatient, fearful, commanding, or frustrated, it can shut down certain kinds of conversations. If a team is facing an adaptive challenge, this can really kill the creativity and learning that we need to engage in to find new solutions. When a leader demonstrates Deliberate Calm and is hopeful, calm, open, and curious, the group can face challenges more creatively.

When leaders provide a foundation of trust, support, and psychological safety, it allows them to challenge and push their teams to do more than they initially think they can. This form of challenging leadership grounded in their trust in the capabilities of the team strengthens team performance and can lead employees to express creativity, feel empowered to make changes, and seek to learn and improve, but *only when a positive, supportive team climate with psychological safety is already in place.*[8] Outside a positive team climate, challenging leadership may feel like a threat and shift team members into protection.

Leaders can foster psychological safety among their teams using these four steps:

1. REFRAME MISTAKES

What good looks like

- Acknowledge that mistakes happen.
- Avoid showing anger when mistakes happen.
- Help team members correct mistakes.

What great looks like

- Share your own mistakes vulnerably and often.
- Remind team members frequently that our work is complex and that we should expect mistakes.
- Reframe mistakes as steps in a longer journey, as valuable feedback and data we can work with, and as an opportunity to learn.

2. ENCOURAGE ALL VOICES

What good looks like

1. Every time there's a big decision, explicitly ask, "Are we ready to move forward?" and make sure everyone says "yes."
2. Avoid using discrediting language when somebody shares (e.g., avoid saying thing like "yes, but . . ." or "There is a lot of context that you don't know").

What great looks like

- Actively avoid the "sunflower" effect, where others align with the view of the leader.
- Remind the team frequently of the power of having everyone share. Note that, in our complex world, leaders don't have all the answers and everyone has a unique and useful part of the answer. Ask people to share their thoughts as well as their feelings and underlying beliefs or assumptions.
- Invite participation in neutral, nonthreatening ways (e.g., "What could be a viewpoint we are missing? Are there any blind spots we missed?") and pause long enough for people to speak up.
- Set up formal team mechanisms to encourage sharing of ideas (e.g., have a standing "devil's advocate meeting" to pressure-test plans and ideas).
- Fill silences with questions instead of comments.
- Explain why certain points of view were not incorporated into a final decision; share context and the decision-making process with the team transparently.

3. APPRECIATE CONTRIBUTIONS

What good looks like

- Proactively and frequently acknowledge the good job that team members are doing.
- Say "thank you" when people speak up, or go above and beyond the norm.

What great looks like

- Make recognition part of your team's language and norms.
- Give special thanks to people who bring up uncomfortable, hard issues, recognizing contributions to the open group dynamic as much as problem solving.
- Be specific about any action that you celebrate, and the impact it had on you.
- Acknowledge the points that others make during a meeting (e.g., "To build on Cara's point . . . ").

4. COACH TEAM MEMBERS TO HELP AND SUPPORT EACH OTHER

What good looks like

- Encourage peer recognition (e.g., set a team norm to write a two-minute thank-you note every day).
- Remind team members that it is everyone's role to enhance the experience of others on the team.

What great looks like

- Develop norms encouraging team members to give their views.
- Coach team members to support each other (e.g., ask them to ask

> deep questions to really understand what their team members are bringing to the discussion).
> - Provide feedback and coaching to individual team members on their contributions to psychological safety.

RAISING TEAM AWARENESS

In addition to having a foundation of psychological safety, teams that are in unfamiliar territory in one or more significant ways and are seeking novel solutions in an Adaptive Zone context can practice Dual Awareness in order to collaborate effectively and access a state of learning. This requires team members to gain individual and collective awareness of what is happening in their environment and how it is affecting their internal state and team dynamic.

Stop the Domino Effect of Protection

When the team arrives at their next meeting, they are surprised to see a chart on the whiteboard that Elizabeth has begun filling out. The columns contain their names, formal roles, mindsets about leadership and success, and traits they discussed at the Origin Stories dinner. There are blank columns titled "Trigger" and "Emotion/Protection Behavior."

Once they are all seated, Elizabeth addresses the team. "Before we get to today's agenda, I want to do an exercise that I call 'The Domino Effect,'" she says. "We've talked about what happens when you're in a state of protection, but what do you know about what causes you to shift into this state?"

Most of us are unaware of our triggers that shift us into protection. A trigger can be an event, a person, something that someone says, or anything that our brain consciously or unconsciously interprets or predicts is a threat. It is incredibly valuable to gain awareness of these triggers, as well as how we typically react in protection. In a team setting, it is just as important to know what can trigger your team members into protection and how they react so that you can break this cycle by adjusting your own behavior accordingly.

On all teams, there is a dance that occurs as individuals dip in and out of protection and exhibit behaviors that push others in and out of protection as well. We rarely pay attention to what state we are in as individuals or as a team, even when we are making critical decisions, but it's far more effective to make decisions and ask for commitments when the team as a whole is in a state of learning. If one of us is in learning but someone else on the team is in protection, the other person will not be open to what we have to say. In these cases, self-awareness is not enough. We must observe not only ourselves but our full teams through that skylight in the ceiling and notice the signs that they are in protection. Then we can take action to help them shift.

Elizabeth asks if anyone can name one of their triggers. Chad goes first. "It really bothers me when people show up to a meeting but then don't participate or seem to check out," he says. "When they stop listening and turn away or look at their phones, it feels completely disrespectful, as if everyone else's time and opinions don't even matter."

"Okay, great," Elizabeth says as she writes "checking out" in the "triggers" column next to Chad's name. "And how do you typically react when it seems like someone is checking out or ignoring you?"

Chad smiles. "Well, I'm sure it's not the best," he says, "but I get mad and usually just talk louder, be provocative at a loud volume. Like, maybe I can force them to hear what I'm saying."

Elizabeth nods and writes it down. "Who else?"

"I get really flustered when people ask me things I don't know," Roberto says. "I feel exposed and uncertain, and think I should already have an answer. My behavior gets really defensive. I go on counterattack and challenge the person asking the question."

"Oh, defensiveness is such a trigger for me," Latha says. "I feel angry and frustrated when people are putting their own interests ahead of the interests of the team. When I see people getting defensive about their territory or people, I think they're just concerned for themselves and not a team player."

"And how do you react? What's the behavior that goes with that feeling?" Elizabeth asks.

Latha sighs. "I usually just try to confront it and call it out. But there have definitely been times when it made the situation worse because the way I called it out was fueled by my anger and frustration."

"Listen, there's no shame in how we act when we're in protection," Elizabeth reminds them. "Of course, we want to reduce those moments and gain the ability to choose a better response. But these are natural reactions. It's all part of the process and is actually a sign that the situation we're facing matters."

Mark speaks up next. "I didn't fully put this together until recently," he says, "but I get triggered by other people's big emotions, especially yelling, anger, aggression, or talking over others. I feel angry. And I either go on the attack or I shut down," Mark adds. "In my personal life, I often get aggressive back, but at work I'm more likely to get overwhelmed and shut down and disengage."

"Sorry, Mark, I must be triggering you all the time," Giovanna says. "My trigger is when I feel like I'm not being heard or my views are being dismissed. Whenever I start feeling like I can't influence people or a situation, I start feeling powerless and out of control and it freaks me out. So I start trying to take control, and it probably comes off as pushy and belligerent."

"That's exactly it," Elizabeth says, looking back at the whiteboard. "In a team setting, one person's protection behavior is often someone else's trigger. Just look at this. Roberto gets triggered if you push him with a hard question that he doesn't know the answer to. His protection response of defensiveness will trigger Latha, whose protection response is to confront him. But this will potentially push him even harder. Then their argument will trigger Giovanna to start

NAME	FORMAL ROLE	SUCCESS FOR ME IS...	STRENGTHS
Giovanna	Commercial and customer	Continue to grow by delivering for customers, keeping them satisfied and loyal.	Determination, grit, resilience, optimism
Chad	Manufacturing	Implement predictable long-term plans so we can reliably deliver products on time and on budget.	Creative problem solver, analytical
Latha	Distribution and logistics	Make just-in-time delivery work, ensuring on-time delivery.	See big picture, integrator, systems thinking
Mark	Procurement and sourcing	Procure needed materials at lowest cost.	Communication, influence, motivational win-win negotiation
Roberto	Quality	More robust quality processes and organization so we can minimize variability and eliminate defects.	Perfectionist, analytical, data, root cause

feeling like she's losing control of the meeting, and possibly Mark as well, when things start getting emotionally charged. Giovanna's protection reaction of taking control and talking over people will further trigger Mark. He will shut down and disengage, if he hasn't already, which triggers Chad to start getting loud. And on and on

EDGE	TRIGGERS	PROTECTION REACTIONS
Stubborn, over-react, try to control things	Feeling out of control; people not listening, feeling disrespected or ignored	Takes over, interrupt, get directive, tell people what to do
Sometimes analyzing the problem too much and not taking action	Checking out, not engaging	Gets mad Talks louder, provokes
Focus on the macro issues, but micro interactions can seem transactional	Not being a team player—getting defensive, playing politics and hidden agendas	Gets frustrated Confronts, calls people out
Try to please everyone, but blame others or the situation if it doesn't work	People who are rude, pushy, or loud	Gets angry Disengages, shuts down
Allow perfect to be the enemy of good enough; can focus on being right rather than taking action	Not knowing the answer	Gets flustered Argues, gets defensive, challenges the person asking the question

it goes in a *downward spiral of protection*. The business content is now almost irrelevant as your colliding icebergs derail the entire discussion. All it takes is for one person to get triggered to start the domino effect."

Help Each Other Shift into Learning

This type of domino effect happens in teams, families, and all sorts of groups. Each of us shifts into protection several times a day, and of course we are most often triggered by other people or our own interpretations of their behavior. This is part of our human conditioning, and we should not be afraid or ashamed of it. In fact, just as our own protection moments are signals of opportunities for growth, in a team context they are signs that we have an opportunity for deeper understanding and mutual learning.

Awareness is key. Once we know that this is happening, we can take steps to change it. One thing we can do is find out what helps our team members shift out of protection and into learning. Then, when we notice that one of us is exhibiting protection behaviors, we can break the cycle by requesting a break and giving everyone a chance to cool down or by helping another person shift into learning by exhibiting the behavior that we know will help them. Elizabeth adds a column to the whiteboard that reads "Helpful Behaviors," and the team goes around and shares their thoughts about what actions help them shift into learning.

If everyone on the team agrees to it, it is also helpful to gently point it out when we notice that one or more people are shifting into protection. We call this a *skylight moment*. A team member can simply raise their hand and ask for a skylight moment. This is a cue for the team to take a few breaths, get a drink of water, and think about how the current team mindset and behaviors are or aren't serving us in the moment.

It is often helpful for one team member to explicitly take on the role of observer to help raise the team's awareness. According to psychologist David Kantor's "Four Player Model," developed as part of his theory of structural dynamics, people in a group take on one of four roles: *Movers* suggest actions or decisions around the content of the issue; *Followers* support a mover and their move; *Opposers* resist or go against a move; and *Bystanders* are observers who take no position with respect to the content of problem or the moves people are making.

For example, if Giovanna suggests that she and Latha meet for coffee, and Latha says, "Yes, let's meet up, but I don't want to get coffee. Let's take a walk, instead," Latha is following Giovanna's move to meet up, opposing the suggestion that they meet for coffee, and making her own move that they go for a walk.

Individuals can move fluidly among these four roles.[9] However, teams often get stuck in certain patterns. For instance, some teams with strong personalities can fall into a pattern of moves and countermoves, with everyone pulling in different directions and no one reacting to other moves by either following or opposing.

One of the most helpful things that someone on a team can do is to play an active bystander role. An unhelpful bystander will stay silent or check out or hold back, but active bystanders raise the team's awareness by observing what is happening, noticing patterns, asking curious questions, and pointing out relevant interpersonal dynamics and habits. In particular, the bystander can ask questions that point the team toward double loop learning.

In our current team, Elizabeth has been playing the role of bystander. She has no point of view on the content of the problem itself. She is simply observing and making suggestions about the team process.

But we do not actually need an outsider for this, as long as we make sure that we are each effectively playing each of these different roles at different times. Sometimes we make a move, sometimes we explain why we are opposed to a course of action, sometimes we voice our agreement and actively follow the decisions we support, and at other times we step out of the content and notice the broader dynamics of the situation and the team from the skylight as an active, constructive observer.

Check In and Check Out

To raise team awareness, it is also helpful to begin each team meeting by taking a moment to set an intention and get aligned on the problem we're trying to solve and the benefit we are trying to create for the company. Connecting to the team purpose, even briefly like this, motivates us to embrace challenges as a positive form of stress.[10, 11] Then, it helps to talk about how we want the meeting to go and what we want to accomplish, and openly discuss what might trip us up. Each team member can answer a few questions about how we're feeling, what we want to get out of this meeting, and if there's anything that might keep us from being fully present.

It is also helpful to end meetings with the same intention and by talking about how the meeting went. We can ask if there's anything that was left unsaid and if we are fully aligned on the things we agreed on. This will help make sure we are moving forward as a unit without any lingering questions or misunderstandings.

A WHOLE THAT IS GREATER THAN THE SUM OF ITS PARTS

Elizabeth has given the team a tremendous number of resources to access a state of learning, even amid their high-stakes adaptive challenge. With no time to lose, they begin implementing as many of these practices as possible. During meetings, they focus on observing what state they are in and suggest skylight moments whenever they sense that one or more team members are shifting into protection. At first, this only happens after things have already gotten heated and they need a fairly lengthy break to calm down. Then they begin to catch themselves more quickly. They even start laughing together as they all jump to be the first one to raise their hand when one of them is triggered. Meanwhile, Giovanna focuses on creating psychological safety for the team. Slowly but surely, she can see that the team is opening up their collective iceberg and operating from a more effective learning mindset.

Their initial breakthrough happens in a meeting that starts like many others. The team is trying to work together more collaboratively, but they are still feeling stuck, unable to resolve the still mounting supply chain and product quality issues.

"Again, what is the real problem we need to solve here?" asks Chad. "I know I must sound like a broken record, but we still haven't gotten to the root of the problem."

"As long as we're being broken records," says Roberto, "let me add my agreement and my suggestion to start investing now in data, analytics, and quality processes both for QC and QA. We simply don't have the data and insights we need to answer your question, Chad."

Giovanna is biting her tongue, feeling the urge to intervene and get the meeting back on track. Then she notices that Latha looks annoyed and pauses, reminding herself that trying to take control hasn't been working. She internally reframes this as an opportunity to help empower the team. Knowing that Latha is a big-picture thinker, Giovanna asks, "Latha, what do you think?" Latha looks a bit surprised. "Sorry, I didn't mean to call you out," Giovanna says, "but you look frustrated. I think we're all feeling that right now. I also know you have a great way of taking a step back and helping us think about these things more strategically. If we peel back your surface-level frustration, what is really bothering you? And can you reframe that in a way that might help us get unstuck?"

The team is quiet while Latha thinks for a moment. "Well, initially I noticed that I was feeling frustrated with Roberto," she says. "I was aware that I had an urge to roll my eyes, thinking to myself, *Oh boy, there he goes again, trying to just get more budget*. And then I was frustrated with myself for being judgmental and not assuming positive intent."

"Okay, thank you for that honest response," says Giovanna, a little worried that this is not helping at all. She is doing her best to neither criticize nor take over and give it a bit more time to see how this might play out. "So, now go ahead and assume positive intent. How do you want to respond differently?"

After a fifteen-second pause and reflection, which feels like an eternity to Giovanna as she is trying to lead in a new and unfamiliar way, Latha finally says, "Chad, you keep saying we aren't zeroed in on the root causes and we need more data. And Roberto, you keep saying that we don't have the data and insights that we need to solve this. Let's assume that what you're both saying is true. Where does that leave us? I know part of the issue is that we haven't invested in the data and analytics and processes, but that would only help in the future anyway. How do we tackle this here and now when we don't have the data?"

Giovanna's heart sinks, thinking that her new approach didn't work at all. They are right back to square one *again*. She feels a strong urge to grab on to one problem they might be able to solve, even if it's not the biggest one, and start doling out action items to make some progress. But she knows this is her reactive tendency and that it hasn't been working. Instead, she tries to do the same thing that she just asked Latha to do: practice awareness to connect with and reframe what is really bothering her.

"Team, is there any way to take Latha's provocation to heart and actually do something constructive?" Giovanna is afraid that the answer is no, but she reminds herself that this is just a few minutes down a blind alley. Maybe something good can come of it. At the very least, the team will see that she is trying to lead differently.

The team thinks about Giovanna's question and Latha's challenge. "We know we don't have the data we need, but does the data exist?" asks Chad. "That's not a rhetorical question. I've been focused on the data that we have, which isn't sufficient to help us figure this out. But is there data out there in the world that we don't have and could get?"

Mark jumps in. "Hey, after our last meeting, when we aligned on our shared aspiration, I've been thinking about some of the things I could do to help, like fostering more of a trusted partnership with our suppliers. Given how we've been beating up on them lately, if they do have insight into their own quality problems, I'm pretty sure they're not proactively bringing us all the data. Maybe we can change that."

A lightbulb goes off for Giovanna as well. "Now that you say that, I'm not sure we have all the data from our customers, either."

Latha adds, "Some of our logistics and distribution partners might also have data. We get reports on damaged and late shipments, but we've never asked for any raw data or even what data they have."

Giovanna is starting to feel more comfortable asking questions that she doesn't know the answer to and allowing time for the team to think deeply. She asks, "Where else might there be data that we don't have but could get?"

"I just remembered something," Chad finally says. "The other day, I was in the plant talking to an operations supervisor. He had no hard data, but he said he's noticed over the last few months that when components came in on this specific kind of pallet framed by two-by-four wood planks, they tended to have problems later on. The wooden pallets that this supplier usually ships the components on are framed with four-by-four planks, and those components seem to work fine. He didn't know why and couldn't prove anything. But what if he was right? And beyond this specific issue, there might be more important data that only exists in people's heads. We could still get to it if we ask the right people the right questions. I never thought of it this way, but that's still data of a sort, and it might be helpful to us."

As the discussion continues, the team realizes that there is potentially a lot more data and insights out there to be found and brought to bear. "You know," says Mark at the end of the meeting, "we said that we want more trust-based partnerships. What if we asked them to partner with us around the data and solicited their ideas and invited them to help solve the problem?"

Giovanna is intrigued. "When you say 'them,' who do you mean?"

Roberto is excited now and jumps in. "Why not all of them? Partners, suppliers, customers. We all want to solve this, right?"

After the meeting, the team keeps exploring this idea. They decide to work with employees, suppliers, partners, and customers, eventually holding several collaborative working sessions to discover the full extent of the problems. Within a month, they have finally identified the root cause of the issues: Some of the company's newer products were designed to be smaller, more packed with digital features, and more sensitive in terms of their measurements and calibrations. They required new, smaller, and more sensitive components, sourced from existing and new suppliers.

To meet the new design specifications, several suppliers had to change their designs, start up new production lines, or use contract manufacturers in their own supply chains. The resulting components tended to work extremely reliably in the lab and looked fine on inspection, but they were fragile and susceptible to damage. The fragility of these components combined with expanded shipping routes, more customers and customer applications, and new logistics partners who optimized for speed and on-time delivery but handled the products less delicately, all conspired to create a perfect storm of product failures and ripple effects of related problems that further obscured the root cause of the issue.

With this critical discovery, the team continues operating as a unit. They are slowing down and creating a shared reality by listening fully to each other, taking a long-term perspective, and looking at the levers of the complicated system that they need to collectively manage, rather than attempting to manage individual pieces on their own. This helps them grow more aligned on what they need to deliver. Perhaps the biggest change occurs within Giovanna, who grows as a leader by focusing on how she can create psychological safety and help the team function effectively as a whole rather than as a group of individuals.

Collaborating openly with their partners requires the team to exhibit new levels of vulnerability and courage, of humility and curiosity, of collaboration and trust. And the team's ability to continue demonstrating dual awareness and deliberate calm, not only individually but also as an aligned and high-performing learning team, allows them not only to resolve a very thorny set of issues but to eventually come out on the other side with even stronger customer and business partner relationships.

TRANSFORM YOUR TEAM'S COLLECTIVE ICEBERG

Just like individuals, teams often have underlying limiting mindsets that can keep them from working together effectively and prevent them from reaching their full potential. Transforming the way teams interact and collaborate requires a fundamental shift in these mindsets.

To start, choose a team that you are a part of. This can be at work, with friends or a volunteer effort, or even within your family. Then reflect on a behavior you have observed that is limiting the team's performance and how you can help create change. Use the following questions to guide this reflection:

- What is the situation or challenge?
- What are the limiting ("from") team behaviors? And the consequential result?
- What emotions go along with those behaviors?
- What could alternative ("to") behaviors be? And what would become possible as a result of these new behaviors?
- What emotions go along with those behaviors?
- What mindsets and beliefs are limiting the team's performance, underlying the "from" behavior?
- What mindset would be more beneficial to the team and support the desired behavior?
- What concrete steps can I take to enable this change?
- What experiments can I recommend to the team to improve their performance?

PART IV

THE DELIBERATE CALM PROTOCOL

CHAPTER 10

YOUR PERSONAL
OPERATING MODEL

If your dreams don't scare you, they're not big enough.
—ELLEN JOHNSON SIRLEAF

An important step toward practicing Deliberate Calm is to consciously design your life so it is easier to remain grounded and present no matter what is going on around you. Your personal operating model is that design. It is comprised of the choices you make every day about how to spend your time and energy, how you bring awareness to yourself and what is going on around you, how you show up in your life and relationships, and what you prioritize to make your life work for you.

In the appendix, we will present a four-week protocol for you to begin developing your Deliberate Calm muscle. Before you begin, it is important to lay a solid foundation of habits and practices that will make it easier for you to train and build this muscle. Think of it as training for a marathon. Before you begin the actual training protocol, you would prepare by setting up the rest of your life, getting enough sleep, eating well, and so on. Your personal operating model is the setup of your life, and the four-week protocol will serve as your training. Practicing Deliberate Calm in the midst of volatility is certainly a marathon.

Whether you have been intentional about creating it or not, you already have a personal operating model. Even if it was not designed consciously, it's worth considering what is in your personal operating model currently and how well it is or isn't working for you. Taking the time to become aware of your strengths and weaknesses and what areas or roles of your life you may want to change will help you demonstrate Deliberate Calm as you face adaptive challenges.

The personal operating model you create today is not permanent. It will and should evolve as your circumstances change, as you grow and learn, and as you require new types of support over time. For example, when you are in a high-stakes Adaptive Zone context, you might need to make a change in your priorities and how you focus your time and energy. Other life changes like starting a new job, getting married or divorced, losing a loved one, having children or having them leave the nest, and experiencing setbacks, challenges, and triumphs often require updates to our personal operating model to help serve our evolving life needs and opportunities.

In the busyness and overwhelm of a challenging environment, we often don't take a step back to adapt our personal operating model to what the new situation requires. But when your context evolves and you continue functioning from the same old personal operating model, there is a potential for mismatch. We have seen this occur many times throughout the book, as leaders struggled, got burned out, or responded ineffectively when approaching new, adaptive circumstances with their outdated personal operating models.

We recommend revisiting your personal operating model every week or so to begin with and then every few months or whenever you find yourself approaching a time of significant change. Think of this as a dynamic tool instead of a set of commitments that you stubbornly pursue even as your context changes. After all, Deliberate Calm is all about making choices with awareness of external and internal dynamics, adapting, and discovering new ways of learning and leading as our circumstances evolve.

THE FOUR PERSONAL OPERATING MODEL PILLARS

The personal operating model will help you assess four pillars of your life and how they can support you in developing Dual Awareness and Deliberate Calm: your awareness, your purpose, your energy, and your relationships.

When going through the reflections below, you can use the following template.

 AWARENESS

- DUAL AWARENESS PRACTICE AND 5 LEVELS OF AWARENESS
- REFRAMING TO ACCESS ADAPTIVE ZONE PRACTICE

 PURPOSE

- KNOWING AND CONNECTING TO YOUR PURPOSE
- LIVING "ON PURPOSE" (TIME, DECISIONS, ORIENTATION OF YOUR LEARNING)

 ENERGY

- AWARENESS AND MANAGEMENT OF YOUR ENERGY
- RECOVERY ACROSS PHYSICAL, MENTAL, EMOTIONAL, SPIRITUAL, AND SOCIAL PRACTICES

 RELATIONSHIPS

- DEEPENING CONNECTIONS – 1:1, IN TEAMS, IN COMMUNITIES
- TRANSFORMING CONFLICT INTO LEARNING (INQUIRY AND ADVOCACY, DELIBERATE CALM, PSYCHOLOGICALLY SAFE LEARNING TEAMS)

FIGURE 10.1: Personal Operating Model Framework

Awareness

This pillar supports your strength of bringing Dual Awareness to your experiences, your ability to recognize if you are in the Familiar or Adaptive Zone, how high the stakes are that you are facing, awareness of your inner state, and particularly when you are in the Adaptive Zone, whether you are in a state of learning or protection. This pillar is also about recognizing that we can't always be in learning, nor should we try to be. We need to build in time for reflection, recovery, recreation, and performance, and we need to acknowledge that it is natural to occasionally fall into a state of protection.

As we learn and grow, we become more at ease with our inner talk and mindsets even when they are not "helpful" or "adaptive." As written in so many other spiritual and leadership guides, making

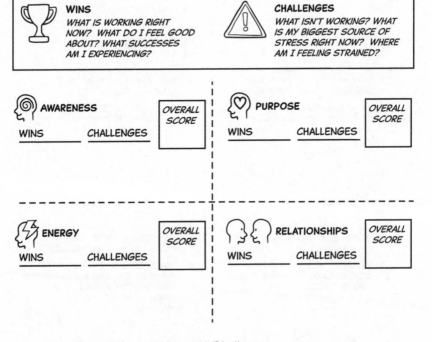

FIGURE 10.2 Current State: Wins and Challenges

the unconscious conscious and the unintentional more deliberate and choiceful is a large part, if not the largest part, of moving closer to living a life of incredible impact, purpose, and fulfillment. We hope that working on this pillar of your personal operating model will not only make the other pillars easier but will also bring you some relief and ease in the midst of the rapidly changing and uncertain world we live in.

To assess your current level of awareness in different situations, ask yourself the following questions:

- Think back to a couple of the more demanding, high-stakes moments you experienced in the last week. What was the situation? What zone do you think it was in: Familiar or Adaptive?
- What were the stakes, both in terms of what others might say the stakes were "objectively" (what was concretely at stake) and how the stakes felt to you subjectively (the pressure you were under, regardless of objective reality)?
- What was your internal state? What were you thinking and feeling? Were you in learning or protection or something else (relaxed, autopilot, recovery, performance, execution)?
- Do you think your inner state was an optimal match for the situation? If not, what was the extent of the mismatch and what might have been more helpful?
- At what level of awareness do you think you were during the flow of the action?
  - Level 1: Unaware—I was not aware that they happened.
  - Level 2: Delayed—I became aware after the moment happened.
  - Level 3: Perceptive—I was aware but not able to effectively respond to the situation in the moment.
  - Level 4: Resilient—I was aware in the moment and able to respond after a short pause or time-out.

- Level 5: Adaptive—I was aware and able to pivot from "protection" to "learning" in the moment (Dual Awareness in action).
- In the past week or so, what are the moments you remember when you experienced the following internal states?
  - Relaxation or recreation
  - Recovery
  - Performance execution
  - Learning
  - Protection
  - Possibly moving toward danger
- Identify the mindset you were operating from in one learning and one protection moment. You can do this by asking, "Why did I feel and behave this way?" Then repeat the "why" question three times.

  As a reminder, here are the seven protection and learning mindset pairs:
  - Fixed or Growth Mindset
  - Expert or Curious Mindset
  - Reactive or Creative Mindset
  - Victim or Agent Mindset
  - Scarcity or Abundance Mindset
  - Certainty or Exploration Mindset
  - Safeguard or Opportunity Mindset
- What impact did your levels of awareness and the states you were in this week have? There is no right or wrong answer here. Whatever comes up is good.
- Having reflected on the above, what's your overall score to this pillar? On a scale of 1 (my awareness levels are limiting my potential, keeping me away from what I want to achieve, and negatively impacting my life) to 10 (I feel that I have developed

Dual Awareness and am able to be Deliberate Calm when I need it, and my awareness levels are actively improving my life), rate your awareness practice. Note this for checking in a month, two months, and six months to see your progress.

- How would improving your awareness benefit your life? What would it enable you to do? How would it affect your impact at work, in your relationships, and in your energy and fulfillment levels?
- What is one thing you can do this month to practice awareness? You can start small and simple. For example, the following activities will help you develop awareness:
  - At the start of the week, look at your agenda and identify the potential Adaptive Zone challenges.
  - Experiment with awareness reminders. For example, wear a bracelet that reminds you to check in with how you feel and whether you are in protection or learning or another state.
  - Set reminders on your smartphone or watch to check in with yourself and perform short breathing exercises.
  - Do short meditation exercises that build your awareness muscle.
  - Start keeping a daily journal in which you write down an end-of-day reflection.

Purpose

This pillar holds your purpose, as well as who and what is most important to you, including your values, the principles you live by, your family, and your career.

Right now, you may not have an answer to the question "What is your purpose?" If so, let's look at some ways to uncover your purpose. You can start by reflecting on your values. Whether or not you are able to articulate your overarching purpose in life, we all have things that we believe in and that matter to us and ways in which we want to show up in the world, perform, and connect with other people. Those are your values, and they are directly connected to your purpose. If your purpose is our dot on the horizon, living and working in accordance with your values is how you are going to get there.

Even if you already feel connected to your purpose, it can be helpful to reflect on your values so that whatever direction life takes you in, you remain conscious of how you want to engage and respond. Then you can set intentions about how you are going to show up and perform in ways that are aligned with your values. Just like connecting to your larger purpose, this is an emotional regulation technique. You feel more in control and decisive when you are acting with intention. This can help you stay grounded in the face of challenges or the unknown.

Considering all of the values listed below, please select the ones that are critical to how you live your life:

- Mastery
- Safety of family
- Integrity
- Autonomy
- Equity
- Success
- Being trustworthy
- Pleasure
- Recognition
- Awareness of environmental issues
- Adventure
- Stability
- Avoiding shame
- Caring for friends and family
- Justice
- World peace

- Being understanding
- Independence
- Harmony
- Power
- Tradition
- Conservation
- Enjoyment
- Ambition
- Excitement
- Reputation
- Safety of community
- Influence
- Being supportive
- Indulgence
- Choice
- Respecting authority
- Avoiding embarrassment
- Status
- Spirituality
- Open-mindedness
- Loyalty
- You can add anything else that comes up for you

Once you have chosen your values, allocate 100 points total across the values you selected, based on how much each value matters to you.

Next, think about in which of the following areas of your life you currently see your values playing a significant role:

- Family
- Work
- Spirituality

- Friends
- Community

Interests/Hobbies

Building on what you've learned about what matters to you, what would you describe as your individual purpose? Here are just a few examples:

- My purpose is to make my community a safer and more inclusive place through my everyday work.
- My purpose is to clean up and preserve the environment for future generations to enjoy.
- My purpose is to improve the lives of my family members and friends by being a supportive parent and caring friend.

Now that you've framed or recalled your purpose, let's take a moment to assess your current state wins and challenges. What's working well right now, and where do you have a feeling that you may want to make a shift?

To help focus the reflection, the following questions may help you understand to what extent you are currently living your purpose across work and nonwork activities. Please rate how frequently you engage in the following behaviors. For each sentence, please choose never, rarely, sometimes, often, or always.

- My purpose guides the decisions I make—never, rarely, sometimes, often, always.
- I search for meaning and purpose in key moments of my life—never, rarely, sometimes, often, always.
- I try to find meaning and purpose in everyday experiences—never, rarely, sometimes, often, always.

- I search for experiences that are significant to me—never, rarely, sometimes, often, always.
- I refer to my values, or what matters to me, to help make decisions—never, rarely, sometimes, often, always.
- My purpose influences my decision-making process—never, rarely, sometimes, often, always.
- I am able to work toward my purpose at my current organization—never, rarely, sometimes, often, always.

Having reflected on the above, what's your overall score to this pillar? On a scale of 1 (I am very unclear of my purpose and values, I don't reflect on it in my day-to-day life, and the decisions that I make are not guided by it) to 10 (I know my purpose, I know what matters to me, I revisit it regularly, and it guides my decision-making on a daily basis), rate your purpose alignment practice. Check in in a month, in two months, and in six months to note your progress.

Now take a moment to think about how you can focus more on your purpose and on living your life according to your values. What behaviors, habits, or practices can you experiment with? Remember, if you want to create real change, you have to focus on behaviors and actions. Get tactical. What specifically will you do differently? One suggestion is to focus on just one specific behavior in the next month—for example, making sure that you spend at least an hour each day working on a project of some sort that is squarely "on purpose."

Energy

This pillar holds your well-being and recovery and the physical, mental, spiritual, emotional, and social practices that help recharge your batteries.

As we have discussed in detail, taking care of your energy and planning your recovery holistically is essential for your well-being, your adaptability, and your ability to shift into learning even in the midst of challenges or the unknown. However, our habits often lead us to prioritize just one or two methods of recovery above a well-rounded recovery plan, or to give up the activities that energize and recharge us precisely when we need them the most.

Now is the time to commit to a regular recovery practice to keep your batteries charged. This is not selfish or indulgent! As leaders, it is especially important to model good recovery habits for our teams. Perhaps one of the most important things we can do as leaders is to set the right tone. The energy we bring to each interaction is observed and often mimicked by others. "Do as I say, not as I do" will absolutely not cut it when it comes to role-modeling energy and recovery.

While each person's needs for recovery are highly individual, holistic recovery includes adequate sleep, exercise, nutrition, authentic connection, activities that you find personally fulfilling, introspection, focus, rest, and activities that connect you to your purpose. Please note that this is general advice for the average person. Please consult with your doctor to address any specific needs and before making any changes to your nutrition or lifestyle.

A DAY IN THE LIFE

Below is an example of how a busy human can nonetheless live a balanced day. You will see that the goal is not intensity but rather weaving in moments of recovery throughout your day.

MINDFUL WAKE-UP

Resist the urge to reach for your phone! Spend at least twenty minutes on a nonwork morning routine.

MORNING ROUTINE

Bring some intention setting and movement into every morning. For example, when brushing your teeth, take a deep breath and smile, then set an intention for the day ahead. What do you want to do? Who do you want to be? You might take a few minutes to do a little physical activity, like stretching, while waiting for your coffee to drip or for your water to boil.

MOVEMENT WHILE WORKING

Consider if you really need to be at your desk for that next meeting or if you could do it while walking instead.

FREQUENT BREAKS

Make sure to move every two hours, whether it is to get a glass of water or to do a few breathing exercises, and stretch. In fact, set a reminder.

UNINTERRUPTED WORK BLOCKS

Schedule a few uninterrupted hours during the day (or at least one!) to focus on work that requires real brain power and creativity. Block this time on your calendar so that you don't fill it with meetings or emails. In fact, close your email so you are not tempted to read and answer incoming messages.

DAILY APPRECIATION

Consider which of your friends, family members, or colleagues would benefit from a quick text, email, or call. Send them a quick note and let them know you are thinking about them.

RUTHLESS PRIORITIZATION

We are all different, but our productivity generally starts to slow down after six to eight hours of real work. Near the end of the workday ask yourself, "What really has to get done today? What can be delayed until tomorrow or even deleted from the to-do list?"

NON-NEGOTIABLE RECOVERY

Whether it is dinner with a loved one, a fitness class, a yoga session, or some quiet time by yourself, block out times on your calendar for the things *you* need to stay well.

KINDNESS AND SELF-COMPASSION

Life does not always go the way you hoped. Every day may have curveballs that make it hard, and the work you prepared may not turn out the way you expected. If this is something you struggle with, consider integrating a practice of self-compassion to navigate through these moments.

NIGHTLY GRATITUDE

In the evening, write down or say three things that you are grateful for and why you are grateful for them. Be specific and try to mention new things each day.

TIME FOR BED

Put your phone in another room (physical alarm clocks still work). Avoid emails, news, or stressful discussions at least one hour before bed.

Now that you have a better idea of what holistic recovery looks like for you, ask yourself the following questions:

- What recovery practices are currently working well for me?
- What recovery practices are no longer working for me or where do I have challenge areas?

- Having reflected on the above, what's your overall score to this pillar? On a scale of 1 (I have not integrated recovery practices in my day-to-day life) to 10 (I have integrated recovery practices in my day-to-day life, and I am able to flexibly stick to them), rate your purpose alignment practice. Note this for checking in one month, two months, and six months to see your progress.

- What is most important for me right now when it comes to managing my energy? What is the one thing I can do for a month to help me in this area?

Relationships

This pillar holds all the roles you play in the different types of relationships in your life—at work with colleagues and team members, in your personal life with family members, friends, community members, and so on. It also holds the role you play in groups of people—teams at work, your family as a whole, communities you are a part of such as religious groups and volunteer organizations, and even groups of friends. Finally, there are the roles that others play with you, whether or not you have cultivated and tapped into a network of relationships that help you thrive, not only in terms of the roles you play but also the roles you want and need others to play in your life.

While we have focused primarily on our roles and relationships as leaders in this book, we have also seen how conflict among our various roles as leaders, partners, parents, community members, and friends can drain our batteries and leave us depleted. It's also clear that our hidden icebergs affect us not just at work but also in every part of our lives. And when we get swept away by our emotions in one area, we are more likely to do so in others. We have seen time and time again how facing high-stakes adaptive challenges at work can lead us to exhibit protection behaviors at home and vice versa. It is therefore important to be aware of and reflect on how you want to show up in each area of your life and how you want to balance each of the roles you currently play so they are aligned with your priorities.

Start by listing the relationships that are most alive for you right now (for example, the relationship you have with those you manage, your children, your spouse, your close friends). It's easy to forget how many relationships we are actively involved in. Naming them will help make your priorities clearer and, as a bonus, remind you of the wealth of social connection in your life. Also name the groups of people you actively play a role in (for example, your team(s) at work, church groups, and circles of friends).

Next, ask yourself the following questions:

- How am I showing up in each one of these relationships? What is working well?
- Where are the ways I'm showing up not consistent with how I want to show up? Which relationships feel strained or missing from my focus?
- Who do I most want to spend time with and why?
- Who am I excited to have in my life ten years from now? Why?
- Do I have enough friends, and do I spend enough time with the friends who energize me?
- Do I have people in my life who help and support me and fulfill my needs for affiliation, recreation, love, achievement, agency, and autonomy?
- What do I need to change in order to bring a better version of myself to certain relationships in my life?
- Having reflected on the above, what's your overall score to this pillar? On a scale of 1 (I am not happy how I manage my relationships and the communities I am part of, it's hard to show up the way I want to, and I am not tapped into a network that supports my growth)

to 10 (I am very happy with how I manage my relationships and the communities I am part of, I am able to show up the way I want to, and I am tapped into a network that supports my growth), rate your purpose alignment practice. Note this for checking in a month, two months, and six months to see your progress.

- What is the one thing I want to focus on in my relationships or communities for the next month by bringing awareness, trying a new way of relating or communicating, or operating from a new mindset?

YOUR IDEAL WEEK VERSUS YOUR CURRENT WEEK

You are hopefully gaining a good sense of what is and isn't working in your current personal operating model. But what does this mean moving forward? Take some time to map out what an ideal week would look like for you. This should not be a vacation week but rather a typical week in which everything goes according to plan and you're not thrown any curveballs. (We know that is very atypical!) Go through and literally plan out your imaginary ideal week, keeping these questions in mind:

- What would your daily routines look like?
- How would you spend your time? What is your ideal balance of meetings, focused work, working with others, working alone, recreational activities, time with friends and family, and so on?
- What awareness practices would you engage in and how often?
- In what ways would you connect to your purpose?
- What activities would you prioritize?
- How would you recover?
- How would you show up in your personal and professional lives?
- Who would you spend the most time with?

Now compare this ideal week to a typical week in your current life.

- How similar are these two weeks? In what ways are they different?
- What are some small shifts you can make in the near term in order to close the gap between your ideal week and your typical week?
- What are some bigger changes you can commit to making in the longer term to close the gap?

SET YOURSELF UP FOR SUCCESS

Reflection and planning are important, but in the real world, they will only get you so far. It's easy to slip into old patterns as you face day-to-day challenges and new pressures. Remember these tips for making your changes stick:

IT'S A TEAM EFFORT: No one's operating model works in a vacuum. Ask those around you to help you remain accountable. Choose a partner to share your operating model goals with and check in with that person regularly, maybe even as often as daily. This can be a trusted colleague, a friend, or maybe even your spouse. When you share your intentions with this buddy, be open to feedback and suggestions. Others can often see things that are difficult for us to notice, such as blind spots or progress that we may take for granted.

ALIGN YOUR TIME WITH YOUR INTENTIONS: Many leaders find it helpful to engage their calendars in this work. Block time to reflect and strengthen your awareness. Block time for recovery. Block time for on-purpose work. Don't assume relationship and teamwork will "just happen." Dedicate time to it. This is important work that deserves prioritization. Another tip: end every day with dedicated prep time for the next day. How can tomorrow have some dedicated blocks for awareness, purpose, recovery, and relationships?

TRY SMALL STEPS, AND RITUALIZE TO CREATE A FEEDBACK LOOP: Big changes are daunting and inspire procrastination and defeat. Try small steps and habits and include a few nonnegotiables that are the minimum achievements you want to integrate come rain or shine. For example, if you find that you need a major energy and recovery overhaul, don't set a goal to recover like a professional athlete in all areas. Instead, start small by setting an intention to take at least two five-minute breaks every day to do a mini-meditation or get some movement and see how it affects you.

In addition to starting small, creating a feedback loop by checking in frequently with yourself (and maybe your accountability buddy) and refining your wins, challenges, and intentions is another way to make real progress. Acknowledge, celebrate, and savor what has worked—no matter how small. Over time, you may also want to explore using this personal operating model thinking with your team. What matters most is that *you* take ownership for your personal operating model.

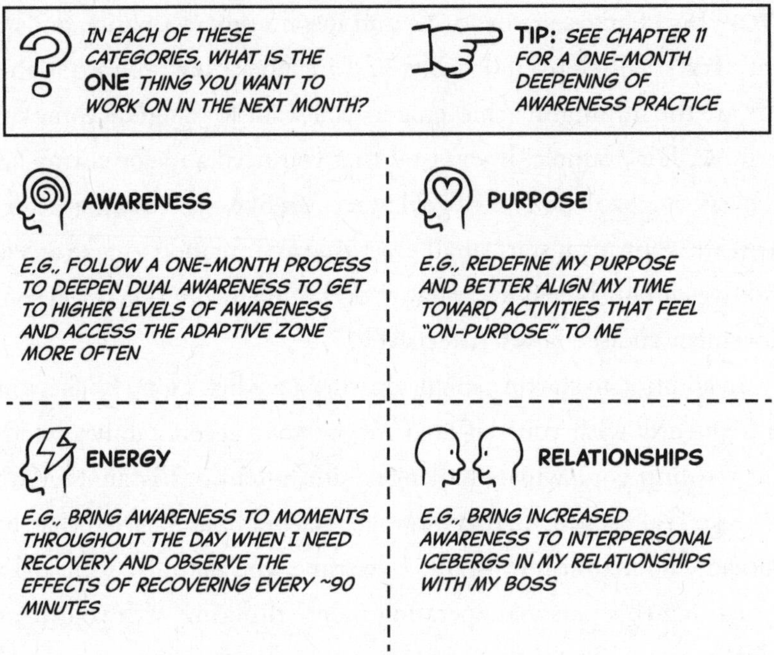

 IN EACH OF THESE
CATEGORIES, WHAT IS THE
ONE *THING YOU WANT TO
WORK ON IN THE NEXT MONTH?*

 TIP: *SEE CHAPTER 11
FOR A ONE-MONTH
DEEPENING OF
AWARENESS PRACTICE*

 AWARENESS

*E.G., FOLLOW A ONE-MONTH PROCESS
TO DEEPEN DUAL AWARENESS TO GET
TO HIGHER LEVELS OF AWARENESS
AND ACCESS THE ADAPTIVE ZONE
MORE OFTEN*

 PURPOSE

*E.G., REDEFINE MY PURPOSE
AND BETTER ALIGN MY TIME
TOWARD ACTIVITIES THAT FEEL
"ON-PURPOSE" TO ME*

 ENERGY

*E.G., BRING AWARENESS TO MOMENTS
THROUGHOUT THE DAY WHEN I NEED
RECOVERY AND OBSERVE THE
EFFECTS OF RECOVERING EVERY ~90
MINUTES*

 RELATIONSHIPS

*E.G., BRING INCREASED
AWARENESS TO INTERPERSONAL
ICEBERGS IN MY RELATIONSHIPS
WITH MY BOSS*

FIGURE 10.3: Intentions for the Next Month

CONCLUSION

One can choose to go back toward safety or forward
toward growth. Growth must be chosen again and
again; fear must be overcome again and again.
—ABRAHAM MASLOW

In 2018, Canadian prime minister Justin Trudeau said, "The pace of change has never been this fast, but it will never be this slow again." In our increasingly VUCA—volatile, uncertain, complex, and ambiguous—world, old methods are crumbling and new ones seek to emerge, and as leaders we must continuously adapt to create a new reality that we will be proud to leave for the next generation. For each of us, this adaptation may play out in different levels in our lives: in our families, in our teams and organizations, in our countries, and in the world.

None of us knows what disruption or change is lurking around the corner. But we do know that as the world changes, it will continue to become more and more important for us to adapt and more and more difficult to do so. What the world needs now are leaders who can also be learners even in the most challenging circumstances. To become this type of learning leaders, we must expand our consciousness so we can break through the habits that keep us tied to the past, see the world with fresh eyes, and open up new ways of relating to each other and the changing world.

This means that it will never be easier than it is today to start practicing Deliberate Calm. Doing so will help you unlock the adaptability paradox so that you can learn, adapt, thrive, and succeed no matter what is going on around you or what challenges you may face. If you are not currently in the midst of a disruption or crisis, it may seem like there is no reason to start practicing Deliberate Calm now, but this is actually the perfect time to start building this muscle to prepare for the future's unknown. If you are currently facing a major change or challenge, it may seem like you have no time to integrate new practices into your life. But there is always enough time to pause before reacting and to make a deliberately calm choice, and in this context, slowing down now means speeding up later. We encourage you to start applying these techniques however you can right now, no matter what is going on for you personally or professionally.

Think back to Captain Sullenberger, whose story we used to open this book. He had mere seconds to decide whether to follow the existing playbook and return to the airport or to adapt to the situation he was facing and try something new, and he made those seconds count. You now possess all of the tools you need to master your emotions and leverage all of your resources to choose the best possible response regardless of what you are facing.

With this in mind, we hope that you will choose to begin the four-week Deliberate Calm Protocol right away to build your practice and prepare yourself for whatever life has in store. The word "practice" is key. You will not do this perfectly today, at the end of four weeks, or probably ever, nor do you need to. We certainly don't! But accepting and embracing your humanity is a key part of the process.

As you move forward, we encourage you to share what you've learned. Simply practicing Deliberate Calm will have an impact on those around you. You also have the opportunity to teach these skills to others, creating a ripple effect among your family, your teams, your community, and ultimately the world. We wrote this book grounded in the optimism that with greater awareness, we can rise together to meet the challenges of the future with compassion, confidence, and hope. Thank you for choosing to be a part of this movement.

FOUR WEEKS TO DELIBERATE CALM

The best time
to plant a tree
was years ago.
The second-best
time is today.

—CHINESE PROVERB

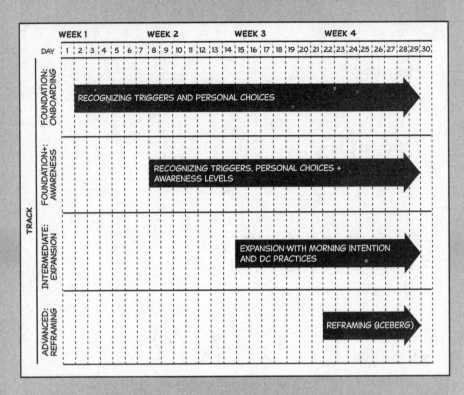

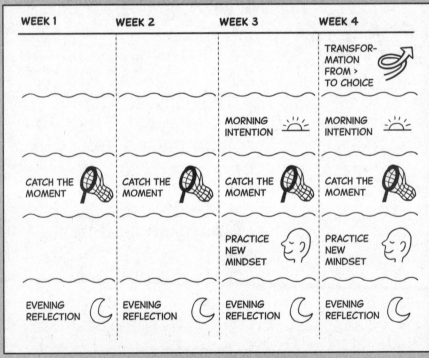

Now that you have your foundational personal operating model in place, it is time to begin building your Deliberate Calm muscle. Over the next four weeks, you will engage in practices that will help you gain awareness of your context and what the situation demands from you, make better conscious choices, respond effectively to challenges, and transform at a deeper level so you are less likely to shift into protection no matter what is going on around you. You can choose to start this protocol immediately or after spending some time living from your new personal operating model. Either way, you should begin this protocol when you feel strong and excited to begin something new. Creating new habits takes time.[1,2,3] We propose starting with the four-week protocol and continuing the journey after.

During each week of the protocol, you will focus on gaining awareness around your personal triggers and how you respond in the moment. During Week 2, you will also work on recognizing what level of awareness you are currently operating from. During Week 3, you will add Deliberate Calm practices to further your progress. During Week 4, you will work on the transformative process of reframing your iceberg. While Deliberate Calm is a lifelong practice and not something that you can complete within four weeks, by the end of this period you should see a marked difference in your ability to practice Dual Awareness and remain significantly calmer and more at choice in the face of challenges and the unknown.

WEEK 1
FOUNDATION/ONBOARDING

This week, you will work on becoming more aware of the moments when you shift into a state of protection so you can start to realize how often this happens and why, as well as how it impacts your thoughts, feelings, and behavior. With practice, you will be able to catch yourself shifting into protection in real time. Later in the protocol, we will add Deliberate Calm tools to help you pivot from a state of protection to learning in these moments and even to anticipate them so you can remain in a state of learning no matter what is going on around you.

DAILY PRACTICES

1. Catch the Moment

Your goal this week is to catch or become aware of four "trigger moments" each day. These are moments when you feel a strong emotion and the impulse to react emotionally. This means you are likely in a state of protection. This can happen in any context, from high-stakes adaptive moments to everyday low-stakes moments in the Familiar Zone.

After each trigger moment, write down a brief summary of what happened, how you felt, what you were thinking, and your resulting behavior. You can either keep a journal with you or take notes on your phone to capture these moments. Please do this every day. While your goal is to catch four of these moments each day, it is okay if you have more or fewer than four.

To give you an idea, here is an example:

MOMENT: I was loading the dishwasher with my wife, and she gave me "instructions" on how to do it better.
FEELING: Irritated
THOUGHTS: This is so not important. Who cares how to load the dishwasher?
BEHAVIOR: Switch off and withdraw.

2. Evening Reflection

Each evening, you will complete a ten-minute reflection on those trigger moments, how they influenced your behavior, and why. Taking time for reflection is critically important throughout this protocol and beyond. It is a powerful way to process what happened during the day and to create space to listen to your inner world with some distance between you and the trigger moment. What moments were difficult and why, how did you feel, and why did you respond the way you did? Reflection helps you see the big picture and your own reactive behavior and its drivers.

> **For this week, take ten minutes each evening to reflect and answer the following questions:**

Which one of these trigger moments was the most stressful for you?

_____

_____

_____

_____

In one sentence, describe what you believe was the trigger in this moment. It may be something that someone said, a thought you had, a sound you heard, or something you saw.

_____

_____

_____

At approximately what time today did this most stressful moment occur?

_____

Would you describe the thoughts you had in this moment as protective in nature (defensive, scared, angry, negative) or of a learning nature (curious, positive, open to experiences)?

_____

_____

_____

From 1 to 10, how did you feel physically in this moment in terms of the level of energy in your body (1=low energy, 10=high energy)?

_____

From 1 to 10, how pleasant or unpleasant did you feel in this moment? (1=unpleasant, 10=pleasant)?

_____

What emotions did you experience in this moment (for example, excited, enthusiastic, elated, happy, upset, anxious, frustrated, stressed, nervous, tense, sad, depressed, sluggish, bored, calm, relaxed, serene, content, or anything else that comes up for you)?

_____

_____

_____

_____

_____

From 1 to 10, what was your overall response to this situation (1=I moved away from my goals. My reaction was counterproductive and not helpful in achieving what I wanted to achieve in this situation; 10=I moved toward my goals. My reaction was productive and helpful in achieving what I want to achieve in this situation)?

_____

Taking a step back and reflecting on the situation you were in, what do you think the situation called for? Was this a Familiar Zone situation, asking you to focus on what you already know, or was this an Adaptive Zone situation that required something new?

_____

_____

_____

_____

_____

Apart from the moments you felt triggered, which experiences and situations did you choose to engage with today? Which potential situations and experiences did you choose not to engage with? Why? Which invitations to learn did you accept, which did you postpone, and which did you avoid?

_____

_____

_____

_____

_____

Before ending your nightly reflection, take a deep breath and take a moment to think about this exercise and whether any insights have arisen. Have any patterns become clear to you?

_____

_____

_____

_____

_____

_____

WEEK 1 WRAP-UP

At the end of the week, you will have taken note of around twenty-eight Adaptive Moments and completed seven nightly reflections. Can you spot any patterns emerging among your trigger moments and reactive patterns? For example, did these moments occur at similar times during the day, or when you were engaged in the same activities, or as you interacted with specific people? What about your reactions? Were your thoughts, emotions, and physical sensations similar or different during each moment? How did you behave?

Now, take an extra moment to reflect on the week as a whole. What has come up for you this week? Have you experienced any "aha" moments? It's absolutely fine if you haven't. You are still increasing your awareness day by day, and next week we will go a little deeper.

FOUNDATION + AWARENESS

This week, in addition to catching your trigger moments, you will begin to recognize which awareness level you are operating from during these moments. As you keep practicing, you will likely begin to see your level of awareness rise. However, this is not always a linear process. It is perfectly normal to plateau or even regress at times. Be patient with yourself and trust that you are making progress, even when it isn't obvious to you.

DAILY PRACTICES

Your actions this week will be very similar to Week 1 as you continue to strengthen your Dual Awareness.

1. Catch the Moments

Once again, try to become aware of four trigger moments each day. Then write down what happened, your thoughts, feelings, and behavior soon after the event. You can either keep a journal with you or take notes on your phone.

2. Evening Reflection

Then, you will complete a slightly more in-depth reflection each evening by answering the following questions:

During each of your trigger moments, at what level of awareness did you primarily find yourself operating from?

☐ **AWARENESS LEVEL 1**: Unaware—Not aware of internal state or external zone

☐ **AWARENESS LEVEL 2**: Delayed—Aware after it happens

☐ **AWARENESS LEVEL 3**: Perceptive—Aware but not able to effectively respond in the moment

☐ **AWARENESS LEVEL 4**: Resilient—Aware and able to respond after a short pause or time-out

☐ **AWARENESS LEVEL 5**: Adaptive—Aware and able to pivot effectively from protection to learning in the moment (Dual Awareness in action)

Which one of these trigger moments was the most stressful for you?

_____

In one sentence, describe what you believe was the trigger in this moment. It may be something that someone said, a thought you had, a sound you heard, or something you saw.

_____

_____

At approximately what time today did this most stressful moment occur?

_____

_____

What level of awareness did you experience during this most stressful moment?

☐ **AWARENESS LEVEL 1:** Unaware—Not aware of internal state or external zone

☐ **AWARENESS LEVEL 2:** Delayed—Aware after it happens

☐ **AWARENESS LEVEL 3:** Perceptive—Aware but not able to effectively respond in the moment

☐ **AWARENESS LEVEL 4:** Resilient—Aware and able to respond after a short pause or time-out

☐ **AWARENESS LEVEL 5:** Adaptive—Aware and able to pivot effectively from protection to learning in the moment (Dual Awareness in action)

Would you describe the thoughts you had in this moment as protective in nature (defensive, scared, angry, negative) or of a learning nature (curious, positive, open to experiences)?

_____

_____

_____

From 1 to 10, how did you feel physically in this moment in terms of the level of energy in your body (1=low energy, 10=high energy)?

_____

From 1 to 10, how pleasant or unpleasant did you feel in this moment (1=unpleasant, 10=pleasant)?

_____

What emotions did you experience in this moment (for example, excited, enthusiastic, elated, happy, upset, anxious, frustrated, stressed, nervous, tense, sad, depressed, sluggish, bored, calm, relaxed, serene, content, or anything else that comes up for you)?

_____

_____

_____

_____

From 1 to 10, what was your overall response to this situation (1 = I moved away from my goals. My reaction was counterproductive and not helpful in achieving what I wanted to achieve in this situation; 10 = I moved toward my goals. My reaction was productive and helpful in achieving what I want to achieve in this situation)?

_____

Taking a step back and reflecting on the situation you were in, what do you think the situation called for? Was this a Familiar Zone situation, asking you to focus on what you already know, or was this an Adaptive Zone situation that required something new?

_____

_____

_____

_____

Apart from the moments you felt triggered, which experiences and situations did you choose to engage with today? Which potential situations and experiences did you choose not to engage with? Why? Which invitations to learn did you accept, which did you postpone, and which did you avoid?

_____

_____

Before ending your nightly reflection, take a deep breath and take a moment to think about this exercise and whether any insights have arisen. Have any patterns become clear to you?

_____

WEEK 2 WRAP-UP

At the end of Week 2, you should have noted forty to sixty trigger moments and completed fourteen nightly reflections. It's likely that you will begin to see patterns emerging regarding your triggers and your reactions. Take a moment to make a note of these. Also reflect on the week as a whole. Did you find yourself being triggered more or less frequently than you were during Week 1? Was there any difference in how you experienced your trigger moments and responded in the moment?

You are now halfway through the four-week protocol. You have laid the groundwork for a significant increase in Dual Awareness. Next week, on this fertile ground, you will begin incorporating Deliberate Calm tools so you can learn to pivot from protection to learning in the moment. This is only the beginning!

EXPANSION

This week, you will work on anticipating trigger moments and better responding to what the situation calls for. In other words, you will be practicing Dual Awareness in the moment. You will continue to catch your trigger moments during the day while also predicting what zones you may encounter and which moments are most likely to trigger you. To help anticipate these moments, you will add a morning intention-setting practice.

Intention setting allows you to leverage many of the same physical, mental, emotional, and performance benefits as connecting to your purpose. Just like being connected to a larger sense of purpose, this practice attaches a positive meaning to any stress or tension you may feel. It primes you to adopt a learning mindset and to deactivate the fear response so you are less likely to get swept away by your emotions. This way, you throw a small anchor that holds you steady during trigger moments.

In addition to being a beneficial daily practice, setting intentions about how you want to show up directly before difficult moments can help you stay in learning when it matters most. This practice builds the prediction power in your brain. It can be particularly helpful before entering a negotiation or any meeting or encounter that you know might be contentious or difficult.

Of course, this requires you to be aware beforehand of when you are most likely to shift into protection. It can be helpful to take a few minutes at the start of the day to go through your agenda, identify high-stakes topics, and set an intention for what you want to accomplish and how you want the experience to unfold for yourself and others. This enables you to predict "emotional hot spots" or situations that ask for a learning mindset and provides a bulwark against reactivity.

With your intentions in place, this week you will also work on pivoting from protection to learning in high-stakes moments. As in the first two weeks, you will end each day with a ten-minute reflection practice to continue growing your level of awareness and gaining insight into what drives your behavior. By the end of this week, you will be ready for a transformational exercise to create deeper and more lasting change.

DAILY PRACTICES

1. Catch the Moments

Once again, try to become aware of four trigger moments each day. Then write down what happened, your thoughts, feelings, and behavior soon after the event. You can either keep a journal with you or take notes on your phone.

2. Morning Intention Setting

Each morning, find a quiet space and ten minutes to sit uninterrupted. If at all possible, we recommend doing this before looking at your phone. Answer the following questions about the day ahead:

What is your hope/aspiration/intention for today? What would make it a great day?

_____

_____

_____

Who do you want to be today? How do you want to show up for
yourself and others?

_____

_____

_____

_____

What is this day asking of you? What challenges or opportunities are
inviting you to stay curious and potentially let go of your plans?

_____

_____

_____

_____

What would make this day worthwhile and fulfilling for you?

_____

_____

_____

_____

What are the potentially high-stakes situations or trigger moments you might be facing today? Is there an Adaptive Zone situation you may be engaging in when you want to prioritize staying in learning?

_____

_____

_____

_____

Exploring these potentially stressful or challenging moments, what do you think will be the key factors that cause you to experience stress? Are there ways to reframe the situation that will make it easier to experience the situation differently and respond constructively?

_____

_____

_____

_____

What do these particular situations call for, a focus on execution of what I already know or a focus on keeping an open, learning mind?

_____

_____

_____

_____

Set an intention for the relevant moments during the day. Try to visualize the following:

☐ What do you want to happen?

☐ How do you want to think and feel?

☐ How do you want others to think and feel?

☐ How do you want to show up for this specific moment?

Reflecting on how you want to show up for this specific moment, what can you do ahead of time to feel well prepared for the important moments during the day (for example, taking a quick walk beforehand, making sure you have a nutritious lunch, or taking a moment for a few deep breaths).

_____

_____

_____

_____

_____

_____

3. Pivot from Protection to Learning

This week, when you notice that you are experiencing trigger or adaptive moments, you will start actively trying to pivot from protection to learning by using either physiological tools, reframing, or both. You can experiment by taking a time-out to implement these tools or by trying to shift into learning in the moment. As you practice, you should be able to make this change more and more quickly. Be patient with yourself, as this does take time. There will inevitably be moments when you attempt to implement these tools and get carried away by your emotions anyway. That's okay, as the goal is not to stay in learning all the time.

Physiological Tools

As you notice yourself encountering a trigger or adaptive moment, implementing one or more of these quick and easy interventions can help calm your body down so you can access a state of learning.

- Breathe deeply, with exhalations that are longer than inhalations.
- Zoom out and take in a panoramic view of your surroundings.
- Take a brisk five-to-ten-minute walk.
- Intentionally speak with a lower, warmer pitch to your voice.
- Breathe into your belly (diaphragmatic breathing) instead of your chest.

Reframing

As we have discussed earlier, there are some mindsets that may suit us when we are in the Familiar Zone but lead us to respond less effectively when we are in the Adaptive Zone. Intentionally operating from a learning mindset instead of a status quo/limiting mindset can help you access a state of learning. This week, as you notice yourself encountering an adaptive or trigger moment, try to pivot to one of these learning mindsets.

Growth Mindset—When we are operating from a growth mindset, we believe that we can develop our intelligence and gain new skills over time.

Curious Mindset—With a curious mindset, we are willing to ask questions, explore, and discover. We are eager to learn from trying something new in a state of learning.

Creative Mindset—With a creative mindset, we lead with purpose, empower ourselves and others to explore new possibilities, and experiment our way to innovative solutions.

Agent Mindset—With an agent mindset, we maintain an inner locus of control. We know that within reason, we have the ability to try new things, overcome challenges, and accomplish whatever we put our minds to.

Abundance Mindset—With an abundance mindset, we see that resources are plentiful and do not need to be competed for. Challenges are potentially win-win situations looking to be discovered. This is an especially useful mindset to adopt when facing a negotiation.

Exploration Mindset—With an exploration mindset, we are open to possibilities outside our original plan. We do not know what the future holds, so we believe that the best way to succeed is to plan ahead but remain flexible and curious as we go, keeping our eyes open for unforeseen opportunities.

Opportunity Mindset—With an opportunity mindset, we are looking for potential opportunities instead of possible pitfalls and believe that we can make something great happen.

4. Evening Reflection ☾

This week, you will complete a slightly more in-depth reflection each evening by answering the following questions:

During each of your trigger moments, at what level of awareness did you primarily find yourself operating from?

☐ **AWARENESS LEVEL 1:** Unaware—Not aware of internal state or external zone

☐ **AWARENESS LEVEL 2:** Delayed—Aware after it happens

☐ **AWARENESS LEVEL 3:** Perceptive—Aware but not able to effectively respond in the moment

☐ **AWARENESS LEVEL 4:** Resilient—Aware and able to respond after a short pause or time-out

☐ **AWARENESS LEVEL 5:** Adaptive—Aware and able to pivot effectively from protection to learning in the moment (Dual Awareness in action)

Which one of these trigger moments was the most stressful for you?

_____

In one sentence, can you describe what you believe was the trigger in this moment? It may be something that someone said, a thought you had, a sound you heard, or something you saw.

_____

_____

_____

At approximately what time today did this most stressful moment occur?

_____

What level of awareness did you experience during this most stressful moment?

☐ **AWARENESS LEVEL 1:** Unaware—Not aware of internal state or external zone

☐ **AWARENESS LEVEL 2:** Delayed—Aware after it happens

☐ **AWARENESS LEVEL 3:** Perceptive—Aware but not able to effectively respond in the moment

☐ **AWARENESS LEVEL 4:** Resilient—Aware and able to respond after a short pause or time-out

☐ **AWARENESS LEVEL 5:** Adaptive—Aware and able to pivot effectively from protection to learning in the moment (Dual Awareness in action)

Would you describe the thoughts you had in this moment as protective in nature (defensive, scared, angry, negative) or of a learning nature (curious, positive, open to experiences)?

_____

_____

_____

_____

_____

From 1 to 10, how did you feel physically in this moment in terms of the level of energy in your body (1=low energy, 10=high energy)?

_____

From 1 to 10, how pleasant or unpleasant did you feel in this moment (1=unpleasant, 10=pleasant)?

_____

What emotions did you experience in this moment (for example, excited, enthusiastic, elated, happy, upset, anxious, frustrated, stressed, nervous, tense, sad, depressed, sluggish, bored, calm, relaxed, serene, content, or anything else that comes up for you)?

_____

_____

_____

_____

_____

From 1 to 10, what was your overall response to this situation (1=I moved away from my goals. My reaction was counterproductive, and not helpful in achieving what I wanted to achieve in this situation; 10=I moved toward my goals. My reaction was productive and helpful in achieving what I want to achieve in this situation)?

_____

_____

Were you able to use physiological tools to be more effective? What worked and what didn't work?

_____

_____

_____

_____

Were you able to use reframing techniques to be more effective? What worked and what didn't work?

_____

_____

_____

_____

Taking a step back and reflecting on the situation you were in, what do you think the situation called for? Was this a Familiar Zone situation, asking you to focus on what you already know, or was this an Adaptive Zone situation that required something new?

_____

_____

_____

Apart from the moments you felt triggered, which experiences and situations did you choose to engage with today? Which potential situations and experience did you choose not to engage with? Why?

Which invitations to learn did you accept, which did you postpone, and which did you avoid?

_____

_____

_____

Before ending your nightly reflection, take a deep breath and take a moment to think about this exercise and whether any insights have arisen. Have any patterns become clear to you?

_____

_____

_____

_____

WEEK 3 WRAP-UP

By the end of this week, you should have noted sixty to eighty trigger moments and completed twenty-one evening reflections. Take a moment to reflect on the week. What patterns keep coming up? When you attempted to pivot from protection to learning, how often did you succeed? Which techniques worked and which ones didn't? Did you notice whether or not you were able to catch the trigger moments more and more quickly? With the increased awareness and tools that you have gained so far, next week you will work on shifting a behavior that is not currently serving you. This is when the real transformation begins.

LEVEL UP

This week, you will identify a behavior you want to change, discover the underlying limiting mindset that is driving this behavior, develop a more enabling mindset to support your desired behavior, and create moments to practice operating from your new learning mindset.

ONETIME TRANSFORMATION EXERCISE: FROM-TO

Unlike the other exercises that you complete every day, you will do this one just once, at the beginning of Week 4.

Start by looking back at the past three weeks. By now, patterns should be recognizable. Take some time to reflect on your triggers, and then answer the following questions:

What are the patterns among the triggers that keep coming up for you?

_____

_____

_____

_____

_____

What are the patterns among the reactive behaviors you exhibited during trigger moments? These can be things that you do, such as yelling, complaining, criticizing, checking out, or becoming aggressive. Or they can be things that you don't do, such as holding back from sharing your opinions, avoiding giving direct feedback, or failing to take responsibility.

_____

_____

_____

_____

_____

In your evening reflections, you noted when your reactions moved you away from your goals. What did you do or not do in those moments? It is likely that you have identified one or two patterns among unhelpful behaviors.

_____

_____

Choose one behavior that keeps coming up in relation to the results that are important for you, for example, giving feedback, micromanaging, or not taking accountability.

This week, you can make a choice to change that behavior by discovering and changing the underlying mindset that is driving it. Ask yourself the following questions:

What behavior am I exhibiting that is getting in the way of my goals?
(This is the behavior you want to move away from.)

_____

_____

_____

_____

_____

What situation(s) am I in when I typically exhibit this behavior? Is this
the Familiar or Adaptive Zone? What does the situation call for?

_____

_____

_____

_____

_____

What are my feelings in this situation?

_____

_____

_____

_____

_____

What thoughts go through my mind in this situation?

_____

_____

_____

_____

What is the mindset I am operating from that is leading to these thoughts, feelings, and behaviors?

_____

_____

_____

_____

How is this mindset serving me?

_____

_____

_____

_____

How is this mindset not serving me?

_____

_____

_____

How would my life be different if I no longer operated from this mindset?

_____

_____

_____

_____

What am I afraid will happen if I change this behavior?

_____

_____

_____

_____

What is the worst thing that can happen if I change this behavior?

_____

_____

_____

_____

What is most likely to happen if I continue to behave this way?

_____

_____

_____

_____

What is a more enabling mindset I can choose to operate from in this situation?

_____

_____

_____

_____

_____

If I imagine myself back in this situation with this new mindset, what feelings and thoughts come up? How are these different from before?

_____

_____

_____

_____

_____

What behavior would I naturally exhibit based on these thoughts and feelings? (This is the behavior you want to move to.)

_____

_____

_____

_____

_____

If I continued showing up in this new way, what would likely be the result?

_____

_____

_____

_____

_____

What are some small experiments I can do to practice operating from this mindset and exhibiting this new behavior?

_____

_____

_____

_____

_____

DAILY PRACTICES

1. Catch the Moments

Once again, try to become aware of four trigger moments each day. Then write down what happened and your thoughts, feelings, and behavior soon after the event. You can either keep a journal with you or take notes on your phone.

2. Morning Intention Setting

> **Each morning, find a quiet space and ten minutes to sit uninterrupted. If at all possible, we recommend doing this before looking at your phone. Answer the following questions about the day ahead:**

What is your hope/aspiration/intention for today? What would make it a great day?

_____

_____

_____

_____

_____

Who do you want to be today? How do you want to show up for yourself and others?

_____

_____

_____

_____

_____

What is this day asking of you? What challenges or opportunities are inviting you to stay curious and potentially let go of your plans?

_____

_____

_____

_____

_____

What would make this day worthwhile and fulfilling for you?

_____

_____

_____

_____

What are the potentially high-stakes situations or trigger moments you might be facing today? Is there an Adaptive Zone situation you may be engaging in when you want to prioritize staying in learning?

_____

_____

_____

_____

Exploring these potentially stressful or challenging moments, what do you think will be the key factors that cause you to experience stress? Are there ways to reframe the situation that will make it easier to experience the situation differently and respond constructively?

_____

_____

_____

_____

_____

What do these particular situations call for, a focus on execution of what I already know or a focus on keeping an open, learning mind?

_____

_____

_____

_____

_____

Set an intention for the relevant moments during the day. Try to visualize the following:

- [ ] What do you want to happen?

- [ ] How do you want to think and feel?

- [ ] How do you want others to think and feel?

- [ ] How do you want to show up for this specific moment?

Reflecting on how you want to show up for this specific moment, what can you do ahead of time to feel well prepared for the important moments during the day, for example, taking a quick walk beforehand, making sure you have a nutritious lunch, or taking a moment for a few deep breaths.

_____

_____

_____

_____

3. Practice Operating from Your New Mindset

Your new behaviors may not come naturally at first. That's okay. Continue practicing until it begins to feel more organic. That's how you create a habit.[4, 5, 6] Look for moments this week, ideally at least once a day, to intentionally practice exhibiting your new behavior and operating from your new enabling mindset. Think about what supports you might need to succeed at this and how you can create more and more opportunities to practice.

4. Evening Reflection

This week, you will complete an in-depth reflection each evening by answering the following questions:

Were you able to practice your desired mindset and behavior today? What went well? What did you learn? Does the new mindset you tried out feel true to you, or do you want to adapt it?

_____

_____

_____

_____

What will be the next moment when you can practice your new mindset and behavior?

_____

_____

_____

_____

During each of your trigger moments, at what level of awareness did you primarily find yourself operating from?

☐ **AWARENESS LEVEL 1**: Unaware—Not aware of internal state or external zone

☐ **AWARENESS LEVEL 2**: Delayed—Aware after it happens

☐ **AWARENESS LEVEL 3**: Perceptive—Aware but not able to effectively respond in the moment

☐ **AWARENESS LEVEL 4**: Resilient—Aware and able to respond after a short pause or time-out

☐ **AWARENESS LEVEL 5**: Adaptive—Aware and able to pivot effectively from protection to learning in the moment (Dual Awareness in action)

Which one of these trigger moments was the most stressful for you?

_____

_____

_____

_____

In one sentence, describe what you believe was the trigger in this moment. It may be something that someone said, a thought you had, a sound you heard, or something you saw.

_____

_____

_____

_____

At approximately what time today did this most stressful moment occur?

_____

What level of awareness did you experience during this most stressful moment?

☐ AWARENESS LEVEL 1: Unaware—Not aware of internal state or external zone

☐ AWARENESS LEVEL 2: Delayed—Aware after it happens

☐ AWARENESS LEVEL 3: Perceptive—Aware but not able to effectively respond in the moment

☐ **AWARENESS LEVEL 4:** Resilient—Aware and able to respond after a short pause or time-out

☐ **AWARENESS LEVEL 5:** Adaptive—Aware and able to pivot effectively from protection to learning in the moment (Dual Awareness in action)

Would you describe your thoughts in this moment as protective in nature (defensive, scared, angry, negative) or of a learning nature (curious, positive, open to experiences)?

_____

_____

From 1 to 10, how did you feel physically in this moment in terms of the level of energy in your body (1=low energy, 10=high energy)?

_____

From 1 to 10, how pleasant or unpleasant did you feel in this moment (1=unpleasant, 10=pleasant)?

_____

What emotions did you experience in this moment (for example, excited, enthusiastic, elated, happy, upset, anxious, frustrated, stressed, nervous, tense, sad, depressed, sluggish, bored, calm, relaxed, serene, content, or anything else that comes up for you)?

_____

_____

_____

From 1 to 10, what was your overall response to this situation (1=I moved away from my goals. My reaction was counterproductive, and not helpful in achieving what I wanted to achieve in this situation; 10= I moved toward my goals. My reaction was productive and helpful in achieving what I want to achieve in this situation)?

_____

Taking a step back and reflecting on the situation you were in, what do you think the situation called for? Was this a Familiar Zone situation, asking you to focus on what you already know, or was this an Adaptive Zone situation that required something new?

_____

_____

_____

_____

Apart from the moments you felt triggered, which experiences and situations did you choose to engage with today? Which potential situations and experience did you choose not to engage with? Why? Which invitations to learn did you accept, which did you postpone, and which did you avoid?

_____

_____

_____

_____

_____

Before ending your nightly reflection, take a deep breath and take a moment to think about this exercise and whether any insights have arisen. Have any patterns become clear to you?

_____

_____

_____

_____

WEEK 4 WRAP-UP

Whether or not you were consistently successful in operating from your new mindset and exhibiting more effective behavior during trigger moments, you have gained so much information about yourself over the past four weeks. You have learned what external circumstances are most likely to push you into a state of protection. You have learned how you are likely to respond internally during those moments. And you have learned how the behaviors you exhibit as a result impact your external circumstances. This connection between your external context and your internal state is the foundation of Dual Awareness. With this awareness, change is inevitable. It may happen more slowly or with more hiccups than you would like, but if you keep moving forward and listening to those whispers from inside you, you will continue to grow, learn, and evolve.

Your four-week protocol has come to an end, but the journey continues. Take some time to reflect on the past four weeks and everything you have learned, and to think about how you want to move forward. Which practices will you continue with every day, and which ones will you revisit as circumstances change or you feel stuck in any area of your life? Remember, as the world continues to change around you and challenges arise, only you are accountable for your behavior, for your decisions, and for creating your life's experience. This does not mean that you are to blame when things go wrong. It means that no matter what, you always have an opportunity to make things right.

ACKNOWLEDGMENTS

First and foremost, we must thank Jodi Lipper, our amazing writing partner, without whom this book would not have been possible. We had three very different authors, each with his or her own ideas and thoughts that were often complementary but sometimes challenging. Jodi was at the center, and expertly and synergistically wove it all together. This talent, as well as her ability to make complex concepts simple for the reader, made all the difference. We are grateful for her hard work and dedication, for her collaboration, and for our friendship, which grew throughout this process.

A number of our colleagues, among them Michael Park, Scott Rutherford, Daniel Pacthod, and Robert Lewis, as well as our entire "Launch" innovation committee at McKinsey, provided the resources and support to explore and build a client offering focused on adaptability and resilience amid volatility and uncertainty, including Deliberate Calm. In particular, thanks to Bob Sternfels, who provided his personal coaching and support to innovate and build a new kind of leadership journey, which has now touched tens of thousands of leaders around the world.

Thank you especially to all the folks who rolled up their sleeves to build the adaptability journey for leaders, among them Sasha Zolley,

Kate Lazaroff-Puck, Johanne Lavoie, Annie-Lou St-Amant, Marino Mugayar-Baldocchi, Cara Volpe, Ashley Kellner, and Alex Wood.

Thank you to our leadership who made this book possible: Kevin Sneader, the former MP of McKinsey & Company; Raju Narisetti, the leader of global publishing and chief editor of McKinsey & Company; and our practice leadership, who leaned in, in various ways, to support this effort: Michael Park, Dana Maor, Patrick Simon, Chris Gagnon, Mary Meaney, Bill Schaninger, Amadeo Di Lodovico, Brooke Weddle, Arne Gast, Gemma D'Auria, and Michael Lurie.

We are grateful for Erik Mandersloot and Andrew St. George for their support in the initial phase of the book, as well as the whole Aberkyn and McKinsey & Company community of facilitators of transformation who bring this work alive with our clients.

The first time we wrote about Deliberate Calm was in the article "Leadership in a Crisis," written with Gemma D'Auria. In that article, we discussed five specific things leaders must do to help their organizations navigate volatility and uncertainty as the COVID-19 crisis unfolded. One of those was, of course, Deliberate Calm. This article was a remarkable collaborative effort, supported by many folks on our Organizational Science team who helped do the research to identify those five characteristics, and back them up with empirical evidence. Thank you to Davis Carlin, Randy Lim, Ruth Imose, Kim Rubenstein, Marino Mugayar-Baldocchi, and Laura Pineault, among many others.

The follow-up article, "How to Demonstrate Deliberate Calm in a Crisis," was a collaboration with our dear editor Barbara Tierney, along with a supporting cast of colleagues, including Priyanjali Arora, Laura Pineault, and Roberto Rodriguez.

Then came "Psychological Safety, Emotional Intelligence, and Leadership in a Time of Flux."

Thanks to Bill Schaninger, Amy Edmondson, and Richard Boyatzis.

Finally, the article "Future Proof: Solving the 'Adaptability Paradox' for the Long Term," was a collaboration with Ashish Kothari, Johanne Lavoie, Marino Mugayar-Baldocchi, Sasha Zolley, Kate Lazaroff-Puck, and Laura Tegelberg.

Thank you to the following people for their help finalizing the book: Marino Mugayar-Baldocchi, for his contributions on the adaptability research journey over the years; Kate Lazaroff-Puck, for her contributions to the adaptability solutions and translations into the implementation of this work; and Nick Massios, who speedily designed high-quality illustrations for the book.

We are grateful for the entire team at Harper Business, especially Hollis Heimbouch and Kirby Sandmeyer, for believing in the book, for their wonderful collaboration from start to finish, and for their challenges, which always made our work better. Thanks, too, to the production team, the PR and marketing teams, and everyone who worked behind the scenes to help bring this book to life. Special thanks also to Tracy Locke (publicity), Laura Cole and Amanda Pritzker (marketing), Jocelyn Larnick (production), Nancy Singer (design), and Milan Bozic (the jacket).

A huge thank-you to our literary agent Lynn Johnston for her enthusiasm and expert help and advice throughout every stage of the process.

The authors wish to thank their families for their patience and support during the many hours over weekends, nights, and holidays that we spent on this work:

JACQUI: I'd like to thank my husband, Nicholas, and our amazing twins, Josephine and Samuel, who mean the world to me. They have always supported me, and I could not have achieved this milestone without them. They are my teachers and represent what truly matters to me every single day. I also would like to thank my parents and sisters, who have been foundational to my life journey and are always there for me, no matter what. I am grateful and full of love for all of you.

AARON: I'd like to thank my kids, Kailey and Blaze, who have been with me on a personal journey of volatility, uncertainty, and loss since we lost their mother to addiction several years ago. They've also been with me in our ongoing journey of healing and renewal, along with my wife, Naina. And, of course, the newest member of the family, my son Zoravar, who brings me joy every day. A special thanks to Blaze, who pointed out that we needed to change the subtitle of the book by asking, "Dad, shouldn't you learn first, and then lead once you've actually learned something, instead of the other way around?"

Thanks, too, to some of the great minds who have shaped my work: Morton Deutsch, Harvey Hornstein, Caryn Block, Richard Martell, Walter Mischel, Carol Dweck, and especially W. Warner Burke.

MICHIEL: I'd like to thank my wife, Christine, for her unwavering support to help me grow and expand, and for creating the space for writing this book. I'd like to thank my children, Itse, Douwe, and Yoostje for teaching me about empathy, love, and commitment.

We are grateful for everything this book, the journey, and the people involved have brought us!

*If I have seen further, it is by standing
on the shoulders of Giants.*

—ISAAC NEWTON

NOTES

Introduction

1. M. M. Capozzi, S. Dietsch, D. Pacthod, and M. Park, "Rethink Capabilities to Emerge Stronger from COVID-19," McKinsey and Company, November 23, 2020, https://www.mckinsey.com/business-functions /people-and-organizational-performance/our-insights/rethink-capabilities -to-emerge-stronger-from-covid-19.
2. M. Dondi, J. Klier, F. Panier, and J. Schubert, "Defining the Skills Citizens Will Need in the Future World of Work," McKinsey Global Institute, June 25, 2021, accessed June 30, 2021, https://www.mckinsey.com /industries/public-and-social-sector/our-insights/defining-the-skills -citizens-will-need-in-the-future-world-of-work.
3. M. Kleine, "No Eureka! Incentives Hurt Creative Breakthrough Irrespective of the Incentives' Frame," Max Planck Institute for Innovation & Competition Research Paper No. 21-15, May 18, 2021.
4. K. P. De Meuse, "A Meta-Analysis of the Relationship Between Learning Agility and Leader Success," *Journal of Organizational Psychology* 19, no. 1 (2019): 25–34.
5. E. H. O'Boyle Jr., R. H. Humphrey, J. M. Pollack, et al., "The Relation Between Emotional Intelligence and Job Performance: A Meta-Analysis," *Journal of Organizational Behavior* 32, no. 5 (2011): 788–818.

6. J. Brassey, N. Van Dam, and A. Van Witteloostuijn, *Authentic Confidence: Advancing Authentic Confidence Through Emotional Flexibility: An Evidence-Based Playbook of Insights, Practices, and Tools to Shape Your Future*, 2nd ed. (Zeist, The Netherlands: VMN Media, 2022).
7. J. Brassey, A. V. Witteloostuijn, C. Huszka, T. Silberzahn, and N. V. Dam, "Emotional Flexibility and General Self-Efficacy: A Pilot Training Intervention Study with Knowledge Workers," *PloS One* 15 (10) (2020): e0237821.

Chapter 2: The Zones

1. J. Baker and B. Young, "20 Years Later: Deliberate Practice and the Development of Expertise in Sport," *International Review of Sport and Exercise Psychology* 7, no. 1 (2014): 135–57, doi: 10.1080/1750984X.2014.896024.
2. "Pressure-Driven Meltdowns Are Surprisingly Common in Elite Tennis," *Economist*, September 11, 2021, https://www.economist.com/graphic -detail/2021/09/11/pressure-driven-meltdowns-are-surprisingly -common-in-elite-tennis.
3. Kleine, "No Eureka!"

Chapter 3: The Brain-Body Connection

1. C. Pert, "The Wisdom of the Receptors: Neuropeptides, the Emotions, and Bodymind," *Advances in Mind-Body Medicine* 18, no. 1 (2002): 30–35.
2. E. A. Mayer, "Gut Feelings: The Emerging Biology of Gut–Brain Communication," *Nature Reviews Neuroscience* 12, no. 8 (2011): 453–66.
3. D. Goleman, *Emotional Intelligence: Why It Can Matter More Than IQ* (New York: Bantam Books, 2005).
4. L. F. Barrett, *How Emotions Are Made: The Secret Life of the Brain* (Boston: Houghton Mifflin Harcourt, 2017).
5. D. Mobbs, R. Adolphs, M. S. Fanselow, et al., "On the Nature of Fear," *Scientific American*, October 10, 2019, https://www.scientificamerican .com/article/on-the-nature-of-fear/.
6. W. K. Simmons, J. A. Avery, J. C. Barcalow, et al., "Keeping the Body in Mind: Insula Functional Organization and Functional Connectivity Integrate Interoceptive, Exteroceptive, and Emotional Awareness," *Human Brain Mapping* 34, no. 11 (2013): 2944–58.

7. M. E. Raichle and D. A. Gusnard, "Appraising the Brain's Energy Budget," *Proceedings of the National Academy of Sciences* 99, no. 16 (2002): 10237–39.

8. A. J. Crum and E. J. Langer, "Mind Set Matters: Exercise and the Placebo Effect," *Psychological Science* 18, no. 2 (2007): 165–71, doi: 10.1111/j.1467-9280.2007.01867.x, PMID: 17425538.

9. S. W. Porges, *The Polyvagal Theory: Neurophysiological Foundations of Emotions, Attachment, Communication, and Self Regulation*, Norton series on interpersonal neurobiology (New York: W. W. Norton, 2011).

10. A. Lembke, *Dopamine Nation: Finding Balance in the Age of Indulgence* (New York: Dutton, 2021).

11. N. Farb, J. Daubenmier, C. J. Price, T. Gard, C. Kerr, B. D. Dunn, and W. E. Mehling, "Interoception, Contemplative Practice, and Health," *Frontiers in Psychology* 6 (2015): 763.

12. S. S. Khalsa, R. Adolphs, O. G. Cameron, H. D. Critchley, P. W. Davenport, J. S. Feinstein, and N. Zucker, "Interoception and Mental Health: A Roadmap," *Biological Psychiatry: Cognitive Neuroscience and Neuroimaging* 3, no. 6 (2018): 501–13.

Chapter 4: What Lies Beneath

1. S. David, *Emotional Agility: Get Unstuck, Embrace Change, and Thrive in Work and Life* (New York: Avery, 2016).

2. E. Kwong, "Understanding Unconscious Bias," NPR, July 15, 2020, interview with Pragya Agarwal, author of *Sway: Unravelling Unconscious Bias*, https://www.npr.org/2020/07/14/891140598/understanding-unconscious-bias?t=1644782049157; P. Agarwal, *Sway: Unravelling Unconscious Bias* (New York: Bloomsbury Sigma, 2020).

Chapter 5: Purpose

1. J. Emmett, G. Schrah, M. Schrimper, and A. Wood, "COVID-19 and the Employee Experience: How Leaders Can Seize the Moment," McKinsey and Company, June 29, 2020.

2. A. Alimujiang, A. Wiensch, J. Boss, et al., "Association Between Life Purpose and Mortality Among US Adults Older Than 50 Years," *JAMA Network Open* 2, no. 5 (2019): e194270.

3. S. Musich, S. S. Wang, S. Kraemer, et al., "Purpose in Life and Positive Health Outcomes Among Older Adults," *Population Health Management* 21, no. 2 (2018): 139–47, doi: 10.1089/pop.2017.0063.

4. V. E. Frankl, *Man's Search for Meaning: An Introduction to Logotherapy* (Boston: Beacon Press, 1946).

Chapter 6: Recover Like an Athlete

1. P. L. Ackerman and R. Kanfer, "Integrating Laboratory and Field Study for Improving Selection: Development of a Battery for Predicting Air Traffic Controller Success," *Journal of Applied Psychology* 78, no. 3 (1993): 413–32.

2. K. A. Ericsson, R. T. Krampe, and C. Tesch-Romer, "The Role of Deliberate Practice in the Acquisition of Expert Performance," *Psychological Review* 100, no. 3 (1993): 363–406.

3. R. F. Martell, "Sex Bias at Work: The Effects of Attentional and Memory Demands on Performance Ratings of Men and Women," *Journal of Applied Social Psychology* 21, no. 23 (1991): 1939–60.

4. A. M. Gordon and S. Chen, "The Role of Sleep in Interpersonal Conflict: Do Sleepless Nights Mean Worse Fights?" *Social Psychological and Personality Science* 5, no. 2 (2013): 168–75.

5. M. E. Raichle and D. A. Gusnard, "Appraising the Brain's Energy Budget," *Proceedings of the National Academy of Sciences* 99, no. 16 (2002): 10237–39, doi: 10.1073/pnas.172399499.

6. A. Huberman, *Maximizing Productivity, Physical and Mental Health with Daily Tools*, podcast, Huberman Lab, https://hubermanlab.com /maximizing-productivity-physical-and-mental-health-with-daily -tools/.

7. N. Kleitman, "Basic Rest-Activity Cycle—22 Years Later," *Sleep* 5, no. 4 (1982): 311–17.

8. Huberman, *Maximizing Productivity, Physical and Mental Health with Daily Tools*.

9. M. K. Wekenborg, L. K. Hill, J. F. Thayer, et al., "The Longitudinal Association of Reduced Vagal Tone with Burnout," *Psychosomatic Medicine* 81, no. 9 (2019): 791.

Chapter 7: Developing Dual Awareness

1. J. Luft and H. Ingham, "The Johari Window: A Graphic Model of Interpersonal Awareness," *Proceedings of the Western Training Laboratory in Group Development* (Los Angeles: University of California, Los Angeles, 1955).

2. L. Festinger, "Cognitive Dissonance," *Scientific American* 207, no. 4 (1962): 93–106.

3. J. Brassey, N. Van Dam, and A. Van Witteloostuijn, *Authentic Confidence. Advancing Authentic Confidence Through Emotional Flexibility: An Evidence-Based Playbook of Insights, Practices and Tools to Shape Your Future*, 2nd ed. (Zeist, The Netherlands: VMN Media, 2022).

4. A. Huberman, "Reduce Anxiety & Stress with the Physiological Sigh/ Huberman Lab Quantal Clip," YouTube video, https://www.youtube .com/watch?v=rBdhqBGqiMc.

5. M. van Mersbergen, "Viva La Vagus!" *Choral Journal* 55, no. 3 (2014): 61–67, https://www.memphis.edu/vecl/pdfs/viva_la_vagus.pdf.

6. S. R. Covey, *The 7 Habits of Highly Effective People: Powerful Lessons in Personal Change*, 25th anniversary ed. (New York: Simon & Schuster, 2004).

7. The Curious Advantage, https://curiousadvantage.com/.

Chapter 8: When Icebergs Collide

1. E. S. Bromberg-Martin and T. Sharot, "The Value of Beliefs," *Neuron* 106, no. 4 (May 2020): 561–65, doi: 10.1016/j.neuron.2020.05.001.

2. A. Huberman, *Controlling Your Dopamine for Motivation, Focus, and Satisfaction*, YouTube, https://www.youtube.com/watch?v=QmOF0crdy? RU&t=6789s.

3. R. Burton, *On Being Certain: Believing You Are Right Even When You're Not*, reviews, comments, https://www.rburton.com/_i_on_being_certain _i___believing_you_are_right_even_when_you_re_not_63166.htm.

4. D. Weitz, "The Brains behind Mediation: Reflections on Neuroscience, Conflict Resolution and Decision-Making," *Cardozo Journal of Conflict Resolution* 12 no. 471 (2010).

5. C. Argyris, R. Putnam, and M. M. Smith, *Action Science* (San Francisco: Jossey-Bass, 1985), https://actiondesign.com/resources/readings /action-science.

Chapter 9: Deliberate Calm Teams

1. J. Burnford, "Building Authentic Courage: The Essential Foundation for Successful Diversity and Inclusion," *Forbes*, February 1, 2020, https://www.forbes.com/sites/joyburnford/2020/02/01/building-authentic-courage-the-essential-foundation-for-successful-diversity-and-inclusion/?sh=30768a308623.

2. N. Inui, *Interpersonal Coordination: A Social Neuroscience Approach* (Cham, Switzerland: Springer, 2018).

3. Burnford, "Building Authentic Courage."

4. G. Redford, "Amy Edmondson: Psychological Safety Is Critically Important in Medicine," AAMC, November 12, 2019, https://www.aamc.org/news-insights/amy-edmondson-psychological-safety-critically-important-medicine.

5. C. Duhigg, "What Google Learned from Its Quest to Build the Perfect Team," *New York Times Magazine*, February 28, 2016, https://www.nytimes.com/2016/02/28/magazine/what-google-learned-from-its-quest-to-build-the-perfect-team.html.

6. C. Argyris, "Double Loop Learning in Organizations," *Harvard Business Review*, September 1977, https://hbr.org/1977/09/double-loop-learning-in-organizations.

7. B. Heger, "Psychological Safety and the Critical Role of Leadership Development, McKinsey and Company," *Brian Heger HR* (blog), February 16, 2021, https://www.brianheger.com/psychological-safety-and-the-critical-role-of-leadership-development-mckinsey-co/.

8. A. De Smet, K. Rubenstein, G. Schrah, et al., "Psychological Safety and the Critical Role of Leadership Development," McKinsey and Company, February 11, 2021, https://www.mckinsey.com/business-functions/people-and-organizational-performance/our-insights/psychological-safety-and-the-critical-role-of-leadership-development.

9. Kantor Institute, https://www.kantorinstitute.com/approach.

10. Inui, *Interpersonal Coordination*.

11. Ibid.

Appendix: Four Weeks to Deliberate Calm

1. A. Huberman, *The Science of Making and Breaking Habits*, podcast, Huberman Lab, https://hubermanlab.com/the-science-of-making-and-breaking-habits/.
2. P. Lally, C. H. Van Jaarsveld, H. W. Potts, and J. Wardle, "How Are Habits Formed: Modelling Habit Formation in the Real World," *European Journal of Social Psychology* 40, no. 6 (2010): 998–1009.
3. W. Wood and D. Rünger, "Psychology of Habit," *Annual Review of Psychology* 67 (2016): 289–314.
4. Huberman, *The Science of Making and Breaking Habits*.
5. Lally, Van Jaarsveld, Potts, and Wardle, "How Are Habits Formed: Modelling Habit Formation in the Real World."
6. Wood and Rünger, "Psychology of Habit."

FURTHER READING

Barrett, L. F. "That Is Not How Your Brain Works." *Nautilus*, November 18, 2021. https://nautil.us/issue/98/mind/that-is-not-how-your-brain-works.

Brassey, J., A. De Smet, A. Kothari, et al. "Future Proof: Solving the 'Adaptability Paradox' for the Long Term." McKinsey and Company, August 2, 2021. https://www.mckinsey.com/business-functions/people-and -organizational-performance/our-insights/future-proof-solving-the -adaptability-paradox-for-the-long-term.

Brassey, J., and M. Kruyt. "How to Demonstrate Calm and Optimism in a Crisis." McKinsey and Company, April 30, 2020. https://www.mckinsey .com/business-functions/people-and-organizational-performance/our -insights/how-to-demonstrate-calm-and-optimism-in-a-crisis.

Brassey, J., N. Van Dam, and A. Van Witteloostuijn. *Authentic Confidence. Advancing Authentic Confidence Through Emotional Flexibility: An Evidence-Based Playbook of Insights, Practices and Tools to Shape Your Future*, 2nd ed. Zeist, The Netherlands: VMN Media, 2022.

Chatman, J. A., D. F. Caldwell, C. A. O'Reilly, and B. Doerr. "Parsing Organizational Culture: How the Norm for Adaptability Influences the Relationship Between Culture Consensus and Financial Performance in High-Technology Firms." *Journal of Organizational Behavior* 35, no. 6 (2014): 785–808.

Crum, A. *Science of Mindsets for Health and Performance*. Podcast, Huberman Lab. https://hubermanlab.com/dr-alia-crum-science-of-mindsets-for-health-performance/.

Damasio, A. "How Our Brains Feel Emotion." Big Think. https://www.youtube.com/watch?v=KsSv1KzdiWU&t=258s.

Haver, A., K. Akerjordet, and T. Furunes. "Emotion Regulation and Its Implications for Leadership: An Integrative Review and Future Research Agenda." *Journal of Leadership & Organizational Studies* 20, no. 3 (2013): 287–303.

Huberman, A. *The Science of Making and Breaking Habits*. Podcast, Huberman Lab. https://hubermanlab.com/the-science-of-making-and-breaking-habits/.

Huberman Lab. https://hubermanlab.com.

Khalsa, S. S., R. Adolphs, O. G. Cameron, et al. "Interoception and Mental Health: A Roadmap." *Biological Psychiatry: Cognitive Neuroscience and Neuroimaging* 3, no. 6 (2018): 501–13.

Kosner, A. W. *The Mind at Work: Lisa Feldman Barrett on the Metabolism of Emotion* (blog). *Dropbox*, February 10, 2021, https://blog.dropbox.com/topics/work-culture/the-mind-at-work--lisa-feldman-barrett-on-the-metabolism-of-emot.

Lembke, A. *Understanding and Treating Addiction*. Podcast, Huberman Lab. https://hubermanlab.com/dr-anna-lembke-understanding-and-treating-addiction/.

Lindquist, K. A., T. D. Wager, H. Kober, et al. "The Brain Basis of Emotion: A Meta-Analytic Review." *Behavioral and Brain Sciences* 35, no. 3 (2012): 121.

Narain, C. "A Conversation with Joseph LeDoux." *Cold Spring Harbor Symposia on Quantitative Biology* 79 (2014): 279–81. http://symposium.cshlp.org/content/79/279.full.

Quigley, K. S., S. Kanoski, W. M. Grill, L. F. Barrett, and M. Tsakiris. "Functions of Interoception: From Energy Regulation to Experience of the Self." *Trends in Neurosciences* 44, no. 1 (January 2021): 29–38.

Robson, D. "Interoception: The Hidden Sense That Shapes Wellbeing." *Guardian*, August 15, 2021.

Stanford Profiles. "Alia Crum, Associate Professor of Psychology." https://profiles.stanford.edu/alia-crum.

Van der Kolk, B. A. *The Body Keeps the Score: Brain, Mind, and Body in the Healing of Trauma*. New York: Viking, 2014.

Wheal, J. "Explaining Neurochemistry and Emotions: An Interview with Lisa Feldman-Barrett, Ph.D." *Neurohacker Collective*, March 4, 2021. https://neurohacker.com/explaining-neurochemistry-emotions-an-interview-with-lisa-feldman-barrett-ph-d.

Yeow, J., and R. Martin. "The Role of Self Regulation in Developing Leaders: A Longitudinal Field Experiment." *Leadership Quarterly* 24, no. 5 (2013): 625–37.

INDEX

ABOUT THE AUTHORS

JACQUELINE (JACQUI) BRASSEY (PhD, MAfN) is McKinsey's chief scientist and director of research science in the area of People & Organizational Performance and an affiliated leader of the McKinsey Health Institute. Previously she led the learning and development of McKinsey's top six hundred most senior leaders, among others, and served on the Firm's global Learning Leadership Team. Furthermore, she is a researcher at VU Amsterdam, founder and leader of the Lab for Sustainable Human Development and Performance, and an adjunct professor at IE University in Spain. She serves as a supervisory board member of Save the Children and as an advisory board member of the Master in leadership and development in organizations at Maastricht University in the Netherlands. Jacqui has more than twenty years of experience in business and academia and before joining McKinsey & Company spent most of her career at Unilever, both in the Netherlands and in the United Kingdom. Jacqui holds degrees in both organization and business sciences, as well as in medical sciences. She has a bachelor's degree in international business and languages from Avans University of Applied Sciences, graduated cum laude with bachelor's and master's degrees in policy and organization sciences from Tilburg University, a PhD in economics and business from Groningen University, and a joint master's degree in affective neuroscience from Maastricht University and the University of Florence. She has coauthored and presented more than fifty articles, books, podcasts, and scientific papers. She has worked and lived in five countries, loves running, cycling, hiking, and a good glass of wine, and currently lives with her South African–Dutch family in Luxembourg.

AARON DE SMET joined McKinsey and Company in 2003; he has led the firm's thinking on organizational health and leadership. His articles in *McKinsey Quarterly* are among its most-read and he is a member of the master faculty of the Change Leaders Forum and of the Organizational Agility Forum, which he helped establish. He leads McKinsey's thinking on organizational health and was on the team that developed the Organizational Health Index (OHI) and OrgLab. Aaron has a PhD in social and organizational psychology from Columbia University, where he specialized in organizational dynamics, culture, leadership, and strategic change. He also has an MBA and a BA in psychology. He lives in New Jersey with his family.

MICHIEL KRUYT is currently CEO of Imagine.one, with a mission to create systemic transformation toward a more sustainable and equal planet. Before joining Imagine, Michiel was a partner and one of the leaders of the Organization Practice of McKinsey and Company, and cofounder and former managing partner of Aberkyn, a pioneer specializing in performance transformations, culture change, and executive team and leadership development. For the first fifteen years of his career he worked for Unilever in marketing, sales, and general management roles in the Netherlands, Italy, and the United States. He is a member of the board of the nonprofit Urban Consciousness Center De Roos in Amsterdam. Michiel, his wife, Christine, and their three children live just outside Amsterdam.